Trevor Colbourn

THE LAMP
OF EXPERIENCE

Whig History and the
Intellectual Origins of the
American Revolution

Trevor Colbourn

LIBERTY FUND

Indianapolis

This book is published by Liberty Fund, Inc., a foundation established to encourage study of the ideal of a society of free and responsible individuals.

The cuneiform inscription that serves as our logo and as the design motif for our endpapers is the earliest-known written appearance of the word "freedom" (*amagi*), or "liberty." It is taken from a clay document written about 2300 B.C. in the Sumerian city-state of Lagash.

Library of Congress Cataloging-in-Publication Data
Colbourn, H. Trevor.
The lamp of experience : Whig history and the intellectual origins of the
American Revolution / Trevor Colbourn.
p.   cm.
Includes bibliographical references (p.   ) and index.
ISBN 0-86597-158-7 (cloth). — ISBN 0-86597-159-5 (pbk.)
1. United States — History — Revolution, 1775–1783 — Causes.   2. Statesmen —
United States — Books and reading — History — 18th century.   3. Great Britain —
History — Study and teaching — United States — History — 18th century.   4. Great
Britain — Politics and government — Historiography.   5. United States —
Intellectual life — 18th century.   I. Title.
E210.C58   1998
973.3′11 — DC21
97-3351

LIBERTY FUND, INC.
8335 Allison Pointe Trail, Suite 300
Indianapolis, IN 46250-1687

98 99 00 01 02 C 5 4 3 2 1
98 99 00 01 02 P 5 4 3 2 1

For Douglass

Contents

Preface to the Liberty Fund Edition: 1943 and All That

Much has happened in the more than thirty years that have passed since *The Lamp of Experience* was first published by the Institute of Early American History in 1965. Many who helped shape that volume have passed on—notably, Douglass Adair (to whom *The Lamp of Experience* was properly dedicated), Lyman Butterfield, Julian Boyd, Dumas Malone, Millicent Sowerby, Edwin Wolf II, and John H. Powell. It is a depressingly long list. But this new edition allows for the confirmation of earlier acknowledgments and obligations and also permits some brief reflections on the strange history of a book about history.

Born in Australia (his parents were there at the time), the author was educated in England (European diplomatic history with the late William Medlicott) and secured his graduate degrees in Williamsburg and Baltimore. In Williamsburg, at the College of William and Mary, a young assistant professor named Adair introduced a much younger exchange student named Colbourn to Thomas Jefferson and took seeming delight in asking questions only the questioner could answer. Certainly migration to Baltimore was not an immediate solution: Colbourn's arrival at The Johns Hopkins University in 1949 coincided with his discovery that the Hopkins colonialist, Charles Barker, had decided to abandon his study of the American Revolution for *Henry George* (1955), also a conservative revolutionary to be sure. But the late Charles Barker was a generous spirit who readily agreed to the creation of a very informal advisory committee for his errant graduate student, which soon included Douglass Adair, Dumas

Malone, Lyman Butterfield, and Adair's very scholarly friend, Caroline Robbins. All were generous with their time and all knew Jefferson rather well. The outcome, spurred by the incentive of reemployment at Penn State in 1953, was a doctoral dissertation on Thomas Jefferson's use of history. In turn this dissertation generated a paper given at the American Historical Association convention in 1955, which in turn led to an article in the 1958 *William and Mary Quarterly.*

What next? Lyman Butterfield thought the author's approach to Jefferson had promise but needed substantial expansion. And so the subject of Thomas Jefferson provided the material for chapter 8 and the seed for the further inquiry that became *The Lamp of Experience.* Such growth owed much to the encouragement provided by Caroline Robbins, who allowed the author a summer in her extraordinary private library. Shelf after shelf of the writings of her seventeenth- and eighteenth-century "Commonwealthmen" illustrated the relevance of England's Real Whigs for the leaders of the American Revolution. Frequent visits to the Library of Congress's Rare Book Room and a year combing the shelves of the Library Company of Philadelphia reinforced that message.

Thus far the emergence of *The Lamp of Experience* was far from unusual except for the time taken by its author in writing it. Perhaps his colleagues were too patient. Certainly there were other studies under way and other books already published that advanced the understanding of the intellectual origins of the American Revolution. Some books seem to await the appearance of other books before they take shape. This is particularly true for our understanding of the era of the Revolution, for which 1943 emerges as a seminal historiographical turning point. In the midst of World War II the United States had good reason to celebrate the bicentennial of the birth of Thomas Jefferson and laid plans for the publication of *all* the available papers of that great spokesman for democracy. Begun by Julian Boyd and Lyman Butterfield, this ambitious project has outlived both men. Butterfield, to be sure, deserted Jefferson for the Adams family and editing on a less comprehensive scale. He did, however, live to complete his *Diary and Autobiography of John Adams* (1961) and his *Adams Family Correspondence* (1963) and to see similar projects emerge as a tribute to most of the Founding Fathers.[1]

Plans were also laid for a unique catalog of the magnificent private library Jefferson sold to the Congress in 1815. In charge of this noble enterprise was a battle-axe of an Englishwoman, Millicent Sowerby, who, like her one-time colleague, Ed Wolf, was a rare-book specialist. Wolf later took charge of the Library Company of Philadelphia and made Benjamin Franklin's collection into an available and very special resource for students of eighteenth-century America. Millicent Sowerby pursued her task with deliberate speed (1952–59) but rewarded her impatient admirers with so much more than an inventory of Jefferson's greatest library: she told us when he acquired his books and, if possible, what he thought of them. This was, wrote Douglass Adair in his *William and Mary Quarterly* review, "a bio-bibliography," and "a marvelous guide to the intellectual world of Jefferson."

Caroline Robbins was the other willful Englishwoman who made very special contributions to our understanding of the intellectual world of the seventeenth and eighteenth centuries. Sometime Chair at Bryn Mawr College, she is still justly venerated for her pathfinding *The Eighteenth-Century Commonwealthman* (1959), dedicated to her famous brother.[2] Both *The Lamp* and Bernard Bailyn's *Ideological Origins of the American Revolution* appeared six years later, and both were enormously indebted to Robbins and her writings on the "Commonwealthmen." Even Jonathan Clark, whose interpretations of the ma-

---

1. For example: George Washington, James Madison, Alexander Hamilton, John Marshall, Benjamin Rush, Benjamin Franklin, and James Wilson; not included is Aaron Burr or, as yet, John Dickinson. The *New York Times* provided the down payment on the *Jefferson Papers.*

2. (Lionel) Lord Robbins, author of The Blueprint for Higher Education in Post-War Britain.

terial do not always agree with those of Robbins, concedes in *The Language of Liberty* (1994) the "meticulous scholarship" exhibited by his compatriot. Well he might.

But 1943 offered more than a new commitment to the American past in the form of plans for the publication of the Founding Fathers' papers and the identification of their books. It was also the year that saw several additional happenings of historical consequence: Columbia University published Adrienne Koch's doctoral dissertation, "The Philosophy of Thomas Jefferson"; Merle Curti successfully made the case for the larger world of ideas in his *The Growth of American Democratic Thought;* and his friend Ralph Henry Gabriel signed off on the extraordinary doctoral dissertation submitted by the young Douglass Adair at Yale, "The Intellectual Origins of Jeffersonian Democracy: Republicans, the Class Struggle, and the Virtuous Farmer." Curti's book remains very much in print, but, strangely, the Adair manuscript long remained just that, a manuscript. Strangely, because the list of interlibrary borrowers could well be mistaken for a "Who's Who" among early American historians. Indeed, Adair offered that as his excuse: "Everyone who should read the book has already borrowed it from Yale." Instead of creating more reasons for celebrating 1943, such as revising his dissertation for publication, Adair devoted more and more of his considerable energies to his relationship with The College of William and Mary as cosponsor of the *William and Mary Quarterly* (from 1946 to 1955). This was an association that brought fame to both Adair and the college.

It is tempting to suggest that the Adair–*William and Mary Quarterly* alliance accounts for much of the new scholarship that emerged in the 1950s and 1960s. This would be an exaggeration—Irving Brant's first *Madison* volume appeared as early as 1941—but Adair influenced many by commissioning articles from such other talented colleagues as Peter Laslett, Adrienne Koch, and Jack Pocock and by writing quite a few himself.[3] Caroline Robbins was the best-known partner in

---

3. See Trevor Colbourn, ed., *Fame and the Founding Fathers* (N.Y., 1974), v–vi.

his exploration of "English Classical History," and theirs was indeed a remarkable scholarly liaison. Few studies of early American history published during these two decades lacked an acknowledgment of the assistance given by Adair. The late Page Smith remarked of Adair, "I have never known anyone who was so much a source of ideas and inspiration to others." Smith's outstanding biography of James Wilson (1956) confirms Adair's contribution. So do Robbins's book on the Commonwealthmen and Elisha P. Douglass's book *Rebels and Democrats* (1955), a splendid study that probably appeared before its time and failed to secure its due attention. The list is long.

Another very special study of political ideas appeared as early as 1953. Clinton Rossiter's magnificent *Seedtime of the Republic* arrived six years before Robbins's publication and anticipated many of Robbins's, Bailyn's, and Colbourn's conclusions. They all seem to agree that the leaders of the American Revolution were "conscious conservatives." Rossiter was arguably the first to make that case. According to one reviewer, *Seedtime* was a welcome guide to pre-Revolution intellectual history but was guilty of overload—Rossiter sought to provide too much information. That strange complaint did not apply to Rossiter's excellent treatment of Richard Bland, Jonathan Mayhew, or Benjamin Franklin. Rossiter, a Cornell political scientist and a fine historian, later gave us *1787: The Grand Convention* (1966) before taking his own life—as did Adair but for very different reasons.

Of course there is some danger in suggesting any one year (1943) as the turning point in our acquaintance with the American Revolution. As our absorption with the extraordinary quality and quantity of the new studies descended on us by the end of World War II, we ran the risk of overlooking contributions made by earlier scholars—such as Moses Coit Tyler—nearly a century ago. It was Tyler who asserted the Revolution was "pre-eminently . . . caused by ideas" and enabled Robert Middlekauff three decades later to remind his colleagues that "the intellectual history of the American Revolution has long received study." Actually Adair was not only among the first to challenge the then prevailing view of Charles A. Beard and Frederick

Jackson Turner but was also among the first to consider the classical legacy of the Founding Fathers and their inheritance from the seventeenth-century English republicans. There were few like Tyler a century ago, like Carl Becker seventy years ago, or like Randolph G. Adams and Charles H. McIlwain, who made 1922 a rather fine year for the history of ideas.

Randolph G. Adams earned his doctorate with a dissertation that argued for the ideological origins of the Revolution. In his *Political Ideas of the American Revolution* (1922) he actually claimed the colonists explored their rights as Englishmen, an idea also considered by Charles H. McIlwain. Indeed, McIlwain attempted a constitutional justification for the Revolution. But neither study matched Becker's success, possibly because Becker gave so much more attention to ideas even if he overstated his case for John Locke. Just ten years later Becker gave us his classic *The Heavenly City of the Eighteenth-Century Philosophers,* wherein he depicted history as a subject to substantiate the perfectible nature of man.

Other contributing new studies at this time included Benjamin Wright's *American Interpretations of Natural Law* (1931) and Charles Mullett's *Fundamental Law and the American Revolution* (1933); both were preceded by Vernon Louis Parrington's *The Colonial Mind* (1927). Parrington was a progressivist and an enthusiast for Turner's frontier thesis but had little grasp of the ideology of the colonial leadership. And yet "the philosophic mind" meant something to Parrington, and he sensitized a generation to the possibilities of intellectual history.

Perhaps Gilbert Chinard, a French scholar, was best attuned to such opportunities. He busied himself producing biographies of Thomas Jefferson and John Adams (1929 and 1933, respectively). More significant were his editions of Jefferson's Commonplace Books (1926 and 1927). Chinard's transcription of Jefferson's law notebooks furnished the first public glimpse of the Virginian's sustained interest in feudalism, law, and history. Twenty years later Marie Kimball, perhaps Jefferson's ablest biographer (before Dumas Malone in 1948), was able to demonstrate the political relevance of Jefferson's note-taking—and when and where it took place. Indeed, Chinard and Kimball were among the first to suggest the significance of Jefferson's reading and the British Real Whigs, later explored by Clinton Rossiter and Caroline Robbins.

Where have such endeavors brought us? We now have books by several generations of historians who have shed new light on our Revolutionary past and who have illumined aspects of British history that relate to America's past in ways never previously appreciated. Many of the principal contributors to our once new perspective have died, retired (not usually early retirement), or found new challenges. John (Jack) Pocock, a student of the late Herbert Butterfield at Cambridge, has retired, thereby deserting Jack Greene at Johns Hopkins. Bernard Bailyn has most reluctantly retired from Harvard. Gordon Wood remains at Brown, having impressed many with *The Creation of the American Republic* (1969) and surprised many more with his second book, *The Radicalism of the American Revolution* (1992). Edmund Morgan has yet to stop writing—or halt—new editions of *The Birth of the Republic*. Caroline Robbins is happily still with us but ailing. Pauline Maier's splendid *From Resistance to Revolution* (1972) is still available, thanks to a new (1992) edition from W. W. Norton. It was Norton that published *The Lamp of Experience* in a paperback edition (long unavailable) and *Fame and the Founding Fathers* (1974), the collection of Adair articles edited by Trevor Colbourn and enhanced by a contribution from Caroline Robbins and Robert E. Shalhope, "Douglass Adair and the Historiography of Republicanism." Shalhope also wrote "Toward a Republican Synthesis: The Emergence of an Understanding of Republicanism in American Historiography," which appeared in the *William and Mary Quarterly* in 1972. Both articles are unusually enlightening; however, an Englishman, Colin Bonwick, may have provided the best update on just where these new studies have brought us. His book *The American Revolution* (1991), although brief, is remarkably encompassing and current in its scholarship.

Robert Middlekauff (now back at Berkeley), widely applauded for *The Glorious Cause: The American Revolution, 1763–1789* (1982), was one of the generous reviewers of *The Lamp of Experience*. In that review he noted how Becker and Morgan to some extent "placed American thought in the long tradition of natural rights."[4] He noted also how Caroline Robbins "demonstrated the persistence of a seventeenth-century revolutionary tradition as expounded and amplified by the 'Real Whigs.'" The author, Middlekauff noted, chose to extend and amplify suggestions made by Caroline Robbins; indeed, "He has done much more."

Middlekauff went on in the review to describe what he meant by "much more." He describes the reconstruction of colonial tastes in history (ancient, medieval, seventeenth- and eighteenth-century), which "must have been a difficult job demanding patience and energy." He shows how Americans "used the past selectively to illustrate contentions about political principle and rights." He does this so well that to read further "is to become convinced." Middlekauff concluded by praising the author's research ("so thorough"), judgment ("so balanced"), and craftsmanship ("so excellent"). This is, says Middlekauff, "a balanced and clear-headed book."

The author is hardly likely to disagree with such sentiments but is tempted. The putative confession goes as follows: problems of causation remain difficult for historians; *The Lamp of Experience* tried to avoid the contention that a colonist adopted a particular political position because he read a particular book. But the author remains persuaded that the history read by the Revolutionary generation at the very least made it easier for them to take on an apparent revolutionary posture—no, not posture, for that does not suggest conviction. The Revolutionary leaders were men of substance—propertied,

---

4. Robert Middlekauff, review of *The Lamp of Experience: Whig History and the Intellectual Origins of the American Revolution,* by H. Trevor Colbourn, *Indiana Magazine of History* (March 1966): 90–91.

educated. They *read*. And what they read made it easier for them to become rebels because they did not see rebels when they looked in the mirror. They saw transplanted Englishmen with the rights of expatriated men. They were determined to fight for inherited historic rights and liberties.

Trevor Colbourn
President Emeritus
University of Central Florida

Preface to the 1965 Edition

The American Revolution has never wanted for attention, but important chapters of the intellectual history of the Revolution have yet to be written. The political philosophy of the Revolutionaries is familiar; their historical justification for independence is not. The eighteenth-century American colonist was born into an environment formed by history as well as philosophy, and for many, history afforded an argument more persuasive, more tangible.

Persuasion was important. Americans were not eager to separate from their mother country. "No man was ever more warmly attached to the Hanover family," confessed George Mason of Virginia, adding that "few men had stronger prejudices in favor of that form of government . . . or a greater aversion to changing it." And John Adams agreed that "revolutions are no trifles. They ought never to be undertaken rashly." Independence was for most a last resort, the final move in defense of traditional English rights now put in jeopardy by a sovereignty-mad British administration.

This study seeks to explore some colonial concepts of the rights of Englishmen to which they laid claim; it explores the sources of such concepts and the historical perspective such sources afforded. The reading habits of the Revolutionaries disclose a remarkable devotion to the study of English history. Books—library books—are in themselves an important species of source material, frequently as revealing as personal correspondence and potentially more honest than a diary aimed deliberately at posterity. Obviously a library catalogue, taken alone, can be a deceptive document: few people have read all the books on their shelves, and ownership of an unread book means little. But in association with other evidence, such as notes, marginalia, citations, recommendations, repeated purchases, books can be evaluated; and then, by reading them, one can re-create the perspective of an earlier age.

The history books read by the Revolutionary leaders did not supply their motivation for political action. The dangers of implying such causation are painfully obvious. The most that can be claimed is that the character of their reading, their particular preferences and comments on them, do inform powerfully on their political thought and final action. Carl Becker once observed that "generally speaking, men are influenced by books which clarify their own thought, which express their own motives well, or which suggest to them ideas which their minds are already predisposed to accept." Even within these limits, the historical reading of eighteenth-century American colonists illuminates much of their political conduct toward the mother country they studied so assiduously.

Americans shared with certain English contemporaries common attitudes toward history and its relevance to England's political, moral, and constitutional condition. Both the colonists' ideas of the past and their employment of those ideas contribute substantially to our understanding of the Revolutionary generation.

The obligations incurred in preparing this study are too numerous to list in detail. But I am particularly indebted to my patient wife, Beryl, John H. Powell, Douglass Adair, James Morton Smith, Russel Nye, Robert H. Ferrell, and Alexander R. Butler for editorial and organizational suggestions. In addition Caroline Robbins and E. Millicent Sowerby have been extraordinarily generous with their time, counsel, and friendship. The assistance furnished by Julian P. Boyd, Lyman H. Butterfield, and Edwin Wolf 2nd has been invaluable. Research has been assisted by generous grants from the Institute of Early American History and Culture, the Library Company of Philadelphia, and the Pennsylvania State and Indiana Universities.

Portions of chapter 8 appeared in the *William and Mary Quarterly,* 3d ser., 15 (1958); portions of chapter 6 derive from the Boyd Lee

Spahr Lecture at Dickinson College, November 1958 (published in *Early Dickinsoniana*, Carlisle, Pa., 1961), and the *Pennsylvania Magazine of History and Biography*, 83 (1959). I am grateful to the Adams Manuscript Trust for permission to print the history listings in John Adams's 1790 catalogue.

Bernard Bailyn's first volume of *Pamphlets of the American Revolution, 1750–1776* (Cambridge, Mass., 1965) came to hand as this study went to press; the relevance of his brilliant introductory essay and his superbly presented pamphlets will be widely appreciated.

H. T. C.

My Notion of a Whig, *I mean of a real* Whig *(for the Nominal are worse than any Sort of Men) is, That he is one who is exactly for keeping up to the Strictness of the true old* Gothick Constitution.

—Sir Robert Molesworth, Preface to François Hotman,
Franco-Gallia (London, 1711)

. . . naked Rights are thin and metaphysical Notions *which few are Masters or Judges of.*

—William Atwood, *The Lord Holles his Remains*
(London, 1682)

I have but one lamp by which my feet are guided, and that is the lamp of experience. I know of no way of judging the future but by the past.

—Patrick Henry (1775)

PART ONE

The English Heritage
and the
Colonial Historical View

CHAPTER I

History and the Eighteenth-Century Colonist

One of John Adams's favorite questions was, "What do we mean by the revolution? The War?" No. "That was no part of the revolution. It was only an Effect and consequence of it." As he told Hezekiah Niles, "the real American Revolution" was the "radical change in the principles, opinions, sentiments, and affections of the people." Effected between 1760 and 1775, this took place "before a drop of blood was shed."[1]

The shift in American sentiment was startlingly rapid and comprehensive. Americans basked in the reflected glory of the British imperial victory in 1763, secure in the knowledge that the French menace was finally removed. Benjamin Franklin noted that the colonies felt closer to the mother country than to one another.[2] Yet fifteen years later Americans were engaged in a bloody war with the very King and country who had won for them their prized security. And in resisting England the colonies found unity: "Thirteen clocks were made to strike together," observed Adams.[3]

---

1. John Adams to Hezekiah Niles, Feb. 13, 1818, Charles Francis Adams, ed., *The Works of John Adams,* 10 vols. (Boston, 1856), X, 282–83, hereafter cited as Adams, *Works.*

2. Cited in Arthur M. Schlesinger, *Prelude to Independence: The Newspaper War on Britain, 1774–1776* (N.Y., 1958), 4.

3. John Adams to Hezekiah Niles, Feb. 13, 1818, Adams, *Works,* X, 283.

How was this radical change accomplished? In large part it was the achievement of literate politicians who enlightened and informed American opinion. A French observer, the Marquis de Chastellux, passed along Benjamin Harrison's engrossing picture of "a number of respectable but uninformed inhabitants" waiting upon their intellectual betters: " 'You assert that there is a fixed intention to invade our rights and privileges; we own that we do not see this clearly, but since you assure us that it is so, we believe it. We are about to take a very dangerous step [against England], but we have confidence in you and will do anything you think proper.' " The American Revolution, the Marquis concluded, was made possible, in Virginia at least, by the popular trust in "a small number of virtuous and enlightened citizens." [4]

David Ramsay, participant in and historian of the Revolution, concurred with this judgment. In his *History of the American Revolution,* published in 1789, he paid eloquent tribute to "the well-informed citizens" who made the Revolution possible. Theirs had been the enormously difficult task of first arousing the people to their danger, theirs the subsequent task of sustaining popular feelings over the years of political crisis preceding the war. "In establishing American independence," Ramsay remarked, "the pen and the press had merit equal to that of the sword." Upon the literary contributions of the Revolutionary leadership "depended the success of military operations." [5]

Both the responsibility and the accomplishment of these "virtuous and enlightened citizens" is difficult to exaggerate. In standing against their mother country the patriot leaders knew they were

4. Marquis de Chastellux, *Travels in North America in the Years 1780, 1781 and 1782,* ed. Howard C. Rice, Jr., 2 vols. (Chapel Hill, 1963), II, 429, 435.

5. David Ramsay, *The History of the American Revolution,* 2 vols. (Philadelphia, 1789), II, 322–23. Possibly Ramsay may yet secure the respect that is his due; see, as grounds for such a hope, Page Smith, "David Ramsay and the Causes of the American Revolution," *William and Mary Quarterly,* 3d ser., 17 (1960): 51–77.

undertaking a hazardous experiment. But they knew the justness of their cause. They were devoted to liberty, but it was liberty based upon "English ideas and English principles." The patriots believed themselves inheritors of the privileges of Englishmen, and "though in a colonial situation," they believed they "actually possessed them."[6] They knew the origins and the history of the rights to which they so persuasively laid claim.

I

To the eighteenth-century colonist, the study of history was a prestigious and a practical pursuit. The Enlightenment furnished arguments for man's ability to re-create, with his God-given reason, a Heavenly City in this world (rather than patiently awaiting the next). Men argued that as Newton had discovered universal physical laws, so must there be universal laws of history, that human nature must be the same everywhere, that similar causes produce similar results, that history can repeat itself—or, *mirabile dictu,* that with the lessons learned from the past, errors might be avoided for the future. Condillac spoke for fixed unchanging principles in history: "Discover these," he told his monarch, "and . . . politics will have no more secrets for you."[7]

The testimonial on history's behalf was overwhelming. Lord Bolingbroke called it "philosophy teaching by examples."[8] John Locke praised it as "the great Mistress of Prudence, and civil Knowledge." Even though he was one of the few political writers of his day who

6. Ramsay, *History,* I, 42.

7. Étienne Bonnot de Condillac, *Oeuvres complètes . . . ,* 31 vols. (Paris, 1803), XXIX, 22–23; quoted in R. N. Stromberg, "History in the Eighteenth Century," *Journal of the History of Ideas* 12 (1951): 302. Stromberg is concerned with the eighteenth century's ideas about history.

8. Henry St. John, Viscount Bolingbroke, *Letters on the Study and Use of History* (London, 1752), 14; see also Wallace K. Ferguson, *The Renaissance in Historical Thought; Five Centuries of Interpretation* (Cambridge, Mass., 1948), 84.

failed to draw upon history to support his contentions, he thought history "the proper study of a Gentleman," and urged others to take "a View of our English Constitution and Government in the antient Books of the *Common-Law*." David Hume thought history was "the greatest mistress of wisdom," and Lord Chesterfield told his grandson he would acquire much credit and reputation by knowing history well.[9]

But history was above all useful. James Harrington regarded knowledge of history as the prerequisite of a politician. James Burgh called history an essential study for statesmen, "the inexhaustible mine, out of which political knowledge is brought up." In his *Thoughts on Education*, a manual popular in the American colonies, Burgh contended that "there is no kind of reading that tends more to settle the judgement, than that of *History and Biography*." Useful, the hallmark of a civilized man, historical study had wide appeal. "Man without learninge, and the remembrance of things past," wrote Sir William Dugdale, "falls into a beastlye sottishnesse and his life is noe better to be accounted for than to be buryed alive."[10]

Colonial judgment settled firmly upon the value of history. "Good History," claimed Benjamin Franklin, could "fix in the Minds of Youth deep Impressions of the Beauty and Usefulness of Virtue of all kinds." History showed the "Advantages of Liberty, Mischiefs of Licentiousness, Benefits arising from the good laws and a due Execution of Justice." John Adams expressed the same thought when he pronounced "a comprehensive Knowledge of Law and History necessary for an American Statesman." Thomas Jefferson throughout his

9. John Locke, *Some Thoughts Concerning Education*, ed. R. H. Quick (Cambridge, 1892), 159, 161; David Hume, *The History of England . . .* , 6 vols. (London, 1754–62), V, 471; Bonamy Dobrée, ed., *The Letters of Philip Dormer Stanhope, 4th Earl of Chesterfield*, 6 vols. (London, 1932), VI, 2630.

10. John Toland, ed., *The Oceana of James Harrington, and His Other Works* (London, 1700), 183; James Burgh, *Political Disquisitions . . .* , 3 vols. (London, 1774–75), I, vi, and *Thoughts on Education . . .* (Boston, 1749), 15; William Hamper, *The Life, Diary, and Correspondence of Sir William Dugdale . . .* (London, 1827), plate III.

life found "a knoledge of British history . . . useful to the American politician."[11]

To understand the peculiarities of the colonists' historical vision, one should recall that history in eighteenth-century England was not only subject to the vagaries of intellectual vogue but was also under heavy political pressures. Two principal views of English history had developed: one, usually the more accurate by the standards of modern scholars, can be called the tory interpretation—although not in any party sense; the other is reasonably familiar as the whig interpretation, although it too existed long before a formal Whig party and continued long after whig politicians opportunistically lost interest in it. The historical whigs were writers seeking to support Parliamentary claims upon the royal prerogatives by exalting the antiquity of Parliament and by asserting that their political ambitions had solid foundation in ancient customs. They presented an idealized version of an Anglo-Saxon democracy, which they usually found overturned by Norman treachery and feudalism. The tory historians preferred instead to see no ancient source for the Parliamentary claims and viewed Anglo-Saxon England as feudalistic, but lacking in Norman stability and order.[12]

---

11. *Proposals Relating to the Education of Youth in Pensilvania* (Philadelphia, 1749), in Leonard W. Labaree, Whitfield J. Bell, Jr. et al., eds., *The Papers of Benjamin Franklin* (New Haven, 1960–), III, 412; John Adams to James Warren, July 17, 1774, Worthington C. Ford, ed., *Warren-Adams Letters*, 2 vols. (Massachusetts Historical Society, *Collections*, 72–73 [1917–25], I, 29; Jefferson to John Norvell, June 11, 1807, Paul Leicester Ford, ed., *The Writings of Thomas Jefferson*, 10 vols. (N.Y., 1892–99), IX, 72.

12. The best short study of the development of whig history (and the tory response) is found in Herbert Butterfield, *The Englishman and His History* (Cambridge, Eng., 1944); more recent and more specialized is J. G. A. Pocock's *The Ancient Constitution and the Feudal Law; A Study of English Historical Thought in the Seventeenth Century* (Cambridge, Eng., 1957), and David Douglas, *English Scholars* (London, 1939) has a brilliant sequel in his *The Norman Conquest and British Historians* (Glasgow, 1946). Also recent, and much indebted to Pocock, is F. Smith Fussner, *The Historical Revolution: English Historical Writing and Thought, 1580–1640* (N.Y. and London, 1962). Caroline Robbins, *The Eighteenth-Century Commonwealthman: Studies in the Transmission, Development and Circumstance of English Liberal Thought from the Restoration of Charles II until the War with the Thirteen Colo-*

In the years of intensive and intensifying political debate preceding the American Revolution, Americans converted the arguments of whiggish historians into intellectual weapons, constantly finding resemblances between historical accounts and contemporary criticism of English society, then applying historical generalizations to the context of American debate over imperial relations.

The origins of whig history invoked by American colonists are obscure, but certainly it began during the reigns of the Tudors. In the sixteenth century Tudor monarchs presided over the rise of the English middle class, which then developed an interest in antiquarian research. This research, conducted under severe handicaps, led to a rediscovery of the feudal limitations on royal power, limitations which took on a new political significance during the seventeenth-century conflicts with the Stuart kings.[13] The Society of Antiquaries (founded in the reign of Elizabeth I and abolished by James I) attempted to discover the antiquity of Parliament. In 1571 the *Modus Tenendi Parliamentum* appeared, purporting to describe Parliament as it existed in the time of Edward the Confessor and encouraging a belief in the pre-Norman existence of the House of Commons. Seventeenth-century whig writers discovered in Tacitus, author of the famed *Germania,* a useful source for contentions that the Saxon *witan* was the original of Parliaments. Tacitus had described how the Saxons chose their kings and generals, how they restricted the authority of those they set up to rule, how frequent assemblies were held for discussion of tribal affairs. "About matters of higher consequence," Tacitus wrote, "the whole nation deliberates," and at regular intervals there were conventions in which the people drafted their own laws.[14] Tacitus contributed to the popular notion of a golden age of political liberty in the past—ancient laws and customs were the best. Liberty did not have to be created; it only needed to be restored.

nies (Cambridge, Mass., 1959), is the pathfinding study of the thought and philosophy of Real Whig writers active between 1660 and 1776.

13. Butterfield, *Englishman and His History,* 9–10.

14. Thomas Gordon, trans., *The Works of Tacitus,* 2 vols. (London, 1728), II, 328–32.

For the whig historians the nemesis of Saxon liberties was feudalism, generally held to have been introduced into England by William "the accursed Norman" in 1066. Hence the idea of a "Norman Yoke." The Conquest deprived Englishmen of their liberty, established the tyranny of an alien king and landlords, and replaced the Saxon militia of Alfred's time with the odious form of holding land of the King in return for military service.[15] The scholar who probably contributed most to English — and colonial — awareness of feudalism was Sir Henry Spelman; at least his books were the oft-quoted bases for subsequent studies on the subject. No whig in the general political sense, Spelman made discoveries highly susceptible to whig employment. Convinced that the Norman Conquest had brought feudalism into England, he believed pre-Norman land tenure had been generally "according to the ancient manner of the Germans."[16]

Contributors to whig historiography came to view Magna Charta as a major chapter in the restoration of English liberties. Here Sir Edward Coke made a significant contribution: in Herbert Butterfield's view, Coke "more than anybody else translated medieval limitations upon the monarchy into seventeenth-century terms . . . his anachronistic sins became a service to the cause of liberty."[17] In his *Second Institutes* Coke presented Magna Charta as an affirmation, not of feudal but of common law; and "the Common Law of England had been time out of mind before the Conquest."[18] Coke's admiration for common law led him to develop the doctrine of an ancient or fundamental constitution which predated Normans and Saxons and owed its being to no man.

15. Christopher Hill, "The Norman Yoke," in *Democracy and the Labour Movement; Essays in Honour of Dona Torr*, ed. John Saville (London, 1954), 11.

16. Edmund Gibson, ed., *The English Works of Sir Henry Spelman* . . . , 2 pts. (London, 1723), pt. II, 57, 5.

17. Butterfield, *Englishman and His History*, 54.

18. Sir Edward Coke, *The Second Part of the Institutes of the Laws of England* . . . (London, 1662), "Proeme"; Coke, *The Reports of Sir Edward Coke, Kt., in English* . . . , 7 vols. (London, 1738), IV, Pt. VIII, Preface. Jefferson owned this edition of the *Reports;* his copies survive in the Rare Book Room, Library of Congress; they are, however, uncatalogued.

Concepts such as these proved enormously useful in the hands of Parliament-men against James I and Charles I. The Restoration of the Stuarts in 1660 brought fresh investigations into the antiquity of Parliament and English liberties from such writers as William Petyt (*The Antient Right of the Commons of England Asserted,* 1680) and William Atwood (*Ius Anglorum ab Antiqua,* 1681). With political success in 1688 came further volumes of historical justification. The constitution was now restored to its original principles, or so some whig historians would have it.

But historical contemplation had become a mainspring of political action. Englishmen in the eighteenth century persisted in this instinctive turning to the past for both an explanation and a solution to present problems. The whig interpretation did not die but took on a new life in the hands of critics who denounced the limitations of the Glorious Revolution and the Hanoverian succession. A group of historical writers, identified by Caroline Robbins as eighteenth-century "Commonwealthmen," sought to maintain the revolutionary tradition of their seventeenth-century heroes, and in an endless stream of essays and histories (vastly more popular in America than in England) they kept fresh the memory and the political techniques of the crusades against the Stuarts. Rarely successful in practical politics, they denounced the whigs in power and regarded themselves as the Real Whigs in the tradition of the martyred Algernon Sidney, condemned as a traitor under Charles II for his unpublished "Discourses on Government," which fixed sole power in Parliament and the people. Men such as Sir Robert Molesworth, Thomas Gordon (the translator of Tacitus), Walter Moyle, and John Trenchard, propagators of the new whig interpretation, formed the bridge between whig writers in the Stuart reigns and such "radical" reformers of the American Revolutionary era as James Burgh, Catherine Macaulay, and John Cartwright.[19] For them all the past was a storehouse, not of

19. Caroline Robbins, *The Eighteenth-Century Commonwealthman,* 3–21.

mere example, but of authoritative precedents. This was the heritage of the eighteenth-century American colonist, raised and educated to think of himself as an Englishman, and eager to learn his history.

II

Books were the high road to history, providing the means to the "comprehensive Knowledge of Law and History" sought by John Adams and his fellow Americans. "How can I judge," asked Adams of his diary in 1761, "how can any man judge, unless his mind has been opened and enlarged by reading?"[20] Reading, which made Lord Bacon's full man, could also make the informed man, the history-conscious man, the American colonist firm in his view of his generation's relationship to the long past, its place in the vivid present and the bright future.

Books were available, books of history ancient and modern, sacred and profane. Would-be American statesmen could find them in bookshops and printers' shops, they could form their own libraries, they could read them in the "public" libraries of subscription companies, in towns large and small. History, particularly English whig history, was ready, on the shelves. In all of the lists of books there was a hard core of titles which served as common denominators and the solid majority of these volumes were either historical or political: often they were both. The more history a colonist read the more whigs he inevitably encountered, not only because of their weight or numbers but also because of their popularity and productivity.

Exposure to an academic library meant an early exposure to English history. Each of the nine colleges in colonial America had its library. Harvard College published library catalogues in which the number of secular historical volumes steadily increased as the eighteenth century advanced. The initial Harvard catalogue, issued in

20. John Adams, Diary, Aug. 1, 1761, Adams, *Works,* II, 131.

1723, included such standard seventeenth-century historical sources as John Rushworth's *Historical Collections,* and subsequent lists added Gilbert Burnet's popular *History of His Own Time* and equally important whig works by Paul Rapin-Thoyras and James Tyrrell. Like many college collections, Harvard's suffered from fire, but it was speedily restocked with the help of the strenuous English whig Thomas Hollis. A student at Harvard on the eve of the Revolution found numerous whig authors represented: Thomas Gordon, author of the *Independent Whig* and *Cato's Letters;* Robert Molesworth, whose *Account of Denmark* revealed the nature of absolutism and portrayed liberty as "the greatest natural blessing mankind is capable of enjoying"; Edmund Ludlow (the regicide), whose *Memoirs* were an arsenal of arguments for republicanism and against standing armies; William Molyneux (friend to Locke), author of *The Case of Ireland,* which not only argued that Ireland was independent of the English Parliament but also elaborated a theory of natural inherent rights of men; and Catherine Macaulay, the anti-Stuart historian.[21]

Harvard's collections were larger than those of any other colonial college, but not larger in the proportionate share given to history. Yale's first library catalogue, 1743, listed many of the same history books; but where history had been at best a minor but interesting part of Harvard's holdings, in Yale's library history comprised the largest single category and continued to do so through successive catalogues.[22] The College of New Jersey's library was small, but again history was handsomely represented; and in 1755 when Governor Jonathan Belcher donated his library to the College, historical works

21. For a review of early college libraries, see Louis Shores, *Origins of the American College Library, 1638–1800* (N.Y., 1934); for more light on Hollis, see Caroline Robbins, "The Strenuous Whig, Thomas Hollis of Lincoln's Inn," *William and Mary Quarterly,* 3d ser., 7 (1950): 406–53; and also her "Library of Liberty—Assembled for Harvard College by Thomas Hollis of Lincoln's Inn," *Harvard Library Bulletin* 5 (1951): 5–23, 181–96. See Appendix II for a listing of Harvard's historical holdings.

22. Yale issued library catalogues in 1743 and 1755; see Appendix II for listing of historical works.

of Burnet, Rapin, Ludlow, and Sidney and both Gordon's *Tacitus* and *Cato's Letters* were added. When fire caused destruction at Princeton, President John Witherspoon donated his personal collection including replacements for the burned volumes of Burnet, Vertot (the historian of revolutions), and Potter (*Antiquities of Greece*), and adding two editions of Tacitus for good measure.[23] Rhode Island College, founded in 1764, issued a catalogue in 1782 which listed the familiar works of Mrs. Macaulay, Bishop Burnet, William Robertson (*History of Scotland*), and Lord Clarendon (*History of the Rebellion*). Fire destroyed the library of the College of William and Mary in 1705 and again during the Revolution; no catalogues were published by either King's College in New York or the College of Philadelphia.[24]

Private libraries collected by the colonists were also full of history books, many of them the latest scholarship from Britain; but since books were expensive, private collections in the early eighteenth century were modest. In Virginia Richard Henry Lee II left his son Thomas a library of three hundred titles; the merchant Thomas Gadsden in South Carolina had one hundred and thirty-five volumes;[25] Thomas Jefferson's father, Colonel Peter Jefferson, willed him forty volumes. As the century advanced private libraries grew. Thomas Jefferson constantly added to his meager literary legacy, becoming one of the most important colonial collectors: at one point his library contained some thirty-two hundred titles comprising about six thousand volumes. Franklin's collection was inventoried at forty-two hundred volumes, and the industrious John Adams col-

23. See Julian P. Boyd's edition of the 1760 *Catalogue* of the College of New Jersey (Woodbridge, N.J., 1949).

24. See Appendix II for listing of historical works in the Rhode Island College catalogue of 1782.

25. Louis B. Wright has surveyed the southern scene in quest of colonial reading tastes. See his *First Gentlemen of Virginia: Intellectual Qualities of the Early Colonial Ruling Class* (San Marino, 1940); "The Purposeful Reading of Our Colonial Ancestors," *ELH: A Journal of English Literary History* 4 (1937): 85–111, and "The 'Gentleman's Library' in Early Virginia," *Huntington Library Quarterly* 1 (1938): 3–61.

lected forty-eight hundred. George Washington thought enough of his library by 1771 to order "a Plate with my Arms engraved and 4 or 500 copies struck." Robert Carter of "Nomini Hall" had some fifteen hundred volumes by the eve of the Revolution; John Mercer's library at "Marlborough" was large enough constantly to attract his younger friend and protégé George Mason. Even less wealthy colonists aspired to a literary estate of sorts: Joseph Smith was a Baltimore County ironmaster; when he died in 1770, his property was worth only £4 but it contained the first volume of Rapin's *History of England,* along with clothes, a pen knife, two razors, and an ink pot.[26]

The size of the library mattered less, perhaps, than the industry of the owner. William Byrd made assiduous use of his fine collection of thirty-five hundred volumes at "Westover," and besides, continually lent his books to interested neighbors.[27] Jefferson loved his carefully chosen books; they were his windows on the world of the past, present, and future. He could not "live without books," he confided to John Adams when both bibliophiles were in their great age. Neither fire nor finance kept him from such "pursuit of happiness." Books were for Jefferson "a necessity of life." Even after parting with

26. Dumas Malone, *Jefferson the Virginian* (Boston, 1948), 32; William H. Peden, Thomas Jefferson: Book Collector (Ph.D. diss., University of Virginia, 1942); George Simpson Eddy, "Dr. Benjamin Franklin's Library," American Antiquarian Society, *Proceedings* 34 (1924): 208; Lindsay Swift, "The John Adams Library," Colonial Society of Massachusetts, *Transactions* 19 (1918), 267–69; *Catalogue of the John Adams Library in the Public Library of the City of Boston* (Boston, 1917); John Adams Manuscript catalogue, 1790, in the Adams Papers, reel 193, microfilm; George Washington to Robert Adam, Nov. 22, 1771, John C. Fitzpatrick, ed., *The Writings of George Washington,* 39 vols. (Washington, D.C., 1931–44), II, 77; Louis Morton, *Robert Carter of Nomini Hall . . .* (Williamsburg, Va., 1941), 215–16; Kate Mason Rowland, *The Life of George Mason, 1725–1792,* 2 vols. (N.Y., 1892), I, chap. 2; George K. Smart, "Private Libraries in Colonial Virginia," *American Literature* 10 (1938): 24–52; Joseph T. Wheeler, "Books Owned by Marylanders, 1700–1776," *Maryland Historical Magazine* 35 (1940): 339.

27. The manuscript catalogue of the Byrd Library reposes in the Library Company of Philadelphia; for just how scattered Byrd's books finally became, see Edwin Wolf 2nd, "The Dispersal of the Library of William Byrd of Westover," American Antiquarian Society, *Proceedings* 68 (1958): 19–106.

his great library in 1815 ("the best collection of its size probably in America") he found time and energy to collect another nine hundred volumes before his death eleven years later. He also took time to suggest a thirty-one-hundred-title library for his University of Virginia, so that students in Charlottesville also could look out the right windows.[28]

Most of the Revolutionary leaders shared what Jefferson called his "malady of Bibliomania."[29] John Adams tried to be financially careful as befitted a good Yankee, but when he was forty he ruefully confessed to his wife, Abigail: "I have been imprudent, I have spent an estate in books." The habit never left him; his purchases and his reading continued throughout his life; even in his eighty-second year he modestly recounted the forty-three books read during the previous twelve months.[30] John Dickinson, moderately wealthy, did not worry so much about his expenditures; he also had the advantage of inheriting the fine library of his father-in-law, Isaac Norris, Jr. His love for reading was constantly his refuge from the world: as a student he reported breathlessly how "I fly to Books, to retirement, to Labour, and every Moment is an Age, till I am immersed in Study."[31] As a

28. Jefferson to John Adams, June 10, 1815, Lester J. Cappon, ed., *The Adams-Jefferson Letters: The Complete Correspondence Between Thomas Jefferson and Abigail and John Adams,* 2 vols. (Chapel Hill, 1959), II, 443; Jefferson to Richard Rush, June 22, 1819, Ford, ed., *Writings of Jefferson,* X, 133; William H. Peden, ed., *1828 Catalogue of the Library of the University of Virginia* (Charlottesville, Va., 1945).

29. Jefferson to Lucy Ludwell Paradise, June 1, 1789, Julian P. Boyd et al., eds., *The Papers of Thomas Jefferson* (Princeton, 1950–), XV, 163.

30. John Adams to Abigail Adams, June 29, 1774, Charles Francis Adams, ed., *Familiar Letters of John Adams and his Wife Abigail, during the Revolution* (Boston, 1875), I, 4; Jefferson to John Adams, Jan. 11, 1817, Cappon, ed., *Adams-Jefferson Letters,* II, 505.

31. John Dickinson to his father, Mar. 8, 1754, H. Trevor Colbourn, ed., "A Pennsylvania Farmer at the Court of King George: John Dickinson's London Letters, 1754-1756," *Pennsylvania Magazine of History and Biography* 86 (1962): 257. For more on the library of Isaac Norris, Jr., see James W. Phillips, "The Sources of the Original Dickinson College Library," *Pennsylvania History* 14 (1947): 110–13. There is in the Historical Society of Pennsylvania a manuscript list of books ordered by Norris for the use of the Pennsylvania assembly (Mar. 16, 1752), which included such items as Petyt's *The Ancient Right of the Commons,* and Thornhagh Gurdon's *History of the High Court of Parliament.*

mature man, he began his most famous work with the observation, "I spend a good deal of [my time] . . . in a library, which I think the most valuable part of my small estate."[32] One of the major penalties paid by William Hooper of North Carolina for his Revolutionary role was the British military spoliation of his books. "My library, except as to law books, is shamefully injured and above 100 valuable volumes taken away," Hooper complained bitterly. This was bad enough, but "what vexes me most of all is that they [the British] have broken several sets of books . . . [so] as to make what remains useless lumber."[33]

Books mattered to the eighteenth-century colonist. Frequently the owner wrote extensive marginal comments—Franklin did, and Dickinson, and Adams, and Jefferson. Sometimes a reader exerted himself to secure an American imprint to make a book more widely available. Jefferson did so in several instances. Sometimes a colonial reader would painstakingly transcribe selections into commonplace books or notebooks; Jefferson, Dickinson, and Mayhew filled wallpaper folios or tiny duodecimes with notes. As authors some colonists would divulge their private reading in lengthy footnotes or references in the text, to both dignify and illustrate their political argument. Dickinson piled citation on citation in his polemical pamphlets. Finally, colonists discussed with their correspondents their hopes and fears, their claims and arguments, commenting on the sources as they proceeded.

If academic and private libraries indicate the intellectual environment of the Revolutionary generation, there is a third source of importance—the eighteenth-century social or subscription library. Franklin inspired such a library for his adopted city of Philadelphia. His and other social libraries show not only the reading opportuni-

32. John Dickinson, *Letters from a Farmer . . . ,* in P. L. Ford, ed., *The Writings of John Dickinson* (Philadelphia, 1895), 307. Ordinarily one would discount such a comment in political propaganda, but it fits perfectly with Dickinson's private disposition, and also shows his anxiety to demonstrate that his opinions are well informed.

33. William Hooper to James Iredell, Feb. 17, 1782, Griffith J. McRee, ed., *The Life and Correspondence of James Iredell . . . ,* 2 vols. (N.Y., 1857–58), II, 5.

ties available to citizens of modest means, but insofar as the members determined contents, these libraries give further indications of colonial reading interests. Franklin's Library Company, founded in 1731, enjoyed remarkable success and issued frequent catalogues to keep pace with its growth. Within ten years of its founding, the Company issued a catalogue with some three hundred and seventy-five titles, in which history proved the largest grouping by far—one hundred and fourteen titles, as compared with sixty-nine for literature. On the eve of the Stamp Act crisis in 1765 the Company ordered numerous additional volumes, including Henry Care's popular *English Liberties,* Walter Moyle's *Tracts* on Greek and Roman commonwealths, and Edward Montagu's *Rise and Fall of Antient Republicks,* all contributors to whig history. On the eve of Independence the Company acquired Obadiah Hulme's famous appeal to Saxon liberties, the *Historical Essay on the English Constitution,* suitably supported by Francis Sullivan's slightly more sober *Lectures on the Feudal Law.* By 1775 the Library Company of Philadelphia had some eight thousand titles on its shelves, the vast majority of which continued to be historical.[34]

"Franklin's Library" was a democratic institution: it served all categories of Philadelphians. A contemporary observer reported astonishment "at the general taste for books prevailing with all ranks of the citizens," adding that the librarian "assured me, that for one person of distinction and fortune, there were twenty tradesmen that frequented this library."[35] A letter in Franklin's *Pennsylvania Gazette* developed the theme: "I am but a poor ordinary Mechanick of this

---

34. Edwin Wolf 2nd, "Franklin and His Friends Choose Their Books," *Pennsylvania Magazine of History and Biography* 80 (1956): 14; Franklin's own account of his Library, in Labaree and Bell, eds., *Franklin Papers, III,* 308–9; Wolf, "The First Books and Printed Catalogues of the Library Company of Philadelphia," *Pennsylvania Magazine of History and Biography* 78 (1954): 1–26; "A Book of Minutes . . . of the Library Company of Philadelphia," I, 214, in MS, Library Company of Philadelphia. See also E. V. Lamberton, "Colonial Libraries of Pennsylvania," *Pennsylvania Magazine of History and Biography* 42 (1918): 193–234.

35. Austin K. Gray, *Benjamin Franklin's Library . . .* (N.Y., 1937), 20.

city, obliged to work hard for the maintenance of myself, my wife, and several small children," announced the writer, and "when my daily labour is over, instead of going to the Alehouse, I amuse myself with the books of the Library Company, of which I am an unworthy member."[36] Since a membership cost "upwards of TWENTY ONE POUNDS" by 1768, the number of poor "mechanicks" drinking in the intoxicating drafts of literary fare can be questioned. But as a contributor to the American intellectual scene, the Library Company was probably without peer. Not only did its membership supply ten signers of the Declaration of Independence, but the Library served as the reference collection for the Pennsylvania Assembly and the Continental Congress.[37]

By 1776 there were more than sixty subscription libraries, but the success of the Philadelphia Library Company has overshadowed the activities of these other institutions. As early as 1737 a catalogue had appeared for the joint library of Saybrook, Lyme, and Guilford in Connecticut, which included the works of Burnet, Vertot, and Rapin. In Newport, Rhode Island, the Quaker merchant Abraham Redwood launched the library named after him, which issued an impressive first catalogue in 1750. Providence, close behind Newport, issued a catalogue in 1768 which disclosed large quantities of whig history. New York established its Library Society in 1754 and published a plump catalogue the next year. This latter collection grew steadily. Although New York's holdings never rivaled those of Philadelphia's Library Company, the destruction during the Revolution of the Society's three thousand volumes—"exterminated by the atrocious vandalism of the British troops"—aroused understandable bitterness.

Smaller towns endorsed Franklin's subscription system for secur-

36. Quoted in Edwin Wolf 2nd, ed., *A Catalogue of Books Belonging to the Library Company* (Philadelphia, 1956), iii.

37. It was into "the library-room" in Carpenter's Hall that George Washington darted upon hearing his nomination as Commander in Chief, according to the report of John Adams. See Diary, Sept. 5, 1774, Adams, *Works,* II, 365.

ing books. Burlington, New Jersey, established a library in 1758 and provided residents access to Sidney, *Cato's Letters,* and the curious but popular *Britain's Remembrancer* of James Burgh. Lancaster, Pennsylvania, founded its Juliana Library Company in 1766, diplomatically dedicating its whiggish catalogue of that year to Lady Juliana Penn.[38]

Probably the most impressive of the libraries south of Philadelphia was that established by seventeen citizens of Charleston, South Carolina, in 1748: within two years the Charleston Society grew to one hundred and thirty subscribers and published a catalogue with such familiar authors as Burnet, Rapin, Potter, Atkyn, Petyt, Gordon, and Vertot. Gifts followed, and the Society's 1770 catalogue showed addition of Rushworth's *Collections* and such historical works as William Blackstone's *Commentaries,* Bolingbroke's *Letters on the Study and Use of History,* Squire's whig *Enquiry into the Constitution,* Dalrymple's *Feudal Property,* and Mrs. Macaulay's *History of England.* When Josiah Quincy visited the Charleston Society's library in 1773, he found a "large collection of very valuable books," and by the time the library was destroyed by fire in 1778, it had grown to six or seven thousand volumes. Today only the catalogues survive to show the remarkable reading opportunities afforded Revolutionary South Carolinians.[39]

38. See Appendix II for the historical works in the Connecticut library, the Redwood Library in 1750, the Providence Library in 1768, the New York Society Library in 1754, the Burlington Library in 1758, and the Juliana Library Company in 1766. For an account of the library societies, see C. Seymour Thompson, *Evolution of the American Public Library, 1653–1876* (Washington, D.C., 1952). See also Carl Bridenbaugh, *Cities in Revolt: Urban Life in America, 1743–1776* (N.Y., 1955), 384–85; Austin B. Keep, *The History of the New York Society Library* . . . (N.Y., 1908), 119–20.

39. Frederick P. Bowes, *The Culture of Early Charleston* (Chapel Hill, 1942), 124–25; M. A. DeWolfe Howe, ed., "Journal of Josiah Quincy, Junior, 1773, Mar. 9, 1773," Massachusetts Historical Society, *Proceedings* 49 (1916): 447; see Appendix II for listing of historical works catalogued in the Charleston Library in 1750. It might be noted that the success of the social library probably came at the expense of commercial circulating libraries; William Rind in Maryland advertised an initial listing of 150 titles, including the customary items of Rapin, Robertson, and Hume; Rind lacked capital, could not increase his stock, and failed. In Boston John Mein stocked equally familiar works— those of Burnet, Ludlow, Vertot—but failed because he gave political offense to John Hancock; Mein is credited with popularizing fiction in Boston, but his 1765 catalogue suggests at least an equal devotion to history. See Charles A. Barker, *The Background to*

Besides the subscription, private, and academic libraries, another important indicator of historical tastes of the eighteenth-century colonist was, naturally enough, the American book trade. Booksellers used all avenues to their object of profit. They resorted to broadsides, liberally distributed catalogues, sale notices, and auctions, which grew increasingly popular. The adventure of bidding stimulated sales by appealing to the hope of a bargain. According to the *Union List* compiled by George L. McKay, fewer than a hundred book auctions took place in the colonial period, but of these, fifty occurred in the quarter-century preceding the Revolution.[40]

Records of the colonial bookdealer and publisher—roles often combined in one person—furnish an abundance of information on readers' habits. Auctioneers listed their merchandise in order of anticipated interest, and history headed the procession. "A very large and valuable collection of books in history, divinity, law, and physic" ran one typical advertisement in the *Maryland Gazette* in 1773. In Philadelphia the sequence was "history, divinity, and miscellaneous literary entertainment."[41] This last advertisement was one of scores run by the energetic and enterprising Robert Bell, who was enamoured with the auction as a means of moving his stock. An astute businessman, he preferred profit before politics. Since he would import or publish whatever he thought would sell, his lists serve as a yardstick for the political interests of his customers; history and law books were his best sellers.[42]

---

the *Revolution in Maryland* (New Haven and London, 1940), 64–66; Bridenbaugh, *Cities in Revolt*, 382; Charles L. Bolton, "Circulating Libraries in Boston, 1765–1865," Colonial Society of Massachusetts, *Transactions* 11 (1910): 196–207. For the historical contents of Mein's 1765 catalogue, see Appendix II.

40. George L. McKay, ed., *American Book Auction Catalogues, 1713–1934: A Union List* (N.Y., 1937).

41. *Maryland Gazette* (Annapolis), July 20, 1775; *Pennsylvania Gazette* (Philadelphia), Sept. 22, 1773. See also, for example, *Connecticut Courant* (Hartford), July 13, 1773; *Pennsylvania Packet* (Philadelphia), Oct. 28, 1771; *Newport [R.I.] Mercury*, Sept. 7, 1772.

42. A useful review of Bell's career is A. Everett Peterson, "Bell, Robert," *Dictionary of American Biography*; see also Bridenbaugh, *Cities in Revolt*, 381–87.

Bell may have improved on the colonial book auction, but he had competition in more conventional operations. Here, too, the successful dealers were those who took the colonial political pulse and stocked accordingly. Some found political demands too great: William Aikman, a Scot who settled in Annapolis in 1773, decided that the colonial drift toward revolution was altogether distasteful. Since this judgment coincided with a miscalculation of the market, he decided to beat a retreat to Jamaica in 1775.[43] Henry Knox was not so troubled and did well with the bookstore in Boston from 1771 until the war attracted him to a military career. In 1773 he published a long *Catalogue of Books Imported and to be sold,* which indicates his judgment of the reading tastes of Bostonians. Equally active in Boston were Joseph Greenleaf and Edes and Gill, the latter publishers of the *Boston-Gazette.* To the south was Hezekiah Merrill, the Hartford bookman who advertised in the *Connecticut Courant;* and in New York lists were published by such dealers as Garrat Noel, Ebenezer Hazard, John Donaldson, Samuel London, and James Rivington.[44] Rivington, publisher of the *New-York Gazetteer,* had reputed Tory sympathies which cost him his press in 1775, but he handled whig publications, including large quantities of history books.[45]

Philadelphia, a hive of bookmen, had more dealers than any other city. Sale lists of William Bradford, Robert McGill, and David Hall disclose their emphasis upon historical publications.[46] And this pattern extended to the south, from Annapolis to Williamsburg, from Williamsburg to Charleston. Dixon and Hunter's *Virginia Gazette*

43. Wheeler, "Booksellers and Circulating Libraries in Colonial Maryland," *Maryland Historical Magazine* 42 (1939): 117.

44. "Henry Knox and the London Book-Store in Boston, 1771–1774," Massachusetts Historical Society, *Proceedings* 61 (1928): 225–304. For a review of his 1773 catalogue and the other dealers' lists, see Appendix II.

45. There is an excellent account of James Rivington's checkered journalistic career in Schlesinger, *Prelude to Independence.* See Appendix II for selections of Rivington's sale lists.

46. The David Hall Letterbooks in the American Philosophical Society are particularly illuminating. See Appendix II.

office doubled as a bookstore,[47] and in South Carolina at least three booksellers advertised stocks of "choice and useful books," most "lately imported from London."[48]

Almost all of the stock was imported, for English publishers could advance books, thus furnishing capital, and there was less risk in importing quantities of books of known reputation. Yet there was less profit in this safe sort of business enterprise, and judicious local publishing could improve both reputation and income. Despite shortages of paper and ink, colonial book printing in the eighteenth century increased. The bulk of American imprints was given over to inexpensive pamphlets, sermons, and almanacs, none of which demanded risk or investment. But as Lawrence C. Wroth observed, "there is no greater mistake possible than for the student of literature to assume that this production of the native press is beneath his notice." By the mid-eighteenth century there were twenty-four presses in ten of the colonies,[49] which produced over thirty-six hundred titles between 1743 and 1760, mainly in the population centers of Boston, Philadelphia, and New York.[50]

Large publishing projects were undertaken with caution, frequently on a subscription basis. The result was the issuance of books expected to be sure-sellers. The availability of reprinted English historical studies assumes importance in this setting. For example, although there were several English editions of Henry Care's *English Liberties* available in America, the book underwent an American edition by James Franklin in Boston in 1721, and another by John Carter in Providence in 1774. Much the same treatment was accorded such works as *The Independent Whig,* which enjoyed Philadelphia editions in 1724 and 1740, and Rapin's *Dissertation on the Rise . . . of the Whigs and Tories,* reissued in Boston in 1773.

47. Jefferson was among the book-buying customers of Dixon and Hunter; see Marie Kimball, *Jefferson: The Road to Glory, 1743 to 1776* (N.Y., 1943), 102.

48. These are listed in Appendix II.

49. Lawrence C. Wroth, *An American Bookshelf, 1755* (Philadelphia, 1934), 4.

50. Bridenbaugh, *Cities in Revolt,* 183.

The energetic Robert Bell was active in the reprint trade. He brought out Blackstone's massive *Commentaries* on a subscription basis between 1771 and 1772; his success can be measured by twenty-two pages of subscribers listed in the fourth volume. He was also successful with William Robertson's *History of the Reign of Charles V*, and followed it with the *Political Disquisitions* of James Burgh. Bell's performance with Burgh is the more remarkable when it is recalled that the *Disquisitions* were published first in London in 1774–75, and Bell's Philadelphia edition appeared in 1775 — with most of the Continental Congress subscribing. "His Excellency, George Washington, Esq.; Generalissimo of all the Forces in America," headed the list, which included Thomas Jefferson, John Adams, John Dickinson, James Wilson, Christopher Gadsden, and Roger Sherman among others. Adams commented, somewhat unnecessarily, that he and his colleagues held Burgh in "high estimation," and he vowed that he would help "make the Disquisitions more known and attended to in several parts of America."[51] Bell was unable to secure support for an American imprint of Hume's pro-Stuart *History of England,* but made up for this misjudgment with an edition of John Cartwright's whiggish pamphlet *American Independence the Interest and Glory of Great Britain* in 1776.

Probably the most successful of English works reprinted in America was the *Chronicle of the Kings of England,* a curious Biblical parody. First reprinted in Newport, Rhode Island, in 1744, then in Boston in 1759, the *Chronicle* enjoyed two American editions on the eve of the Revolution. The last was brought out by Robert Bell (in association with Benjamin Towne) in 1774.[52]

---

51. John Adams to James Burgh, Dec. 28, 1774, Adams, *Works,* IX, 351.

52. Robert Dodsley may have been the author of the *Chronicle,* but no author was ever named in colonial listings until 1791, when Benjamin Franklin was erroneously given credit for the work. [Questions about the authorship of the *Chronicle* appear to have been resolved by Harry Solomon, *The Rise of Robert Dodsley* (Carbondale: Southern Illinois University Press, 1996) — T. C., 1997.]

III

The eighteenth-century colonist did not lack opportunity for satisfying his literary appetite. If he went to college, he could read in the academic library. If he wished to extend his literary horizon beyond the capacities of personal collection, there was usually a library society nearby, or a generous colleague who would lend a volume. But for the typical educated colonist, buying books was as natural as reading them. The colonial book trade made a variety of books available. No reading colonist could long remain in ignorance of the new publications, since larger book dealers advertised in newspapers even outside their native colony.

History was the main field of interest. If law is associated with history—and the colonists so regarded it—history emerges as the largest single category. This was as true of the college library as of the subscription library, of the personal collection of a Jefferson or a Dickinson as of the advertised stocks of a Bell or a Knox. Americans were reading large amounts of history. The catalogues of all kinds of collections prove it. "These libraries," Franklin later observed, "have improved the general conversation of Americans, made the common tradesmen and farmers as intelligent as most gentlemen from other countries and perhaps have contributed in some degree to the stand as generally made throughout the colonies in defence of their privileges."[53]

53. Benjamin Franklin, Autobiography, Albert H. Smyth, ed., *The Writings of Benjamin Franklin,* 10 vols. (N.Y., 1905–7), I, 312.

CHAPTER II

The Colonial Perspective:
Ancient and Medieval

Truth is the eye of history." Polybius said it, Jefferson read it in the two separate editions of Polybius he owned, and American readers studied it in four recent printings of Polybius's *General History.*[1] Citizens of the greatest, the latest of empires, Americans opened Polybius for information about earlier empires—how they rose, how they flourished, how they fell. Polybius, the stiff, earnest moralist, so determined to find the truth, so beguiled with detail, with fact, with simple preachments of virtue, made an irresistible appeal to colonial readers. There was conviction in him, in his details, in his facts.

American readers knew that history was more than an idle tale for winter nights. Their history reading was purposeful, part of their quest for a usable past as a guide to the present and the future. "Before the establishment of the American states," Jefferson wrote to John Adams in retrospect, "nothing was known to History but the Man of the Old World."[2] This Man of the Old World was the pred-

---

1. James Hampton, ed., *The General History of Polybius . . . ,* 3d ed., 2 vols. (London, 1772–73; 1st ed., 1756–61), I, 47. Jefferson owned the 1763–64 Ernesti edition, in Latin, which he had conflated with the third edition of Hampton's English translation, 1762–63, thus creating a unique 8-volume set. See E. Millicent Sowerby, ed., *Catalogue of the Library of Thomas Jefferson,* 5 vols. (Washington, D.C., 1952–59), I, 25.

2. Jefferson to John Adams, Oct. 28, 1813, Cappon, ed., *Adams-Jefferson Letters,* II, 391.

ecessor of the American, the ancestor of the Man of the New; and his history, from ancient times on, should be enlightening for those who searched the past for present purposes.

Americans educated in the eighteenth century early acquired a familiarity with the classics, with civilizations and empires which had produced Greek and Latin literature. Classical allusions, metaphors, and similes peppered their writing and oratory; few were the events in the ancient past with which the American Revolutionary generation was unfamiliar. And yet, in spite of their early exposure to the originals—Virgil, Cicero, Tacitus in Latin, Thucydides in Greek—Americans usually preferred translations, popularizations, secondary surveys. For Jefferson, reading Latin and Greek authors in their original was a sublime luxury, but it was a luxury he managed frequently to resist, as the many uncut pages of his personal copies of the Latin and Greek classics bear witness.[3]

I

Shortcuts to the classics, printed in English, won universal popularity: Charles Rollin's *Ancient History,* for example, was written "for those who do not intend to make very deep researches." Rollin extracted from the Greek and Latin authorities material he judged "most useful and entertaining . . . most instructive." This was all most colonial readers asked. Rollin wanted to reveal "by example rather than precept" the arts of war and peace, the principles of government, and the conduct of life "that suits all ages and conditions." He hoped to assist men in knowing "the manners of different nations, their genius, laws and customs."[4]

However, much of the colonial reading in ancient history was

3. Jefferson to Joseph Priestley, Jan. 27, 1800, Andrew A. Lipscomb and Albert E. Bergh, eds., *The Writings of Thomas Jefferson,* 20 vols. (Washington, D.C., 1903), X, 146.

4. Charles Rollin, *The Ancient History . . . ,* 2 vols. (Boston, 1827; 1st ed., 1730–38), I, i, vi.

supplied not by ancient historians as such but by seventeenth- and eighteenth-century political writers searching for illumination on problems of their own day. For example, Edward Wortley Montagu, regarding himself as an "Old Whig" true to "Commonwealth *Principles,*" demonstrated in his *Reflections on the Rise and Fall of Antient Republicks,* which appeared in 1759, "The principal causes of the degeneracy of manners which reduc'd those once brave and free people [the Greeks and Romans] into the most abject slavery." After all, explained Montagu, "as the British state and the ancient free Republicks were founded upon the same principles, and their policy and constitution nearly simlar, so, as like causes will ever produce like effects, it is impossible not to perceive an equal resemblance between this and our manners." Montagu blamed the collapse of Athens on the luxury and immorality of the citizenry, along with their proclivity for "venal orators, who encouraged that corruption to maintain their influence."[5]

A contemporary of Montagu, Walter Moyle, a political dabbler in antiquarian studies, furnished American readers with two essays on the Greek and Roman commonwealths. "I am," he said, "on the side of liberty." He traced the history of Sparta to show the value of government by consent to a free maritime people who declined to be tyrannized by a clerical faction. He used Roman history to show the political decay brought by luxury and by magistrates remaining too long in office.[6] James Burgh, whose *Britain's Remembrancer* went through three American editions between 1747 and 1759, also fastened upon corruption, vice, and luxury as the reasons for the collapse of empires. A luxurious people were disinclined to do their

5. For a discussion of Montagu's political associates, see Robbins, *Eighteenth-Century Commonwealthman,* chap. 4. Edward Wortley Montagu, *Reflections on the Rise and Fall of the Antient Republicks* (London, 1759), 5–7, 14–15.

6. Walter Moyle, *The Whole Works . . .* (London, 1727), 63, 99–148. Jefferson owned the rare Glasgow edition of 1750. Moyle sometimes had an interesting turn of phrase; the liberty of a government, he suggested, "is as nice as the chastity of a woman . . . if the fair one gives up the outworks, the citadel is not long maintained." Ibid., 98.

own fighting, and by hiring others to do it for them, they invited tyranny and military despotism. All great empires had sunk "under Luxury and Vice." When ordinary citizens wasted their time and money "getting drunk, haunting of Bawdyhouses, seeing Plays, hearing Musick, etc.," the fabric of the empire began to tear.[7]

These remarks certainly applied to Rome, in the opinion of Oliver Goldsmith, novelist turned historian. Rome had risen "by temperance and . . . fell by luxury." Rome was a victim of her own success and victories. Conquest of Carthage was fatal, for Romans felt smugly safe and superior and entered into a decline "from their ancient modesty, plainness, and severity of life." Romans grew accustomed to luxury; they allowed themselves to be bribed into oppression because they dreaded "more the dangers of poverty than of subjection."[8] The men who overcame Roman liberty were military leaders backed by mercenaries. Standing armies were fatal. "The militia of antient Rome made her mistress of the world." But standing armies enslaved that great people, and their excellent militia and freedom perished together.[9]

Whig historians singled out Julius Caesar for particular attention. He was the military despot, the tyrant whose assassination was so laudable if politically futile. Although neither Cato nor Brutus accomplished much by their opposition to Caesar, both were classic heroes of freedom. Cato failed to die gloriously in battle, but in disemboweling himself (to save Caesar the trouble), he died "one of the most faultless characters we find in the Roman history."[10] Joseph Addison's play, *Cato, A Tragedy*, achieved enduring popularity in the

---

7. James Burgh, *Britain's Remembrancer: or, The Danger Not Over* . . . (London, 1746), 7–9, 15. Franklin published the fifth edition of Burgh's *Remembrancer* in 1747, followed closely by his Philadelphia competitor Godhard Armbrister in 1748, and by Benjamin Mecom in Boston in 1759.

8. Oliver Goldsmith, *The Roman History* . . . , 2d ed., 2 vols. (London, 1771; 1st ed., 1769), I, 311–12; II, 29. Jefferson owned the second edition.

9. Burgh, *Political Disquisitions*, II, 400.

10. Goldsmith, *Roman History*, II, 16.

colonies. It was the play with which the first professional drama company opened in Philadelphia in 1749,[11] and it became especially popular after the Stamp Act crisis, appearing in four editions between 1767 and 1787. Cato supplied Lord Bolingbroke with a yardstick to estimate the threat of military despotism: after all, even the great Cato failed to save Roman liberty from the combination of a Caesar and a standing army.[12]

In the histories read by the colonists, Brutus had an acute sense of patriotism. "Love of his country broke all the ties of private friendship," and his murder of Caesar was the destruction of "a tyrant who had usurped the rights of mankind."[13] Brutus was a historical justification for tyrannicide. His failure was his inability to persuade the corrupt Roman populace that their liberties needed immedi-

---

11. Joseph Addison, *Cato, A Tragedy* (London, 1713). The play ran through six editions in England in 1713, and another fourteen by the end of the century, not counting four editions published in Boston and Worcester, Mass., between 1767 and 1787. For the performance in Philadelphia in 1749, see Frederick B. Tolles, "A Literary Quaker: John Smith of Burlington and Philadelphia," *Pennsylvania Magazine of History and Biography* 65 (1941): 329. Nathaniel Ames, publisher of the Almanacs, recorded seeing the play when he was a Harvard student in 1758, and adorned a later Almanac with some slightly altered lines from a eulogy of *Cato:*

> 'Tis nobly done to Stem Taxation's Rage,
> And raise the Thoughts of a degenerate Age,
> For Happiness and joy, from Freedom spring;
> But Life in Bondage is a worthless Thing.

The original, in Addison's *Works,* I, 264, reads:

> 'Tis nobly done thus to enrich the stage
> And raise the thoughts of a degenerate age;
> To show how endless joys from freedom spring,
> How life in bondage is a worthless thing.

See Chester Noyes Greenough, "New England Almanacs, 1766–1775, and the American Revolution," American Antiquarian Society, *Proceedings* 45 (1935): 307. For other admiration of *Cato,* see chap. 7, 187, below.

12. Henry St. John, Viscount Bolingbroke, *Letters on the Spirit of Patriotism: On the Idea of a Patriot King; and on the State of Parties, at the Accession of King George the First* (Philadelphia, 1749), 13. This edition published by Benjamin Franklin and David Hall.

13. Goldsmith, *Roman History,* II, 24.

ate rescue. Against this background, Americans agreed with William Robertson's conclusion that "the Roman empire must have sunk, though the Goths [had] never invaded it, because the Roman virtue was sunk."[14] Greece and Rome declined as they became rich, luxurious, corrupt, licentious; Rome gave way to the Goths because the Goths had retained their virtue—this was an agreeable explanation to American colonists, who, through their English and German forebears, claimed descent from the conquerors of Rome.

II

The American approach to medieval history, to the Goths, or, more popularly, to the Saxon chapter of their history, derived partly from this classical orientation, partly from colonial interest in common law in Saxon times. In a new country, land titles were frequently in question, leading, as David Ramsay observed, to an "infinity of disputes." By the mid-eighteenth century, the profession of law was "common and fashionable."[15] To study law was to study its history. Sir John Vaughan's *Reports* reminded colonial lawyers of the connection of law and history insofar as "much of the Saxon law is incorporated into our Common Law." The virtues of both were duly digested by John Adams: "the liberty, the unalienable and indefeasible rights of man, the honor and dignity of human nature . . . and the universal happiness of individuals, were never so skillfully and successfully consulted as in that most excellent monument of human art, the Common Law of England." In these words Adams echoed the awe and reverence of his generation toward an antique golden age of English history. Blackstone urged lawyers to investigate the "fountains" of their profession, "the customs of Britons and Ger-

14. As quoted by Burgh, *Political Disquisitions*, III, 15. Robertson's *History of the Reign of Charles V* was published by subscription in Philadelphia by Robert Bell in 1770; John Adams, John Dickinson, and Benjamin Rush were among the listed subscribers.

15. Ramsay, *History of the American Revolution*, I, 43.

mans, as recorded by Caesar and Tacitus," wherein lay the common law as developed from the "northern nations."[16]

Tacitus's *Germania* enjoyed a remarkable vogue in the eighteenth century. John Adams read Tacitus frequently. Jefferson would enthusiastically tell any inquiring student to look to Tacitus as "the first writer in the world without a single exception"; his works were "a compound of history and morality of which we have no other example."[17] Tacitus was a convenient authority on many subjects—on Rome herself as well as on the Saxon tribes which emigrated from Germany to England. American admirers were not even obliged to strain their command of Latin, for they could enjoy the pleasures of Thomas Gordon's new English translation, which came complete with moral discourses. Tacitus, Gordon explained, was "an upright Patriot, zealous for public liberty and the welfare of his Country," a "declared enemy to Tyrants," a historian "of extraordinary wisdom," whose work demonstrated that "no free people will ever submit to . . . [tyranny] unless it steal upon them by treachery." It was not surprising that Gordon's new translation was on the first order list of the Library Company of Philadelphia.[18]

History in the *Germania* certainly stirred the blood of readers interested in ancient virtue. Fascinated by the virtues of the splendid Germans, Tacitus wrote at length of their purity, their independence,

16. Edward Vaughan, ed., *The Reports and Arguments of That Learned Judge, Sir John Vaughan . . .* (London, 1706), 358; John Adams, "On Private Revenge," *Boston-Gazette,* Sept. 5, 1763; William Blackstone, *Commentaries on the Laws of England,* 4th ed., 4 vols. (Oxford, 1770), I, 35–36.

17. John Adams to Jefferson, Feb. 3, 1812, Cappon, ed., *Adams-Jefferson Letters,* II, 295; Jefferson to Mrs. Anne Carey Bankhead, Dec. 8, 1808, Jefferson Papers, Massachusetts Historical Society.

18. Gordon, trans., *Works of Tacitus,* I, 11; John Trenchard and Thomas Gordon, *Cato's Letters . . . ,* 4 vols. (London, 1748), I, 192. Note that Jefferson was so fond of Gordon's translation that he had three sets collated with the Latin original, two going to the Library of Congress in 1815, and the other eventually reposing in the private library of the late Arthur Machen of Baltimore. Wolf, "First Books and Printed Catalogues of the Library Company," *Pennsylvania Magazine of History and Biography* 78 (1954): 12.

their democratic inclinations. True, the form of German government was monarchical, but it was an elective kingship, constrained by assemblies of the tribes. Royal authority was neither unbounded nor arbitrary, and the German kings secured obedience by the justice of their rule and the example of their behavior. Their people lived a simple, happy life, "in a state of chastity well secured, corrupted by no seducing shows and public diversions, by no irritations from banqueting." Their private life would be acceptable to the most rigid puritan. The ancient Germans, Tacitus claimed, were "almost the only Barbarians contented with one wife."[19] It became hard to resist the frequently offered conclusion that a corrupted and depraved Roman Empire had little chance of surviving the onslaught of Germanic virtue.

Of contemporary writers on Germanic history the most popular in the colonies was a Frenchman, Paul de Rapin-Thoyras, "a Man of Learning and industry; Honesty and Candour."[20] His *History of England* depicted the English as direct descendants of Tacitus's noble Germans. The fate and influence of these descendants he followed from the time they crossed the Channel to Britain until he concluded his account of English development with the eighteenth century. Rapin not only popularized Tacitus but at the same time also provided a bridge over which Americans could travel from ancient to medieval history. To an impressive roster of American admirers, Rapin in the translation by Tindal was as accessible as Gordon's *Tacitus.* Although crusty John Adams questioned Rapin's impartiality, he respected him; and John Dickinson referred to the *History* continually, in nearly every one of his publications.[21]

Rapin accepted the *Germania* as a basic source. He argued that the

19. Gordon, trans., *Works of Tacitus,* II, xxii, 325–33, 362.
20. Paul de Rapin-Thoyras, *History of England,* trans. Nicholas Tindal, 2d ed., 4 vols. in 5 (London, 1732–47); comment by Sir John Fortescue, *De Laudibus Legum Angliae,* trans. John Glanvil (London, 1741), xvii.
21. *Boston-Gazette,* Feb. 1, 1773.

Anglo-Saxons, who were the very Germans celebrated by Tacitus, continued upon arrival in England their virtuous customs of government, banding together "to assist one another, and act in common for the good of All." They set up a central government with an elected king and witenagemot or parliament, "where the Concerns of the whole nation only were consider'd." Under Alfred, greatest of the Saxon monarchs, "all Persons accused of any Crime were to be tried by their Peers." "This Privilege," he added, "which the *English* have preserved to this day, is one of the greatest a Nation can enjoy." His readers were reminded that Alfred was responsible only for securing a custom "established by the *Saxons* Time out of Mind." Rapin, it might be added, was not an unreserved admirer of the Saxons. While ready to concede the virtues they brought from Germany, he noted that the Saxons also brought over their "reigning Vice," an addiction to strong liquor.[22]

Rapin's description was accepted by other historians contributing to the colonists' portrait of their ancient ancestors. Thomas Lediard, translator of Mascou's *History of the Ancient Germans,* justified his publication by proclaiming it *The History of Our Great Ancestors.* England's laws, customs, and constitution were formed on the German model, according to Lediard, who issued Mascou's work in 1737, the same decade Rapin's appeared. A century earlier Richard Verstegan had written with the same ambition of showing what a renowned and honorable nation the Germans had been, "that thereby it may consequently appear how honourable it is for Englishmen to be from them descended." Nathaniel Bacon, the Cromwellian lawyer, presented the same portrait of Saxons as a free people governed by laws made by themselves. Readers of Bacon's *Historical Discourse* encountered a delightfully balanced and serene Saxon constitution: "a beautiful composure," he called it, "mutually dependent in every part from the Crown to the clown, the Magistrates being all choice men,

22. Rapin, *History of England,* I, 148, 27, 46, 42, 160–61.

and the King the choicest of the chosen; election being the birth of esteem, and that of merit, this bred love and mutual trust." In both the seventeenth and eighteenth centuries, significant political meaning lurked behind Bacon's pious wish to know again "the happiness of our Fore-fathers the ancient Saxons."[23]

There seemed general agreement on Saxon virtues in the histories Americans most often consulted. There was little need of filial piety to arrive at strong convictions on the reality of ancestral liberties. Even that cautious diplomat and statesman Sir William Temple praised the Saxon kings as "just, good, and pious Princes" who governed with such sense and moderation that "no popular Insurrection ever happened in any of the Saxon reigns." David Hume, considered a tory historian because of his affection for the Stuarts, praised Britons and Saxons as lovers of liberty and fighters against despotism. Hume thought the Germans had carried "to the highest pitch the virtues of valor and love of liberty," and it was inevitable that the Saxons "imported into this island [England] the same principles of independence which they inherited from their ancestors." Like most writers Hume based his remarks on "the masterly pencil of Tacitus," but unlike many such admirers he did not believe the Saxons especially democratic in political practices. He denied existence of a popular branch of the Saxon legislature and insisted that the House of Commons could not and should not seek its origins in Saxon times.[24]

Hume was an exception to the historical rule, and the colonial perspective was not changed by his doubts and reservations on the

23. John Jacob Mascou, *The History of the Ancient Germans . . .* , trans. Thomas Lediard, 2 vols. (London, 1737–38), I, xiv, 57, 64; II, 228; Richard Verstegan, *A Restitution of Decayed Intelligencies in Antiquities . . .* (London, 1628), 42; Nathaniel Bacon, *An Historical Discourse of the Uniformity of the Government of England . . . ,* 2 vols. (London, 1647–51), II, 301; I, 112. The publishing history of Bacon's work is curious and reveals the Stuarts' hostility to such political history: the *Historical Discourse* was reprinted secretly with a 1651 date in 1672, and again in 1682; the last edition was suppressed, and reissued after the abdication of James II in 1689.

24. Jonathan Swift, ed., *The Works of Sir William Temple . . . ,* 2 vols. (London, 1750), II, 584; Hume, *History of England,* I, ii, 141–42, 145.

reality of Saxon democracy. His fellow Scot Lord Kames, the jurist and friend of Benjamin Franklin, endorsed the thesis of Saxon liberty. Kames in his popular *British Antiquities* portrayed a Saxon polity appealing to rural Americans: the Saxons, he asserted, were cultivators of corn, farmers whose economy allowed true social democracy; they elected their judges and gave security of tenure; their kings were men whose powers gradually developed, and originally the Saxon king was "no more than but the chief judge."[25] Kames contended that the Saxons migrating from Germany took only such customs and laws as suited their new English circumstances[26]—an observation with point for Americans seeking parallels to their eighteenth-century circumstances.

Americans also liked the conclusions of Henry Care, whose *English Liberties* praised Saxon ancestors for the wisdom of their government, their "excellent Provisions for their Liberties," and precautions against oppression. William Atwood, a seventeenth-century contemporary of Care and later Chief Justice of New York, renewed discussion of the elective nature of the Saxon king, whom he described as nothing more than a splendid general who maintained office and dignity by "hardy actions and tender Usage of his People."[27] George St. Amand, author of one of the many historical essays that flourished in the colonial bookmarket, reiterated this idea of an elective Saxon monarchy. Like Atwood, St. Amand used the *Mirrour of Justices* in contending for Saxon democracy. The *Mirrour,* considered an essential reference for the colonial lawyer's bookshelf, professed to

25. Henry Home, Lord Kames, *Essays upon Several Subjects concerning British Antiquities . . . ,* 3d ed. (Edinburgh, 1763), 196.

26. Kames, *Historical Law-Tracts,* 2d ed. (Edinburgh, 1761), no. 1. Transcribed by Jefferson in Gilbert Chinard, ed., *The Commonplace Book of Thomas Jefferson, A Repertory of His Ideas on Government* (Baltimore, 1926), 99–103.

27. Henry Care, *English Liberties: or, the Free-Born Subject's Inheritance . . .* (London, n.d. [1680?]), 95; issued in a fifth edition in Boston in 1721 and a sixth edition in Providence in 1774. William Atwood, *The Fundamental Constitution of the English Government . . .* (London, 1690), 37–39, 73.

set forth the "ancient laws and usages" whereby Saxons governed themselves before the Conquest. First published in the sixteenth century, it claimed to be a commentary of early Saxon derivation.[28] St. Amand inquired: "Why mayn't we suppose the Book was a Translation of some Manual of the *Saxon* Laws, put into Norman *French,* with such additions as *Horn* [its editor, and a part-time fishmonger] thought proper, to accommodate it to the Usages of the Time he lived in?" Americans accepted the *Mirrour* as a contribution to Saxon history and agreed that the *Mirrour's* pronouncements on Saxon government "ought to be received for Truth."[29]

Obviously many historians who wrote about Saxon history found in it support for the political lessons they wished to demonstrate. Lord Somers was such a man. A Whig statesman who assisted in the arrangements for the offer to William and Mary in 1689, Somers believed people could change their rulers if they were tyrannical, and he was satisfied that history supported this belief. The many American purchasers of Somers's *Judgment of Whole Kingdoms* (its twelfth and thirteenth editions were published in Newport and Philadelphia, respectively) at once knew the purpose of the book: to assure that "their Children's children may know the Birth-right, Liberty, and Property belonging to an Englishman." James Tyrrell, like Somers an associate of John Locke and an admirer of Saxon antiquity, felt that as a participant in the Glorious Revolution of 1688 he should contribute to justification of Parliament's action against James II. After all, Tyrrell asked, had not the Saxon monarchs been obliged to seek the consent of their parliament to all legislation? Algernon Sidney was in the same situation. He was hardly a historian, but he was ready to praise the Saxons as lovers of liberty enjoying a government dominated by their witenagemot. Basing his remarks on that "wise

28. See William Searle Holdsworth, *A History of English Law,* 12 vols. (London, 1903–38), II, 284–90.

29. George St. Amand, *An Historical Essay on the Legislative Power of England. . . .* (London, 1724), 94, 4–5.

author" Tacitus, he noted that Saxon "kings and princes had no other power than was conferred upon them by these assemblies."[30]

As seventeenth-century writers found political satisfaction in this Saxon emphasis, so did writers in the eighteenth century. Among the most influential contributors to the Saxon myth,[31] and from the colonial viewpoint among the most timely in publication, was the anonymous author of the *Historical Essay on the English Constitution,* whose work appeared in London and Dublin in 1771. The author's identity has lately been a subject of some discussion — evidence points to a mysterious Obadiah Hulme — but American readers were content to accept the book for its content. They eagerly digested this summary of Saxon virtues, a veritable handbook on the historic rights of Englishmen. It rounded out the colonists' picture of their Saxon ancestors. "Our Saxon forefathers," according to Hulme, "founded their government upon the common rights of mankind. They made the elective power of the people the first principle of our constitution, and to protect it, they delegated power for no more than one year." Hulme argued for annual Saxon parliaments, which he felt were the quintessence of the Saxon system along with an elective monarchy.[32]

After reading Hulme it was easier to agree with the conclusions of such men as Molesworth and Bolingbroke. According to Molesworth, one of the original Real Whigs, "all Europe was beholden to

---

30. John, Lord Somers, *The Judgment of Whole Kingdoms and Nations . . .* (London, 1710), 8, and title page; issued in Philadelphia in 1773 and Newport, R.I., in 1774. It was brief, to the point, and cheap at sixpence a copy; see also Robbins, *Eighteenth-Century Commonwealthman,* 78–80. James Tyrrell, *Bibliotheca Politica . . .* (London, 1689), 222; Algernon Sidney, *Discourses Concerning Government,* 2 vols. (Philadelphia, 1805), II, 239. Sidney remarked that the Saxons were "lovers of liberty," who "understood the ways of defending it." Ibid., 238.

31. For a discussion of the Saxon myth, see Appendix I.

32. Obadiah Hulme, *An Historical Essay on the English Constitution* (London, 1771), 7, 24, 31. Published anonymously and long ascribed to Allan Ramsay. Also issued in Dublin, 1771. For a discussion of the authorship, see Sowerby, ed., *Catalogue of Jefferson's Library,* V, 205; and Caroline Robbins, "Letter to the Editor," *Pennsylvania Magazine of History and Biography* 79 (1955): 378.

the Northern nations for introducing or restoring a constitution of government far excelling all others." According to Bolingbroke, "the Principles of the *Saxon Commonwealth* were therefore very democratical."[33] The Saxon system epitomized freedom, a freedom consisting of "being subject to no Law but such to which the Person who is bound consents." It was a system "agreeable to the Rules of Reason."[34] This view, expressed in England in the 1720s, became a basic Revolutionary doctrine in America in the 1760s.

One of the many charms of English history for its colonial readers was its occasional ability to furnish evidence of human happiness. They were attracted to the Saxon past because here they found an ancient political utopia; furthermore, one based on attractive economic arrangements. Tacitus wrote about Saxon land tenure as well as Saxon government; and colonial lawyers, concerned with quitrents, land titles, and rights of inheritance, were exposed to magnificently partisan accounts of the land system of their admirable ancestors.

Most of the historians popular in America described an agrarian Saxon society which was distinctly nonfeudal. Primogeniture was not practiced in ancient Germany; inheritance was "unto all their male children," as Richard Verstegan phrased it in 1628. Migrating Saxons took this custom from Germany to England. The great seventeenth-century scholar and antiquary, Sir Henry Spelman, agreed that Saxon land tenure had been allodial in character, "according to the ancient manner of the Germans," so that, owning their land outright, owners disposed of it as they desired, free of rents, encumbrances, or entails. He concluded that feudalism entered England with the Normans. After the Conquest of 1066, Duke William

33. Robert Molesworth, *An Account of Denmark as It Was in the Year 1692* (London, 1694), chap. 4, as transcribed by Jefferson, *Commonplace Book,* ed. Chinard, 212; Bolingbroke, *Remarks on the History of England* (London, 1747), 53.

34. George St. Amand, *An Historical Essay on the Legislative Power of England* (London, 1762), 148.

"divided *all England* among his soldiers," so that "all things resounded with the feudal oppressions, which in the time of the Saxons had never been heard of."[35]

American readers discovered that even when a writer considered feudalism desirable, he often conceded the nonfeudal nature of Saxon England. Spelman's account may well have appeared more persuasive because he preferred the stability made possible by regulated feudalism—subsequent to the worst Norman excesses. This approach was somewhat similar to that later offered by David Hume. In Hume's opinion Norman feudalism introduced into England "the rudiments of Science and cultivation," and served as a corrective to the "rough and licentious manners" of the allodial practices of the Saxons. Hume praised feudalism for its system of primogeniture, but conceded that Norman feudalism was "destructive of the independence and security of the people."[36] Sir John Dalrymple, author of a popular eighteenth-century essay on *Feudal Property,* is another example of a writer who considered feudalism praiseworthy, but denied that the Saxons practiced it. Saxon land tenure, he claimed, was allodial, and descents were free. The Germanic invaders of Britain had found more land than they could use and therefore felt under no constraint to accept feudal restrictions. The Saxon nobility was "allodial, personal, and honorary," and was presided over by a virtually elective monarch.[37]

35. Verstegan, *Decayed Intelligencies,* 57; Gibson, ed., *Works of Spelman,* Pt. II, 5; see also Spelman, *De Terminis Juridicis . . .* (London, 1648), chap. 8, as transcribed by Jefferson, *Commonplace Book,* ed. Chinard, 186: "The feudal law was introduced into England at and shortly after the Conquest."

36. Hume, *History of England,* I, 159–60, 162–63, 201.

37. Sir John Dalrymple, *An Essay towards a General History of Feudal Property . . .* (London, 1757), 18, 320, 336. See also, Jefferson, *Commonplace Book,* ed. Chinard, 149–50; and Pocock, *The Ancient Constitution,* 243–44.

III

The consensus of historical opinion studied in America supported the existence of a nonfeudal Saxon economic system, even though there was division over the merits of an allodial and a feudal system. Any discussion of feudalism inevitably led to a discussion of when and how feudalism came into England. Americans who admired Saxon political and economic freedom were curious to learn the reasons for the destruction of both. If Saxons were so virtuous, why were they vanquished? If allodial ownership was superior to feudal tenure, why was feudalism victorious? Most books Americans studied identified feudalism with despotism and tyranny. If feudalism was such a "barbarous system,"[38] as Mrs. Macaulay described it, there was surely some extraordinary explanation for its success.

The usual answer was to identify the arrival of feudalism with the arrival of the Normans in 1066. According to Jean Louis de Lolme, a favorite of John Adams, "the establishment of the feudal system in England was an immediate and sudden consequence of that conquest which introduced it." Obadiah Hulme, reading the same sources studied in the colonies, concluded that the Norman Conquest brought economic, political, and religious tyranny, "monsters till then, unknown in England."[39] But the whole question was complicated by the political sympathies of the historians who explored it.

Many seventeenth-century English writers felt that modern Parliamentary claims to political responsibility depended at least in part upon unbroken continuity in English development; to admit a break in historical evolution might admit grounds for monarchical pretensions. Sidney was inclined to propose that there had been no true Norman conquest, "neither conquering Norman nor conquered

38. Catherine Macaulay, *An Address to the People of England, Scotland, and Ireland, on the Present Important Crisis of Affairs* (London, 1775), 9. Reprinted in N.Y., 1775.

39. Jean Louis de Lolme, *The Constitution of England . . .* (London, 1880; 1st ed., Amsterdam, 1771), 13; Hulme, *Historical Essay,* 34–40.

Saxon, but a great and brave people composed of both, united in blood and interest in the defence of their common rights." As added political insurance he refuted royalist claims based on even an imagined conquest, insisting that "the rights . . . of kings are not grounded upon conquest. The liberties of a nation do not arise from the grants of princes." William Atwood was equally concerned: admit the conquest and "the Inheritance which everyone claims on the *Laws* will be maintainable only as a naked Right, and *naked Rights are thin and metaphysical Notions* which few are Masters or Judges of."[40]

There were ways of overcoming the embarrassment of a Norman military victory. For example, Isaac Kimber thought that the Saxons fell before Norman arms because of the softening influence of luxury, idleness, and vice; despite this handicap "the *English* fought with as much Valour as the *Normans*." Henry Care argued that the Normans secured power by guile: it was true that the Normans defeated and killed the Saxon King Harold, but Duke William pretended a right to the English crown; William agreed to a compact to observe the Saxon laws and customs; on this understanding the English submitted as partners of the Normans. Unfortunately William then broke his oath, and he and his successors "made frequent Incroachments upon the Liberties of their People." Care's position was restated in the eighteenth century by the Irish law professor Francis Sullivan, who asserted that the Normans had pretended to an oath to support Saxon laws favorable to "the liberties of the people." Once in authority, they "showed how little regard they had to that obligation, and how bent they were on setting themselves free from all restraint, and to destroy all traces of the old Saxon laws." Sullivan acknowledged that the old elective Saxon monarchy continued in outward form, but held that William's election was extorted "by dread of his power." William had obligations to the "hungry adventurers" he had brought with

40. Sidney, *Discourses*, II, 287, 300; William Atwood, ed., *Lord Hollis His Remains* (London, 1682), 293.

him and thus seized Saxon allodial lands and parceled them out to eager Normans in return for pledged allegiance. In this way, Sullivan concluded, feudalism was introduced into England, and hence "the maxim prevailed that all lands in England are held from the king."[41]

William I was no hero to these historians. He was a crafty Norman who had entered into a firm compact with the innocent English, pledging he would "Govern conformably to the Antient Constitution." Yet William knew that "what is Introduced by Force, by Force may be removed." Roger Acherley said it in his essay on *The Britannic Constitution,* and argued that in any case his only victory was a personal one over Harold. Even Lord Somers presented William as "unjustly stiled the Conqueror," a man who secured the English crown "by a free Choice and Submission of the Peers and Body of the People." Thus King William had obligations inconsistent with his subsequent imposition of feudal despotism. If not a Conqueror, he treated the English as conquered people. According to Kimber, William acknowledged from his deathbed that "he had unjustly usurped the Crown of *England.*" For Algernon Sidney this was an unavoidable conclusion. After all, if William had no right by conquest and no right by forced election or ruptured compact, he had no right by inheritance from Edward the Confessor. Sidney reminded his readers that William "was a bastard, and could inherit nothing."[42]

For all the variety among various historical and legal views of the character of the Norman invasion, the preponderant opinion offered American investigators was that after 1066 feudalism and tyranny made their unwelcome appearance in England. Yet all agreed that whatever the Conquest actually was, it did not abrogate the Saxon

---

41. Isaac Kimber, *The History of England, from the Earliest Accounts . . .* , 3d ed. (London, 1762), 66; see also Robbins, *Eighteenth-Century Commonwealthman,* 240. Care, *English Liberties,* 8–9; Francis Stoughton Sullivan, *An Historical Treatise on the Feudal Law, and the Constitution and Laws of England* (London, 1772), 285–90.

42. Roger Acherley, *The Britannic Constitution . . .* , 2d ed. (London, 1741), 168. Somers cited Spelman as his authority, *Judgment of Whole Kingdoms,* 23; Kimber, *History of England,* 75; Sidney, *Discourses,* I, 152.

constitution, since William and his successors had gone through the motions of observance of the Saxon system of Edward the Confessor. Rapin noted that William's son, William Rufus, promised to restore English government to the basis enjoyed before the Conquest and to reestablish Saxon laws.[43] Rufus failed in his pledge, but his promise certainly seemed to imply both that the submersion of the Saxon system was no more than temporary, and that English people expected its reinstatement. Most American students therefore looked upon the Norman arrival as "that period of English history, which contaminated the purity of the English constitution . . . with a despotick spirit; of which time has not been able totally to eradicate."[44]

IV

In American eyes English medieval history settled into a pattern of periodic efforts to reestablish pre-Norman liberties. Most authorities stressed the charters gained from successive Norman and Angevin monarchs, the Magna Charta of 1215 emerging as the most important of such measures of restitution. The best-selling Rapin served well in this respect. He reviewed the background of Magna Charta in his detailed *History of England* and added a summary in his *Dissertation on the Whigs and Tories*.

Rapin's *Dissertation* served as a handy introduction to and summary of political developments in the post-Conquest era. Rapin reminded readers of the Parliamentary system of the Saxons before the arrival of William, "surnamed the *Bastard*." Then he reviewed the dispossession of the English by the Normans. He pointed out that the Norman nobility acquired the same dislike of royal despotism as demonstrated by the Saxons, so that a political alliance developed in which the object was to restore government "to the same state, as in

---

43. Rapin, *A Dissertation on . . . the Whigs and Tories* (Boston, 1773), 8. This essay was originally included in the full *History of England*.

44. Hulme, *Historical Essay*, 43.

the times of the Saxon kings." Faced with this opposition, Norman monarchs found it increasingly desirable to promise a return to ancient Saxon government and laws, and Henry I confirmed his promise in a charter. Unhappily Henry lived up to his commitments in the same fallible fashion as his brother William Rufus, and the most that could be said was that "the rights of the subject received strength from these promises." Stephen and Henry II also found it necessary to bind themselves—more strongly than their predecessors—to restore the Saxon laws, but the political crisis was merely postponed. This came with the challenge to King John, the outcome of which was Magna Charta.[45]

In the colonial perspective Magna Charta was the most important and inspiring of steps backward in the direction of the glorious and virtuous Saxon system. For this view Americans owed much to Sir Edward Coke and John Selden. Certainly Coke was as frequently cited on Magna Charta as Tacitus on the ancient Germans, and in American eyes the reliability of both was self-evident. Coke had approached Magna Charta as "no new declaration" but as a reaffirmation "of the principal grounds of the laws of England."[46] This made the Charter an unrevolutionary document, no detraction for the conservative lawyers who gave it so much of their attention. As Henry Care commented, a public confirmation of Saxon common law could never be construed as a gracious royal concession.[47] Coke's popular interpretation meant new life for the supremacy of common law over royal prerogative, indicating that kings ruled on suffrance or under compact.

Algernon Sidney's commentaries on the Great Charter, though written by a nonlawyer, were much admired by the colonial legal profession. For Sidney the Charter was an assertion of "the native and

45. Rapin, *Dissertation*, 6–9.
46. Coke, *Second Part of the Institutes*, "Proeme." For further recent discussion of Coke and the Charter, see Pocock, *Ancient Constitution*, 44–45.
47. Care, *English Liberties*, 8.

original rights of our nation" and embodied King John's pledge that neither he nor his successors would ever encroach upon such rights. Magna Charta could not and did not give anything to the people, "who in themselves had all." The chief merit of the document was bringing John to admit that there were popular rights "perpetually inherent, and time out of mind enjoyed." (So said Coke in the *Institutes.*) Sidney might deplore John's failure to adhere to his pledge in emulation of William I, who had "engaged his faith, but broke it"; nevertheless the rights persisted and received royal acknowledgement of their priority. Sidney concluded that by breaking the rights affirmed in Magna Charta, a king branded himself "an execrable perjured person" with whom the people would know how to deal.[48]

In the Charter was a historical illustration of the compact theory so honored four centuries later. Roger Acherley summed up Magna Charta as "a Renewal of the *Original Contract,*" and Anthony Ellis in his *Tracts on Liberty* insisted that the Charter's provisions embraced the entire populace. Here, Ellis claimed, was a democratic document in which "the nobility and commonalty acted so much in concert, that there was no less provision made for the privileges of citizens and burgesses, than for the nobility and gentry." This conclusion seemed justified in light of Coke's legal interpretation. According to Henry Care, the famous thirty-ninth chapter of the Charter, with its guarantee of the rights of freemen, deserved to be written in gold. Under this provision "No free man shall be taken or imprisoned or dispossessed . . . except by the legal judgement of his peers or by the law of the land." Englishmen were assured, Care noted, of a trial "by Equals," and Englishmen on both sides of the Atlantic viewed this thirty-ninth chapter as one of their birthrights.[49]

---

48. Sidney, *Discourses,* II, 256.

49. Acherley, *Britannic Constitution,* 152–53; Anthony Ellis, *Tracts on Liberty, Spiritual and Temporal, of Protestants in England* (London, 1767), 335, 443; Care, *English Liberties,* 26 *n.* Chapter 39 of Magna Charta became chapter 29 in the familiar reissue of Henry III in 1225.

The Charter reestablished ancient rights. It also represented a step toward the restoration of what Hulme's *Historical Essay* called "the elective power of the people," natural for a document patterned "in living memory of Saxon liberties." Bolingbroke called the Charter "a rough Building raised out of the Demolitions, which the *Normans* had made, and upon the solid Foundations laid by the *Saxons*." Rapin believed royal power was so curbed "that it was in a manner reduced to the same state as under the *Saxon* kings before the conquest." The Charter became a yardstick to measure misgovernment, and English kings found themselves deposed "for intending to establish an absolute power contrary to *magna charta*." Such was the fate, Rapin commented, of Edward II and Richard II. English monarchs acquired sweeping obligations: since Magna Charta was, as Lord Somers declared, only "an Abridgement of our antient Laws and Customs, the King that swears to it, swears to them all."[50]

Thus the admiration that Magna Charta excited led to extravagance of thought and language. Even a cautious historian like David Hume praised the Charter for bringing "some order and justice into the administration" and charged King John with such minor vices as "cowardice, inactivity, folly, levity, licentiousness, ingratitude, treachery, tyranny, and cruelty."[51] According to the *Historical Essay*, England owed a debt to those barons who in resisting the rapacity of John revived English liberties.[52]

There was some disagreement over the political reality of what Rapin had called "the Charter of Liberties." Some scholars, such as the Restoration historian Robert Brady, felt Magna Charta was misinterpreted by anti-Stuart writers who perverted historical truth for political advantage. Brady complained, if unavailingly, about those "turbulent men, who hold forth to the People, *Ancient Rights and*

50. Hulme, *Historical Essay*, 62, 55, 58; Bolingbroke, *Remarks on the History of England*, 55; Rapin, *Dissertation*, 11; Somers, *Judgment of Whole Kingdoms*, 26.

51. Hume, *History of England*, I, 388–89, 395, 407.

52. Hulme, *Historical Essay*, 68, 125.

Privileges, which they have found in *Records* and *Histories,* in *Charters,* and other Monuments of Antiquity." In his opinion Magna Charta was a minor relaxation of feudal practices which increased baronial and not popular privilege.[53] But American readers had little cause to be impressed with this historical judgment. The overwhelming majority of their historians exalted Magna Charta, making the Brady school seem unimportant and partisan. In the opinion of Francis Sullivan, this historical controversy was a fight "between the favourers of arbitrary power and the asserters of freedom."[54]

V

For colonial readers the accounts of ancient Greece and Rome told of contending liberty and tyranny, in which tyranny prevailed and empire disintegrated. Historical accounts of ancient and medieval England were far less conclusive: although the happy system of the colonists' Saxon ancestors underwent drastic revision at Norman hands, most historians told of strenuous efforts to recapture Saxon liberty. Englishmen who had known utopia in the form of a free, nonfeudal government might know it again. Magna Charta epitomized their Saxon spirit. From the American viewpoint, the question now was England's capacity to complete the Saxon restoration. But the books they studied offered disappointing and ominous answers.

---

53. Rapin, *History of England,* I, 276; Robert Brady, *A Complete History of England . . . ,* 2 vols. (London, 1685–1700), Preface. See also Butterfield, *Englishman and His History,* 77; and J. G. A. Pocock, "Robert Brady, 1627–1700. A Cambridge Historian of the Restoration," *Cambridge Historical Journal* 10 (1951): 188–91.

54. Sullivan, *Feudal Law,* 362.

CHAPTER III

The Colonial Perspective:
Tudors, Stuarts, and Hanoverians

I f for their time Americans were well informed on antiquity and medieval English history, they were no less aware of their more recent past. Appearing more immediate to present problems, recent history embraced the multitude of sins recorded since Magna Charta —those contained in the history of the Reformation, the history of the religious and political developments which impelled Englishmen to establish the American colonies. It was a history which examined England's colonial behavior and described her emerging imperial consciousness. It paid close attention to the seventeenth-century struggle with the Stuart princes and to eighteenth-century Hanoverian politics.

I

The Tudors had certain undeniable attractions for the colonists. Henry VII, to be sure, was unlovable, if only because he was the first monarch to establish a standing army. But his son Henry VIII sundered the English ties with Rome and brought his people to Protestantism. Henry VIII may have been an arbitrary and capricious despot; still, "with all his Crimes and Exorbitancies he was one of

48

the most glorious Princes of his Time." Because Henry brought the Reformation to England, he represented an inscrutable Divine Will. "Providence often brings about the noblest Designs by the most exceptionable Instruments," the historian Laurence Echard reflected. Even the judicious Rapin confessed that while Henry was "to be numbered among the ill Princes," he could not be ranked among the worst.[1]

Henry VIII's daughters were subjects for wider historical disagreement. Queen Mary's efforts to restore England to the Catholic fold meant that few Protestants could view her reign with equanimity. A sympathetic comment came from the royalist historian Sir Richard Baker, who claimed for Mary "a merciful disposition," since she "oftentimes pities the person, where she shed the blood." Baker thought her religion "a deformity," but admired Mary's devotion to it.[2] Few other writers were as kind: Rapin described her temper as "cruel and vindictive," and Echard observed that "God thought fit to punish her with a Barren Womb and an untimely Death." Robert Dodsley in his *Chronicle* summed up Mary's unhappy reign as one which "stinketh of blood unto this day"; her name was "an abomination," and "the vengeance of the Lord overtook her."[3]

Elizabeth could hardly avoid improving this record. Sufficiently intelligent to have been born of a Protestant mother, she sensibly waged war on the Spanish Catholics. Bolingbroke gazed upon Elizabeth with reverence, and likened her to a patriot king—or queen—since "she united the great body of the people in her and their *common interest,* and she inflamed them with *one national spirit.*"[4] Others praised Elizabeth's sense and judgment: this "good and illustrious

---

1. Laurence Echard, *The History of England,* 3d ed., 3 vols. (London, 1720), I, 298; Rapin, *History of England,* I, 849 *n.*

2. Sir Richard Baker, *A Chronicle of the Kings of England . . .* (London, 1670), 324.

3. Rapin, *History of England,* II, 49; Echard, *History of England,* 327; Robert Dodsley, *The Chronicle of the Kings of England* (Philadelphia, 1774), 54.

4. Bolingbroke, *On Patriotism,* 62.

Queen" had the virtues and none of the vices of her "mighty Father."[5]
Sir Richard Baker admired a Queen who "declined being a Mother
of Children, to the end she might be a Mother of her Country."
Elizabeth did not need the love of a husband since "she delighted in
nothing so much, as in the love of her people," which she earned "by
ordaining good Magistrates, and forbearing Impositions."[6]

Some historians had reservations about Elizabeth's political perfection: Thornhagh Gurdon in his widely read *History of Parliament* reminded readers that the Elizabethan House of Commons attempted
to extend their privileges, but the Queen had seemingly forgotten
their historical grounds, and nipped these "new Claims" in the bud.
David Hume, on the other hand, saw in Elizabeth's popularity evidence that she had not encroached upon any liberties of the people.[7]
There was room for uncertainty about the virtues of the Elizabethan
era; but most sources consulted by eighteenth-century Americans
were favorably disposed to the Virgin Queen, in part because the
reign of Mary was so bleak, in part because the succeeding dynasty
made Elizabeth appear admirable.

II

If uncertain about Elizabethan England, Americans had surer views
on the unsagacious Stuarts. Rapin declared that "there is not an impartial historian" of the Stuarts and thought even Rushworth's edition of source materials favored Parliament at expense of the Crown.
Rapin nonetheless arrived at Rushworth's conclusion: James I and
Charles I had been "very fond of arbitrary power."[8]

Stuart history was well represented in colonial collections, with

5. Rapin, *History of England*, II, 56–57; Echard, *History of England*, 375.
6. Baker, *Chronicle*, 420.
7. Thornhagh Gurdon, *The History of the High Court of Parliament* . . . , 2 vols. (London, 1731), II, 391; Hume, *History of England*, V, 2–13.
8. Rapin, *History of England*, II, 347, 370.

fewer than a half-dozen capable writers taking the Stuart side. Isaac Kimber tried to be judicious about James I, who he thought was neither a sound Protestant nor a good Roman Catholic. He thought James, a melancholy contrast to his Tudor predecessor, "had a high Notion of his own Maxims of Government." Echard strove to find a few kind words: James was "eminent for his Chastity, which was remarkable in a Court so loose and luxurious as his own." Echard suggested that the King was "not well us'd" by Parliament, considering his circumstances, but weakened this point by taking James to task for executing Raleigh and observing that during his reign "the Reputation of England began sensibly to sink." Baker's royalist *Chronicle* saw James as "but a continuation of Queen *Elizabeth*," with "the same vertue, though different sexes." Some whig writers questioned Baker's claim, suggesting homosexual relations between James and "a beautiful youth named George Villiers."[9]

But much less attention was given to James I—even as a "fool and a pedant"[10]—than to his son. James died in his bed; Charles I died on the scaffold, the only English king so executed. If a historian's horizon went back to pre-Norman times, and he subscribed to the antiquity of Parliament, he would probably depict Stuart claims as encroachments on popular liberties. If a historian looked back only to the Conquest, then he might emerge as a royalist who, like Hume, attacked the "encroachments of the Commons." Yet it was easy to sympathize with the tragic, foolhardy Charles I. One commentator wistfully observed how much better it would have been if Charles "had been as good a King as he was a Man."[11] Echard found in Charles "the ROYAL MARTYR," who lost more by his kind heart and treacherous friends than "by all the pretended Acts of his Severity and Tyranny." Another insisted that there was never a

---

9. Kimber, *History of England,* 287; Echard, *History of England,* 407–8; Baker, *Chronicle,* 446; Dodsley, *Chronicle,* 57.

10. Dodsley, *Chronicle,* 57.

11. Hume, *History of England,* V, 540; Kimber, *History of England,* 321.

monarch "so formally and solemnly murdered." Charles was "a Prince of great Wisdome, and all Princely Vertues," whose death was lamented by the majority of his subjects.[12] Lord Clarendon, popular as a contemporary historian, wrote of the death of the brave Charles, "wickedly Murder'd in the sight of the Sun." According to this loyal admirer, Charles was "the worthiest Gentleman, the best Master, the best Friend, the best Husband, the best Father, and the best Christian, that the Age in which he liv'd produced."[13]

Hume saw that Charles had *some* vices, but that "his virtues predominated extremely." Charles, Hume added thoughtfully, was "a good rather than a great man" who lacked political prudence, but he was clearly undeserving of so harsh a fate. Hume professed amazement that "among a civilized people, so much virtue in the person of Charles could meet with so fatal a catastrophe."[14]

Mrs. Macaulay, the "incomparable female historian," wrote a nine-quarto volume *History of England* to refute Hume's monarchical prejudices, taking some twenty years for her task. Horace Walpole once suggested that "England will be finished before her history." The work aroused the enthusiasm of colonists: "I never met with a Mind so warmed and engaged in Sentiments of genuine Liberty," was the report of one who visited with the lady before the American crisis, and another declared her "one of the brightest ornaments, not only of her sex, but of her age and country."[15] Mrs. Macaulay resisted any inclination to historical mercy for Charles I. "In the suffering prince," she explained, "we are apt to overlook the designing tyrant, to dwell

12. Echard, *History of England,* 663; Baker, *Chronicle,* 592.

13. Edward Hyde, Lord Clarendon, *The History of the Rebellion* . . . , 3 vols. in 6 (Oxford, 1731–32), III, 259.

14. Hume, *History of England,* V, 540.

15. James Burgh in his *Political Disquisitions,* I, vii, termed Mrs. Macaulay "incomparable," and Horace Walpole's remark is noted in Lucy Martin Donnelly, "The Celebrated Mrs. Macaulay," *William and Mary Quarterly* 3d ser., 6 (1949): 183; entry of May 31, 1772, Franklin B. Dexter, ed., *The Literary Diary of Ezra Stiles,* 3 vols. (N.Y., 1901), I, 319; John Adams to Catherine Macaulay, Aug. 9, 1770, Adams, *Works,* IX, 332.

on his hardship, and forget his crimes." Allowed his way, he would "have destroyed every principle of Liberty in the constitution." No other prince had undertaken so many innovations or schemes against the English constitution. Nor was Charles a gentleman: he was lewd, unchaste, and perhaps father of "one or two natural children." His passion for political power, she claimed, was merely his "predominant vice." Charles met with "the just vengeance" he brought upon himself for his career of "frantic" tyranny, destruction of liberty, and butchery of his subjects.[16]

There was a basic lesson which Americans learned from the political tragedy of Charles Stuart: it was unwise for a king to aim at more power "than the Constitution allow'd." And, as Rapin wrote, Charles demonstrated "how difficult and how dangerous it is for a king of England, to attempt to subvert so well cemented a government."[17] But the miscarriage of the English Republic after the death of Charles I certainly dismayed Americans. Just as there had been anxiety to explain Saxon failure before feudal Normans, there was the problem of explaining the people's inability to rescue their rights in the 1640s and 1650s. Although Mrs. Macaulay admired the Civil War and Interregnum as one of the most heroic periods of English history, replete with some of England's noblest figures, she insisted that Oliver Cromwell was not one of them. He was the evil genius of the revolution, who dispensed with a people's parliament and established despotism with the aid of his army. Cromwell was a usurper, "a master in all powers of grimace and the arts of hypocrisy"—as evil as Charles Stuart.

James Burgh offered the same judgment, terming Cromwell "the mock-patron of Liberty," who took care of the free English constitution with an army of 30,000 men.[18] Colonial readers found these

---

16. Catherine Macaulay, *The History of England . . .* , 9 vols. (London, 1763–83), V, 100 *n*; IV, 418, 424, 435.

17. Kimber, *History of England*, 321; Rapin, *Dissertation*, 19.

18. Macaulay, *History of England*, V, 111, 215; Burgh, *Political Disquisitions*, III, 377.

opinions expressed earlier by Edmund Ludlow, one of the original regicides, a bitter critic of Cromwell. Ludlow denounced Cromwell with a steady sincerity and hoped "men may learn from the issue of the Cromwellian tyranny, that liberty and a standing mercenary army are incompatible." Algernon Sidney believed Cromwell wrecked "the good old cause"; Cromwell was to the English Republic what Caesar had been to the Roman.[19]

Of course Cromwell also received a poor press from royalist writers. Baker treated Cromwell as a usurper, whose abundant vices obscured any merit in his character. Clarendon dismissed Cromwell as "a brave wicked Man," guilty of the crimes "for which Hellfire is prepared." Hume held Cromwell guilty of the "most atrocious" murder of Charles I, and thought him "covered under a mighty cloud of republican and fanatical illusions."[20]

However, not all the writers popular with colonists agreed with this severe judgment. Rapin saw Cromwell as "one of the greatest men of his age," a man attacked by republicans because he tried to temper Parliamentary authority. Bishop Burnet esteemed the Lord Protector, for "when his own designs did not lead him out of the way, he was a lover of justice and virtue, and even of learning." Echard found Cromwell an honest patriot first, a republican afterwards. The failure of the English republican adventure of the 1650s was not entirely due to Cromwell's despotism. Obadiah Hulme accused historians of being too obsessed with Cromwell to realize that the real culprit was the Long Parliament. Readers of Hulme's *Historical Essay* found an attack both upon Charles I for tyranny and upon Parliament for seeking its own perpetuation. The House of Commons, Hulme claimed, "had no more regard, to the ancient form of

---

19. Edmund Ludlow, *Memoirs . . . ,* 3 vols. (London [?], 1698–99), III, Preface; for similar sentiments, see also I, Preface, and 489, 503; Jefferson owned this edition; it survives in the Rare Book Room, Library of Congress, Sidney, *Discourses,* II, 201–2.

20. Baker, *Chronicle,* 625; Clarendon, *History of the Rebellion,* III, 653; Hume, *History of England,* V, 488–89.

government, to the rights, privileges, and franchises of the people, than William the Conqueror, or any other tyrant, since his time." The Commons was responsible for the King's murder, the destruction of the House of Lords, and the enslavement of the whole nation.[21] Concerned with its own privileges, Parliament became incompetent and represented only itself. Tyranny need not be confined to one person, a Charles Stuart or an Oliver Cromwell; an oligarchy, even a Parliament, can be tyrannical.

Then came the Restoration, the cardinal fact of which was the loss of English virtue. Why else would Charles II receive such a welcome from a people who a dozen years earlier had cheered the execution of his father? Mrs. Macaulay diagnosed the occasion for Charles II's return as a popular "fit of passion and despair"; the people "plunged themselves into a state of hopeless servitude" under a despotic dynasty.

Sensing the mood of his people more perceptively than his father had ever done, Charles II gave way to a love of luxury that accorded well with the desires of his many subjects. But one historian saw him as "rather Abandoned, than Luxurious," and Americans were made to see the sensual side to Charles.[22] Dodsley's popular *Chronicle* edified Americans with Charles's sexual propensities, describing how courtiers paraded a host of beautiful women before him, how "he was enamoured of them all; and he put forth his sceptre unto them, and the land was filled with royal bastards." Moreover, "the nation, taking example from the court, ran headlong into all manner of licentiousness and immorality." Dodsley could well conclude with his invitation to curious readers to look to modern "bawdy novels" for details on the gallantries of Charles II.[23]

---

21. Rapin, *History of England,* II, 602; *Bishop Burnet's History of His Own Time . . . ,* new ed., 2 vols. (London, 1850), I, 52; Echard, *History of England,* 725; Hulme, *Historical Essay,* 109–17.

22. Macaulay, *History of England,* V, 390; Echard, *History of England,* 1047.

23. Dodsley, *Chronicle,* 86, 89.

England in the 1680s was thus pictured as a land without virtue, ruled by a monarch without virtue, a king who avoided conflict with his Parliament through the expedient of bribing it into submission. Charles II governed with his pensioned Parliament "in much the same arbitrary manner as William the Bastard did without a parliament."[24] Historians noted the martyrdom of Algernon Sidney, convicted by Judge Jeffries on the basis of the then unpublished "Discourses." Even Hume, who found something to admire in Charles II, criticized the death of Sidney as "one of the greatest blemishes" of the Restoration.[25]

Jeffries attracted wide attention, and most historians served up at least one example of Jeffries' injustice. A favorite story told and retold involved Colonel Kirke, Jeffries' aide, whom the historical mythmakers rendered notorious. Kirke, it was said, liked music to hang men by—especially if their dying spasms kept time with a martial air. Rapin described Kirke's cruelties as "beyond all imagination." Writers enjoyed the *Tosca*-like tale of the young maiden who sought to save her innocent father (or brother, in some accounts) by submitting to Kirke's "brutal lust," after which he showed the swooning girl the gallows which her father adorned. According to the account by Burnet, Kirke's superior, Jeffries, hanged over six hundred after Monmouth's abortive rising against James II. The King, Burnet reported, was deeply pleased with "Jefferies's Campain."[26]

James II did not begin his reign auspiciously. Hume admitted James was "more imprudent and arbitrary than his predecessor." De Lolme considered James "perhaps the guiltiest Monarch that ever existed."[27] One Englishman nodded chivalrously in the direction of

24. Burgh, *Political Disquisitions*, I, 120.

25. Hume, *History of England*, VI, 271–72. Lacking a second witness to an overt act of treason, Judge Jeffries ruled that "*Scribere est agere*," and so accepted Sidney's manuscript "Discourses" as conclusive evidence. See Burnet's *History of His Own Time*, I, 372.

26. Rapin, *History of England*, II, 750, cites Burnet.

27. Hume, *History of England*, VI, 316; De Lolme, *Constitution of England*, 315.

James's daughters, Queens Mary and Anne, and urged that James should be allowed to "fall gently" since he had bequeathed England two great queens whose contribution to the "bulwarks of the Protestant Religion, and the Liberties of *Europe* . . . may well atone for innumerable Failures in their unfortunate Father." More typical was Isaac Kimber's attack on James as "a thorough Bigot to Popery," who would stick at nothing to bring the Pope to England. Dodsley saw James as "a worshipper of the church of Rome," who "bowed the knee unto her idols, and went a whoring after all her abominations." Moreover, Dodsley continued, James "was a zealous bigot to all the absurd and foolish tenets, which the cunning of her priests have invented to delude the ignorant, and enslave the mighty."[28]

III

None of the historians popular in colonial America had other than praise and admiration for the great and Glorious Revolution of 1688. In every test, it was always "the grand Revolution," or "the Epocha of English freedom," when the Stuarts were expelled forever and England was restored to her rights and privileges. William III was "a wise prince,"[29] a "heroic King," sent to England by "the Hand of Providence" to foil "Popery and arbitrary Power."[30] William was the "glorious Deliverer," who achieved the seventeenth-century political program. "He came; he saw; he delivered."[31] Exactly what did William III deliver? And how long enduring, how satisfactory was the product?

English Whigs worked hard both to explain and to justify seating the Dutch prince on the throne. William supported Parliament's

---

28. Echard, *History of England*, 1150; Kimber, *History of England*, 342; Dodsley, *Chronicle*, 90.

29. Dodsley, *Chronicle*, 96.

30. Kimber, *History of England*, 398.

31. Burgh, *Britain's Remembrancer*, 31.

renewed campaign for "ancient *Rights* and Privileges." Nothing new was introduced in 1688—this was a most unrevolutionary revolution. The contract given William and Mary was justified philosophically and historically. William and Mary, declared William Atwood, had become "*our* LAWFUL *and* RIGHTFUL *King* and *Queen*"; they undertook to restore the ancient Saxon system, and were elected part of it.[32] The new monarchs were committed to Parliament's right to approve taxes, and to rule without a standing army.[33] No wonder De Lolme later marveled that 1688 demonstrated that in England "Liberty has at length disclosed her secret to Mankind, and secured an Asylum to herself."[34]

The honeymoon did not last. William had the good sense to work with Parliament on money matters, but a flood of publications reminded Englishmen of the ancient system they were supposedly restoring, including a Saxon-style militia. Yet William believed that military common sense dictated a standing army. It became evident that William III's contribution to England's constitutional recovery was limited. In contemporary and later accounts Americans read of disillusionment with the halfway measures of the new administration. Bishop Burnet—"honest Burnet," Burgh called him—remonstrated with William over the corruption introduced "on pretence of buying off the jacobites." James Ralph, the American who first went to England with Franklin and stayed on to publish *The Use and Abuse of Parliaments,* wrote of the 1690s as a new "scene of iniquity . . . as made the pension-parliament of Charles II seem innocent." Other comments referred to William as a foreigner (like the first William) who came to England "on pretence of delivering us from slavery; and makes it one of his first works to plunge us into the very vice which has enslaved all the nations of the world, that have ever lost their lib-

---

32. Sir Robert Atkyns, *The Power, Jurisdiction and Privilege of Parliament* . . . (London, 1689), 33; Atwood, *Fundamental Constitution,* title page.

33. Dodsley, *Chronicle,* 97–98.

34. De Lolme, *Constitution of England,* 540.

erties."[35] William "was but half the friend to liberty he pretended to be" and "more fond of power than of squaring his government with the principles of the constitution." Compared to "the immortal and blessed Alfred," William was but "a cold-hearted Dutchman."[36]

William's many critics agreed that he had ample assistance in his misgovernment. Neither people nor Parliament remained alert to their danger. Lessons furnished by Cromwell's Long Parliament were forgotten. Obsessed with the tyranny associated with the Stuarts, the people allowed Parliament to slide into sloth and decadence.[37] There was no sensible action to prevent Parliamentary corruption or restore the Saxon system of annual parliaments.

The picture presented the colonial reader was one of recovery and decline—the promising beginning of 1688 was followed by a frustrating eighteenth century. In such history the colonial reader saw a magnificent postmortem on England's last hope for constitutional liberty. There might be a new monarch, but this meant only a new name rather than a meaningful change. Queen Anne, William III's successor, though "a most virtuous, just, and pious Princess," was nevertheless a Queen "easily led by her Favorites."[38] There might be a change in dynasty, but hardly a change in the speed of English political decay. When Thomas Gordon and John Trenchard collaborated on *Cato's Letters* in the 1720s, they selected their pseudonym because Cato had "contended for public Liberty and Virtue." They commented on the current meaninglessness of political parties and political labels and explained the obsession for place and power: "A *Tory* under Oppression, or out of a Place, is a Whig; a *Whig* with Power to oppress, is a *Tory*." Time had been when a Tory was an

---

35. Burnet, like Rapin, reached American readers well recommended: "the good bishop," observed Burgh, was "like a faithful preacher of righteousness." See Burgh, *Political Disquisitions,* I, 403, 419; James Ralph, *Of The Use and Abuse of Parliaments . . . ,* 2 vols. (London, 1744), I, 121; Burgh, *Political Disquisitions,* I, 403.

36. John Cartwright, *To the Commonalty of Great Britain* (London, 1776), xxxi–xxxii.

37. Bolingbroke, *A Dissertation upon Parties . . . ,* 2d ed. (London, 1735), 218–21.

38. Kimber, *History of England,* 410.

extreme royalist; in early eighteenth-century England the desire for power obliterated principle. "No Men upon Earth have been more servile, crouching, and abandoned Creatures of Power, than the *Whigs* sometimes have been," observed Gordon.[39]

Changed conditions made for strange political bedfellows. Bolingbroke (long known as the wildest, wickedest Tory) saw that the 1688 Revolution had altered political landmarks. The Whigs in power were men "who succeeded to the name rather than the principles of this party after the revolution."[40] Bolingbroke's solution to the transformation of England from decay to virtue was a miraculous regeneration through *The Idea of a Patriot King*. He looked, hopefully, for a prince who would "abandon corruption and restore Parliament." Such a person might save a country whose ruin was so advanced. But even this might not be enough. "To preserve liberty by new laws and schemes of government, while the corruption of a people continues and grows, is absolutely impossible."[41] Bolingbroke was troubled by the thought that the elected might well be representative of the electors. When the people, the electors, "became universally corrupt, as well as the elected," he warned, "the fate of *Rome* will be renewed in *Britain*."[42]

From the American vantage point three alarming themes ran through many accounts of recent English history: moral degeneration; political irresponsibility, prelude to new despotism; and a standing army, historic ally of despots. "Liberty cannot be preserved," Sidney had said, "if the Manners of the People are corrupted."[43] Many feared that Sidney's warning was being fatally ignored in eighteenth-century England, that the English had become "the most luxuri-

39. Trenchard and Gordon, *Cato's Letters*, III, 258–59.

40. Herbert Butterfield, *The Statecraft of Machiavelli* (N.Y., 1956), 151–54; Bolingbroke, *Letters on the Study and Use of History*, new ed. (Paris, 1808), 295.

41. Butterfield, *Statecraft*, 151–61.

42. Bolingbroke, *Dissertation on Parties*, as quoted in Burgh, *Political Disquisitions*, II, 135.

43. Quoted by Trenchard and Gordon, *Cato's Letters*, I, 196.

ous people now in the world . . . a people enslaving themselves in luxury."[44] Luxury as a historical theme fascinated many eighteenth-century writers. Distaste for luxury was logical for intellectuals with puritan antecedents or historical recollections of luxury in ancient Greece and Rome. There was a disposition to trace luxury from the misrule of Charles II. The theatrical stage, which had supplied mistresses to Charles, supplied whig writers with awesome lessons in sinful luxury. Burnet's complaint that "our Plays are the greatest debauchers of the Nation" was recited with telling effect. On the eve of the American Revolution, some were still distressed by actresses leading innocents astray, and Burgh attacked "the female dancers, whose immodest curvetting in the air, and exposing of their limbs" was so "fatally alluring to those already familiarized to vice."[45]

The modern get-rich-quick schemes also seemed symptomatic. The mounting national debt burdened future generations and afforded unhealthy speculative opportunities to the present. *Cato's Letters* gave a discussion of the South Sea Bubble, which involved debt and manipulation, and discussion of which allowed for appeal to the fate of innocent sufferers, the widows and orphans: speculators were worms eating at the English body politic, the "sort of Vermin that are bred and nourished in the Corruption of the State."[46]

44. Quoted by Burgh, *Political Disquisitions*, III, 65.

45. Burnet's original comment was "The stage is a great corrupter of the town"; Burnet's *History of His Own Time*, 915; Burgh's paraphrase occurs in his *Britain's Remembrancer*, 28 *n*. Burgh, *Political Disquisitions*, III, 99. Particularly imaginative was one plan to curb immorality and reduce the appalling national debt: since adultery was a major vice, the design called for flaying and curing the hides of convicted guilty gallants; the product should be auctioned for manufacturing purposes, and revenue would "go some considerable length toward paying the debt of the nation." Consider the charms of a pair of gloves from "a blood royal hide" or a pin cushion "made of such rich stuff" that it might sell for a hundred guineas. There might be a problem of oversupply, but speculators who held up the price of corn could deal with the plentitude of adulterers in England. There was no end to such a program: there could be a Hide Office, with its commissioners and clerks, handsomely paid of course, all places filled by ministers grasping for influence and power. But despite such charges, the revenue for the national treasury might be as much "as we are likely to get by taxing our colonies." Ibid., III, 140.

46. Trenchard and Gordon, *Cato's Letters*, I, 17; III, 23, 209–24.

Yet in the view of many, England's moral and economic decline stemmed directly from the fundamental failure of the political system. Political corruption was regarded as more dangerous than other outward manifestations of decay. The "True *Whigs*" deplored extravagance and venality; they worried over virtue; they returned again and again to the basic betrayal of the principles of England's ancient constitution. It was hard not to conclude that all would have been well—at least, much better—had not Parliament coalesced with the King to ignore the constitutional rights of the people. If only Parliament, prone to corruption because of remoteness from the populace, could return to its ancient purity and independence. The political machine built by Walpole was constructed on infrequent general elections and few voters. *Cato's Letters* drew attention to "the little beggarly Boroughs" which were "Pools of Corruption."[47] Hulme noted "the elective power of the people, hath, with the boroughs, been falling into decay, while many of the villages, and some parts of the open country . . . have risen by trade, into great opulence, and magnitude." The industrial revolution was creating an increasingly unrepresentative situation, and "there is not, perhaps, one man in five thousand, who is now represented in parliament, by a member of his own election." A comparison between the miserable eighteenth-century present and the glorious Saxon past was irresistible. "Our ancient parliaments were composed of *The Wise Men of England,* but . . . they have been changed into *The Rich Men of England,*"[48] rich because of susceptibility to "places, pensions, contracts." The man who managed Parliament, Robert Walpole, was "the Archcorrupter," who contaminated the nation with "a venal spirit, and made the generality of our boroughs, rotten to the very heart."[49]

Had England made any political progress since the 1688 Revolution? Not according to James Burgh: "The *Stuarts* meant a tyranny

47. Ibid., III, 18.
48. Hulme, *Historical Essay,* 76, 126.
49. Burgh, *Political Disquisitions,* I, 387, 69.

by one; the *Walpolians* an aristocracy." There was little to choose between the two. Where the Stuarts had been butchers, attacking "the good lady *Britannia* with slaughtering knives," recent England faced "genteeler corrupters" who "endeavoured her destruction by poison held out to her in a golden cup."[50]

If only parliaments were elected more frequently, England's future would be more encouraging. The seventeenth century had seen triennial parliaments, followed in 1716 by a disastrous septennial act. Eighteenth-century historians cited John Milton's criticism of the triennial arrangement as "but the *third* part of one good step towards that which in times past was our *annual* right." They revived the *Mirrour of Justices* to prove "that parliaments by the old laws, ought to be held twice a year"; by 1716 "we are deprived of 13 parts in 14 of our antient privilege."[51] Malachy Postlethwayt in his widely read *Dictionary of Trade and Commerce* observed that "Parliaments . . . were originally annual; and antiently all the people voted." Times had changed, thanks to a House of Commons which had found a way to control "the creative power from whence they derive their authority."[52]

Septennial elections, Americans were told time after time, were the basic source of all England's political problems.[53] Here was the spring from which flowed the destructive mischief of corruption which "hath sapped the foundation of a fabric, whose building was cemented with the blood of our best citizens," a corruption which had "tainted the minds of men with such an incurable degeneracy, that the virtue of our forefathers is become the ridicule of every modern politician." As Hulme reminded his readers, England's Saxon forefathers had "made the elective power of the people the first prin-

---

50. Ibid., 402–3.

51. Burgh's anthology drew frequently on Milton and the *Mirrour*. See ibid., 84–85, 25.

52. Malachy Postlethwayt, *The Universal Dictionary of Trade and Commerce*, 2 vols. (London, 1751–55), II, 413; Hulme, *Historical Essay*, 126.

53. Macaulay, *Address to the People*, 18.

ciple of our constitution." That first principle was now too obviously forgotten: "As standing water soon stinks . . . so a standing house of commons, will ever be a standing pool of corruption." If England would return, not to a mere halfway house of triennial, but to the true Saxon system of *annual* elections, the pool of corruption might be sufficiently stirred up to permit a Parliamentary return to "pristine purity." The nation needed an "ANNUAL CURRENT."[54]

In eighteenth-century England nostalgic writers also faced the menace of standing armies with all their dreadful associations. History had shown that "when a country is to be enslaved, the army is the instrument to be used," and that from the reign of William III there had been a steady increase in the standing army. European ventures under Queen Anne led to dangerous fascination with "great armies and land wars." Arrival of the Hanoverians brought a dynasty "who had no idea of an insular situation, nor of any security, but what depends on numerous standing forces."[55] "He that is armed," Andrew Fletcher, a protégé of Bishop Burnet,[56] reminded his many American readers, "is always master of the purse of him that is unarmed."[57]

There was, in short, diminishing evidence for England's recovery of her constitutional freedom. Loss of the people's militia may have sealed her fate—"we have quitted our antient security" was one cry heard in America.[58] Luxury, corruption, an infrequently elected Parliament—the colonists' portrait of their mother country was painted in dismal hues.

IV

In more recent times the colonist's perspective was determined, perhaps inevitably, as much by politics as by history. The disputes be-

54. Burgh, *Political Disquisitions*, I, 267–486; Hulme, *Historical Essay*, 149–50.
55. Burgh, *Political Disquisitions*, II, 349, 338.
56. See Robbins, *Eighteenth-Century Commonwealthman*, 180–84.
57. Andrew Fletcher, *The Political Works . . .* (London, 1737), 9.
58. Ibid., 39.

tween England and the American colonies occupied a sizable space on the political stage. Americans discovered—with gratification—that many whig writers made injustice to the American colonies a part of a general indictment of England's decadence. While there was disagreement on what should be done, Americans enjoyed a consoling commentary on their mistreatment. Early in the eighteenth century Thomas Gordon and John Trenchard found room in their *Cato's Letters* for discussion of "ways to retain colonies." England faced a choice—either "to keep independence out of their [the colonists'] power," or "to keep independence out of their will." Only "by using them well" could England be sure of her empire.[59]

However, there was more agreement on the necessity of generous treatment than on the colonial title to it. Some argued that the American colonies were economically rewarding and that enlightened self-interest dictated benevolent government. Others, concerned for England's domestic situation, argued that tyranny in the colonies would augur ill for liberties in the mother country. Burgh warned if "the *American* charters may be destroyed, the charters of all the cities [i.e., London], and those by which all crown lands are held, may be annihilated." He contended that Magna Charta and the Bill of Rights belonged as much to Englishmen in America as Englishmen at home, and that an invasion of documented privilege threatened rights of all Englishmen. Americans did not deserve to be attacked "for doing what the Bill of Rights allows every Englishman."[60]

Among the basic rights of Englishmen was taxation by their own representatives. Although native Englishmen had at least a limited voice in Parliament, Americans had no representation there at all. Moreover, the example of the palatinates of Chester and Durham, which had enjoyed assemblies before the Norman Conquest and which were not taxed until granted representation in Westminster, applied to the palatinates of Maryland and Pennsylvania.[61] The books

59. Trenchard and Gordon, *Cato's Letters,* III, 7.
60. Burgh, *Political Disquisitions,* II, 297, 319.
61. Ibid., 304.

that colonists read sparkled with this sort of illustration. William Molyneux gave Americans a variation of the argument for autonomy in his *Case of Ireland,* which appeared in 1698, but became so popular in America that three new editions were issued between 1770 and 1776. Molyneux championed the rights of Irishmen by arguing that Ireland (quite like the American colonies) had never been conquered and should not be treated as if it had been. He claimed Ireland had made "Voluntary Submission" to England in the distant reign of Henry II, and this move led to a compact between the two countries. With reference to Coke's *Institutes* and the *Modus Tenendi Parliamentum,* Molyneux insisted that the Irish "*should enjoy the like Liberties and Immunities, and be Govern'd by the same Mild Laws . . . as the People of England.*" If a people could claim the rights of Englishmen, to tax them without their consent was "little better, if at all, than *downright Robbing.*"[62]

Granville Sharp cheered his American readers by the observation that "all British subjects, whether in Great Britain, Ireland, or the Colonies, are equally free." He could reach no other conclusion. America was no conquered country; feudal tyranny had no historic right in America; Americans possessed full title to all the fundamental rights embodied in English common law. Any other verdict, said Sharp, would be "*Treason against the* Constitution."[63]

Was Sharp right? English government betrayed Sharp's idea of the constitution. Ministerial demand for an American revenue rose steadily, but critics questioned the necessity as well as the justice of taxing the colonies: "Before the taxing of the unrepresented colonies was thought of, the ministry ought to have reduced exorbitant salaries, abated, or abolished excessive perquisites, annihilated useless places, stopped iniquitous pensions . . . and reduced an odious and

62. William Molyneux, *The Cause of Ireland's Being Bound by Acts of Parliament in England, Stated* (Dublin, 1698), 37–38, 150, 48.

63. Granville Sharp, *A Declaration of the People's Natural Right to a Share in the Legislature . . .* (London, 1774), 11, 230.

devouring army, and taxed vice, luxury, gaming and public diversions." Economies of this sort would bring the British treasury "ten times more than *Grenville* could ever expect from taxing, by force and authority, the unrepresented colonies."[64]

Numerous authors offered to anxious colonial readers encouraging examples of resistance. Sir William Temple furnished an inspiring account of Dutch opposition to Spanish tyranny. There was an apparent parallel: George III, like Emperor Charles V, showed little understanding of provincial rights. Both maintained troops long after any need for them. Both encouraged religious strife—Charles V "by erecting new bishoprics along with the introduction of the inquisition." Dutch resistance to oppression was logical for a people "fond of and tenacious of their ancient Customs and Laws." Just as seventeenth-century Spain fell victim to luxury and corruption, so was England succumbing to the same corroding influences.[65] Molesworth had related a similar tale in his celebrated *Account of Denmark;* here Americans learned of another Germanic people who failed to sustain liberties in the face of such forces as a selfish nobility, apathy and ignorance of history among the populace, and a standing army.[66]

While Americans did not lack information about their rights, neither did they lack conflicting suggestions about their proper course of action. Some sources discouraged colonial resistance to English rule and some suggested Anglo-American cooperation to revivify the constitution. William Blackstone wrote magnificently on "the liberties of Englishmen"—which he derived from "a restoration of that antient constitution, of which our ancestors had been defrauded by the art and finesse of the Norman lawyers." But he flatly denied the possibility of such rights crossing the Atlantic to America. And Obadiah Hulme insisted that the colonists were subject to Parliament's authority even if it was corrupt. Colonization was for the

64. Burgh, *Political Disquisitions,* II, 315.
65. Swift, ed., *Works of Temple,* I, 22; Burgh, *Political Disquisitions,* III, 59.
66. Molesworth, *An Account of Denmark,* 124–27.

common good, not for "the particular good of the settlers." Remedy for colonial complaints lay not with dissolution of empire but closer union. Americans should "unite with their brethren in England, to restore, and maintain . . . the English Constitution upon its genuine foundation." There would be no colonial problem if the English government were restored to its historic Saxon character, and some believed a combined Anglo-colonial effort could restore it.[67]

But the vast majority of "True *Whigs*" insisted on American rights regardless of consequences to the empire. What was to be the route to these rights? There were grounds for doubt that they could be achieved through cooperation with England—even among those who advocated this very course. For example, Hulme conceded in his *Historical Essay* that "as things go, there will soon be very little left of the *British* constitution, besides the name and outward form."[68] The historical lesson taught by the whigs seemed to meet with little response in England. But in America the story was different. Forgotten or ignored as prophets in their own country, English whig historians were not without honor in America. Colonial patriots were prepared to determine just what this history taught about the preservation of their rights.

---

67. Blackstone, *Commentaries*, II, 45–53; Hulme, *Historical Essay*, 210.
68. Hulme, *Historical Essay*, 8.

PART TWO

The Revolutionary Use
of History

CHAPTER IV

The New England
Historical Conscience

The Revolutionary generation of New Englanders was deeply absorbed in its historical origins. Just as seventeenth-century New Englanders had been understandably proud of their Puritan faith and the founders of their colonies, so eighteenth-century New Englanders maintained that pride and developed a keen interest in their English origins. Puritan anxiety for the survival of their faith had created a favorable climate for public education in New England. This concern assured more than an educated clergy; it meant an educated—a historically educated—political leadership.

I

Although the clergy had declined in influence by the eighteenth century, they still occupied a position of importance and respect. They worked, lived, and argued with such political figures as John and Samuel Adams, James Otis, and Josiah Quincy, Jr., and with such men the clergy played a vital role in formulating New England political opinion.

One of the more interesting survivals from the seventeenth-century theocracy was the Election Sermon (the first was in 1634, the last probably in 1884), given at the May meeting of the General Court. Since this coincided with the annual Boston convention of the clergy, ministers from all over New England became disseminators of new ideas. According to one scholar, the Election Sermon was second only to the colonial newspapers in successfully propagating political arguments.[1] A clergyman could argue effectively for resistance to tyranny as a sacred duty; a Samuel Adams in the audience would apply the Christian lesson to his secular cause, and be strengthened.

The common denominators to the clergy and the lay politician were significant. The minister went to the same college as his political associate, read the same books, and arrived at many of the same conclusions. The sources cited by the divines in their sermons often read like a directory of "True *Whig*" historians. The classical authors—Tacitus, Sallust (both in the Thomas Gordon translation), Plutarch, and Caesar—were closely followed by Locke and Sidney, Coke and Somers, Burnet and Rapin. Andrew Eliot, of South Church in Boston, admitted that it was Algernon Sidney, the "Martyr to civil Liberty," who first taught him "to form any just sentiments on government," sentiments Eliot developed by reading John Trenchard's *History of Standing Armies* and Marchamont Nedham's familiar *Excellencie of a Free State*.[2] Jonathan Mayhew, of Boston's West Church, was equally attached to Sidney and not only used Gordon's *Tacitus*, but also admired his *Cato's Letters*.[3]

Mayhew was probably the most outstanding of New England's politically minded clerics. A "transcendent genius" according to John Adams, Jonathan Mayhew was an early advocate of "the principles

1. Charles W. Akers, *Called Unto Liberty: A Life of Jonathan Mayhew, 1720–1766* (Cambridge, 1964), 95; see also Lindsay Swift, "The Massachusetts Election Sermon," Colonial Society of Massachusetts, *Transactions* I (1895): 288–451.

2. Alice M. Baldwin, *The New England Clergy and The American Revolution* (N.Y., 1928), 7–8, 11.

3. See, for example, Jonathan Mayhew, "A Circumstantial Narrative," in Mayhew Manuscripts, Letter XII, Boston University.

and feelings" for which the Revolution was undertaken.[4] The problems of religion and life were one and the same to Mayhew. At Harvard he wrote in his notebooks that he was determined to discover "the Affairs, Actions and Thoughts of the Living and the Dead, in the most remote Ages and the most distant Nations."[5] He carefully studied "the Characters and Reign etc of K[ing]. C[harles]. I" for a better understanding of the origins of the Puritan migration. To this end he studied Whitelocke's *Memorials* ("an exquisite scholar") and read the *Memoirs* of "honest Ludlow" the regicide. He admired Milton's account of the English Commonwealth and noted that the rebellion came because "Charles the first had sinned flagrantly and repeatedly" against "the antient form of Government" in England.[6]

The use to which Mayhew put such studies is best seen in his controversial *Discourse Concerning Unlimited Submission,* a sermon delivered on the occasion of the centennial anniversary of the execution of Charles I on January 30, 1649/50. Taking vigorous issue with recent Anglican efforts to portray Charles as a martyred monarch, Mayhew began his refutation with some remarks on the antiquity of English liberties. The English constitution, he asserted, "is originally and essentially free." Roman sources, such as the reliable Tacitus, made it clear that "the ancient Britains . . . were extremely *jealous of their liberties.*" England's monarchs originally held title to their throne "solely by grant of parliament," which meant the ancient English kings ruled "by the voluntary consent of the people."[7]

If Mayhew's history showed him a familiar pre-Norman political

4. John Adams to Hezekiah Niles, Feb. 13, 1818, and to William Tudor, Apr. 5, 1818, Adams, *Works,* X, 288, 301.

5. Mayhew, "Some General Rules for the Improvement of Knowledge," in Harvard College Extracts, Mayhew Manuscripts, Boston University.

6. Mayhew, "Memorandum and Extracts Relating to the Characters of the Reign etc of King Charles I," in ibid.; Bernhard Knollenberg, ed., "Thomas Hollis and Jonathan Mayhew: Their Correspondence, 1759–66," Massachusetts Historical Society, *Proceedings* 69 (1956): 116–17.

7. Mayhew, *A Discourse Concerning Unlimited Submission and Non-Resistance to the Higher Powers: With Some Reflections on the Resistance to King Charles I . . .* (Boston, 1750), 45.

utopia in England, it also proved the right of all men "to vindicate their natural and legal rights." On this principle Tarquin was expelled from ancient Rome; on this principle the conquering and tyrannical Julius Caesar was "cut off in the senate house"; and on this principle Charles I "was beheaded before his own banqueting house," and James II had to flee from the country "which he aim'd at enslaving." All men had rights; but Englishmen had a record for maintaining theirs despite the tyrannical efforts of misguided kings like Charles I.[8]

After forty pages of such historical discourse, Mayhew reached the main point of his sermon: the essential rightness of the execution of an English king. Mayhew did not mince his words. Charles had governed in "a perfectly wild and arbitrary manner," paying no regard to the constitutional limitations upon his royal authority. Charles was a victim of his own "natural lust for power," and the evil influence of wicked councilors. His execution was the deserved fate of a monarch who levied taxes without the consent of his people, who set up arbitrary courts, who "reduced the Sabbath with his Book in favor of sports" and openly encouraged Roman Catholicism. Opposition to Charles could not be treason—in Mayhew's view Charles was no longer a king after his attempt to change a free and happy government into "a wretched, absolute monarchy." Charles had "unkinged himself" long before his trial. England did not execute a monarch, but "a lawless tyrant." The date of January 30 should be "a standing memento that Britons will not be slaves." And lest the political lesson be missed, Mayhew gave due notice that the death of a Stuart tyrant should be "a warning to all corrupt councellors and ministers, not to go too far in advising to arbitrary, dispotic measures."[9]

Mayhew's religious message was overshadowed by his historical discussion. Those interested in theology might discover, if they listened carefully, that Mayhew believed the biblical injunction to sub-

8. Ibid., 12–13.
9. Ibid., 41–54.

mit to higher powers was meant for good rulers only; bad rulers—
like Charles I and his sons—were the devil's ministers, not the Lord's.
Mayhew's religion showed there was no obligation to obey a bad
king; his history showed the positive action that could be taken
against tyranny.

The vigor of Mayhew's presentation established his political reputation. His sermon was published not only in Boston, but in London
as well—in 1752 and again in 1767.[10] In Boston, John Adams remembered long afterward, Mayhew's sermon "was read by everybody."[11]
This included some angry Anglicans who quoted Stuart sympathizers
like Lord Clarendon, or resorted to the argument that a king should
be obeyed because he is a king.[12] Among others who joined the
newspaper controversy over Charles I were Mayhew supporters who
wrote to the *Boston Evening-Post* citing Burnet: Charles I "had a high
Notion of Regal Power, and thought that every Opposition to it was
Rebellion." The same newspaper also published a definition of a good
king: such a monarch "has imprison'd none against the law, granted
no Monopolies to the Injury of Trade, collected no Ship-Money,
rob'd none of their Religious Liberties . . . all which . . . were flagrant in the Tyrannical Reigns of the *Steward-Family*," so well known
for their "violent Attachment to Popery and Arbitrary Power."[13]

Mayhew had indeed (as John Adams noted) revived Puritan "ani-
mosities against tyranny." In his Election Sermon before Governor
William Shirley in 1754, Mayhew returned to his theme that "loyalty and slavery are not synonymous." "Monarchical government," he
declared, "has no better foundation in the oracles of God, than any

10. Richard Baron included Mayhew's sermon in a collection, *The Pillars of Priestcraft
and Orthodoxy Shaken,* published in London in 1752 in 2 volumes and in a 4-volume
edition in 1767. Mayhew was soon widely known in England as a result, and Akers
believes Baron's anthology was the link between Mayhew and Hollis; Akers, *Jonathan
Mayhew,* 143.

11. John Adams to Hezekiah Niles, Feb. 13, 1818, Adams, *Works,* X, 288.

12. *Boston Evening-Post,* Mar. 12, 1750.

13. Ibid., Mar. 5, Apr. 9, 1750.

other."[14] In 1765, with the provocation of the Stamp Act to consider, Mayhew delivered another moving discourse on the virtues of liberty and the iniquity of tyranny. The essence of slavery, he announced, consists in subjection to others—"whether many, few, or but one, it matters not."[15] The day after his sermon the Boston mob attacked Chief Justice Thomas Hutchinson's house, and many thought Mayhew was responsible. Mayhew did his best to disavow any association with the mob's action; violence of this sort, he said, was a poor cloak for "zeal for liberty."[16] The tyranny of the mob was as bad as the tyranny of the British Parliament.

Mayhew's case against England was essentially conservative. He wanted to preserve the constitutional rights belonging to all Englishmen. During the decade preceding his untimely death in 1766, Mayhew read widely on the legal rights of Englishmen in America. His happy correspondence with Thomas Hollis of Lincoln's Inn brought a steady stream of handsome history books to his Boston home. Hollis, as Caroline Robbins has noted, "thought that England had discovered liberty and that it should be shared with other people." A wealthy man, Hollis sponsored fine new editions of Locke, Sidney, and Milton, sending copies to Mayhew.[17] Hollis also arranged for his literary friends to send Mayhew their productions. Catherine Macaulay supplied Mayhew with volumes of her *History of England;* Mayhew read her treatment of the Stuarts "with great pleasure." As Mayhew exclaimed to Hollis, Mrs. Macaulay wrote "with a Spirit of Liberty, which might shame many great Men (so called) in these

14. Mayhew, *A Sermon Preach'd in the Audience of His Excellency William Shirley . . . May 29, 1754* (Boston, 1754), 21, 6–7.

15. The original sermon has not survived; this is drawn from a memorandum in the Mayhew Manuscripts, Boston University. The sermon was given on the afternoon of Aug. 25, 1765; see Akers, *Jonathan Mayhew,* 202–4.

16. Mayhew, *The Snare Broken . . . A Thanksgiving-Discourse . . .* (Boston, 1766), 7. This sermon was dedicated to William Pitt, to whom Hollis sent a copy; see Akers, *Jonathan Mayhew,* 212.

17. Robbins, *Eighteenth-Century Commonwealthman,* 266; see also Francis Blackburne, ed., *Memoirs of Thomas Hollis,* 2 vols. (London, 1780), I, 239.

days of degeneracy, and tyrannysm and oppression." [18] Mayhew also returned to *Cato's Letters* (which he had first read at Harvard) and was so moved at rereading Trenchard's essay on the proper treatment of colonies that he urged Hollis to have the piece reprinted in the London press. Hollis was delighted to respond, and in October 1765 readers of the *St. James' Chronicle* were duly regaled with Trenchard's timely item from the fourth volume of *Cato's Letters*. [19] Londoners thus had an opportunity to agree with Mayhew that Trenchard offered "many things much to the present purpose . . . which look almost like prophecy." [20] Hollis not only kept Mayhew well supplied with reading matter, but also offered observations on the discouraging tone of such books. Mayhew became increasingly worried over the future of the Anglo-American connection. As he confessed to Hollis, "the account which you give me, as well as others, of the political state of Affairs in England, is extremely afflictive to me; and fills me with very gloomy apprehensions." [21]

Mayhew's matured conclusions were most cogently presented in his Thanksgiving Sermon, *The Snare Broken*. Since he died of a stroke shortly after, this was Mayhew's political valedictory. But he died comforted by the news of the repeal of the Stamp Act; he had lived to see a measure of British recognition for colonial constitutional rights. What mattered to Mayhew was that England should continue to respect American liberties. The mother country must recall that her colonists were historically "freeborn, never made slaves by the right of conquest in war." England must remember that the colonists were English and entitled by Magna Charta to fundamental constitutional privileges, confirmed in colonial charters. The Stamp Act, calling for taxation without colonial consent, had clearly violated

18. Mayhew to Thomas Hollis, Aug. 8, 1765, Knollenberg, ed., "Hollis-Mayhew Correspondence," Massachusetts Historical Society, *Proceedings* 69 (1956): 173.

19. See *St. James' Chronicle*, Oct. 1765; Blackburne, ed., *Memoirs of Hollis*, II, 662–66.

20. Mayhew to Hollis, Aug. 9, 1765, Knollenberg, ed., "Hollis-Mayhew Correspondence," Massachusetts Historical Society, *Proceedings* 69 (1956): 176.

21. Blackburne, ed., *Memoirs of Hollis,* I, 243.

the most basic of colonial rights, derived from Magna Charta, colonial charters, and the British constitution. It was now up to aroused Americans to prevent future violations: "History, one may presume to say, affords no example of any nation, country, or people long free, who did not take some care of themselves." Only by being alert would Americans avoid "that ugly Hag Slavery, the deformed child of Satan." Mayhew was happy over the end of the Stamp Act; but he feared complacency, for history supplied too many horrid examples of what could happen to a sleeping people. And yet Mayhew found room for some optimism. "Let us not be insensible of our own felicity," he urged. The chief threat to future happiness lies with the few "evil-minded individuals in Britain" who in the past had ensnared King and Parliament. Americans were not faced with the need for change or innovation; they now knew their rights and liberties, and they knew their historical and constitutional foundation. If innovations came, they would come from England. Americans needed only to hold tight to what they knew they were entitled to.[22]

The Snare Broken enjoyed three editions before the end of 1766. It was a distinguished political testament, written in a language understood by contemporaries and supported by familiar authorities. Mayhew had relied heavily upon such relatively recent writers as Sidney, Milton, and Locke, saying "I liked them; they seemed rational."[23] Mayhew was not a political philosopher.[24] He saw politics as a tool of religion, and he made civil and religious liberty his inseparable goals. "The purpose of the divine mission of Jesus Christ," he said, "is the happiness of man: but that happiness can only result from Virtue, and virtue is inseparable from Civil Liberty."[25] His contributions to the

22. Mayhew, *Snare Broken*, 34, 27, 8–9, 4–5, 35.

23. Ibid., 35.

24. Clinton Rossiter, "The Life and Mind of Jonathan Mayhew," *William and Mary Quarterly*, 3d ser., 7 (1950): 531–58.

25. Mayhew, Sermon fragment in Harvard College Library, cited by Clifford K. Shipton, *Sibley's Harvard Graduates; Biographical Sketches of Those Who Attended Harvard College . . .* (Boston, 1873–), XI, 461.

American Revolution were a religious justification of the movement and a clerical endorsement of the patriot politicians. He reminded his congregation of the antiquity of the rights for which he stood, recalling the principles of the Puritans of the seventeenth century and demonstrating the derivation of New England principles in the eighteenth century. His public recollection of earlier royal tyrants was intended to awaken his people to present dangers. He never forgot the Stuarts. "Four princes," he called them, "whose reigns were all inglorious"; they were men "of great pride and vanity, of arbitrary notions and practices, of little wisdom, policy or discretion." [26] Their Hanoverian successors now presided over "a nation where infidelity, irreligion, corruption and venality, and almost every kind of vice, seems to have been increasing all the time!" [27]

Mayhew was far from alone in his historical interests. James Lockwood, who gave the Election Sermon in 1759, also discussed the justifiable beheading of Charles I and the appropriate removal of James II by a nation then "jealous of their liberties." William Patten in Plymouth County gave a sermon in 1766 on the importance of popular over private good, and illustrated his lesson by pointing to the familiar examples of Charles I and James II; Patten urged his congregation: "Let us be exhorted, to 'stand fast in the liberty' wherewith, both the God of nature, and the british constitution, have made us free." In Providence, Rhode Island, David Rowland celebrated the end of the Stamp Act with a sermon on the early history of English liberty and concluded that "it is our happiness under *English government* to enjoy whatever we have a natural right to." [28]

26. Mayhew, *A Discourse Occasioned by the Death of King George II . . .* (Boston, 1761), 23.

27. Mayhew, *A Discourse . . . Occasioned by the Earthquakes . . .* (Boston, 1755), 66.

28. James Lockwood, *The Worth and Excellence of Civil Freedom and Liberty Illustrated . . .* (New London, Conn., 1759), 12; William Patten, *A Discourse Delivered at Hallifax in the County of Plymouth . . .* (Boston, 1766), 10–11, 18; David S. Rowland, *Divine Providence Illustrated and Improved. A Thanksgiving-Discourse . . . Occasioned by the Repeal of the Stamp-Act* (Providence, 1766), 27, 8–9.

But perhaps the minister who best maintained the political views of Mayhew was Isaac Skillman, of Boston's Second Baptist Church. Skillman gave an enormously popular Thanksgiving Sermon in Boston after the *Gaspée* incident of 1772; his *Oration Upon the Beauties of Liberty, or, the Essential Rights of Americans* earned five new editions within two years. Dedicating his sermon to Lord Dartmouth and calling himself "a British Bostonian," Skillman began by carefully disassociating himself from any criticism of the King: George III, declared Skillman, surely did not mean to attempt tyranny; he must know (as Mayhew claimed Charles I must have known) that a tyrannical monarch ceases to be a king, since as a tyrant he has broken his coronation oath to govern justly. George must certainly recall the fate of Charles I, and should he "tread in the same steps, what can he expect?" Skillman professed the deepest love for his King, but, he said, "I revere the rights of an Englishman before the authority of any King upon the Earth."[29]

According to Skillman the chief enemy of Englishmen was ministerial tyranny. It was up to the King and Parliament to set straight their own house. They should correct mistaken policies and recall their history. They might profit, he suggested, from Burnet's *History of His Own Time* (so "noble, valuable and great") and from restudying the record of monarchical and Parliamentary tyranny in the seventeenth century. History, claimed Skillman, "shews, that an arbitrary dispotic power in a prince, is the ruin of a nation. . . . Every Age and every history furnishes us with proofs, as clear as the light of the morning." History showed Skillman that "it is no rebellion to oppose any King, ministry, or governor, that destroys . . . the rights of the people." George III ruled as much by compact in America as in England. He had no hereditary right, as in Hanover; "it cannot be a parliamentary right, that lies in Britain." It was manifestly not a right

---

29. Isaac Skillman, *An Oration Upon the Beauties of Liberty, or, the Essential Rights of Americans* (Boston, 1772). The authorship of this sermon has been disputed, sometimes being ascribed to John Allen. See Baldwin, *New England Clergy*, 117 *n.*

by conquest—and never would be. George III had contracted to defend colonial religious and civil rights; if he broke his contract the King became the real rebel.[30]

Skillman's use of history, his sources, and his arguments are comparable to Mayhew's. The language is stronger, the threats less disguised, but unlike Mayhew, Skillman had lived to see the Townshend Acts and the Boston Massacre. New England clergymen were keenly exercised over British tyranny because their ancestors had fled England to avoid Stuart oppressions. Their history deepened their sense of alarm. Contemporary England seemed to resemble the corrupted country of Charles II. As Andrew Eliot of Boston, successor to Mayhew in the confidence of Thomas Hollis, confessed, "I tremble for the nation which has so few honest patriots—These few I fear will not be able to Stem the torrent of Ambition Luxury and Venality."[31]

The clergy trembled and they thundered. They feared tyranny, and they feared immorality and spiritual decay. They joined battle with a mother country oblivious of its political and moral obligations, and ultimately separation seemed essential to avoid the contagion of English "swearing, lying, killing, stealing, adultery." The England of their historical admiration was apparently gone forever. "The general prevalence of vice," concluded Samuel Langdon of Portsmouth, New Hampshire, in 1775, "has changed the whole face of things in the British government." Now he saw "a mere shadow of its ancient political system."[32] With singular felicity of phrase, Samuel Stillman,

---

30. Skillman, *Oration*, 5, 28, 10, 26, xiv, x–xi, viii, vii.

31. Andrew Eliot to Hollis, May 13, 1767, Hollis Manuscripts, Massachusetts Historical Society. Jacob Duché echoed Eliot's fears in a prayer before the Continental Congress in 1774: "We rather tremble for the parent state, and would fain keep off from our own borders those luxuries, which may perhaps already have impaired her constitutional vigor." See Duché's *The Duty of Standing Fast in Our Spiritual and Temporal Liberties . . .* (Philadelphia, 1775), in Frank Moore, *The Patriot Preachers of the American Revolution* (N.Y., 1860), 84–85.

32. Samuel Langdon, *A Sermon Preached before the Honorable Congress of the Massachusetts-Bay . . . May 31, 1775* (Watertown, 1775), in John W. Thornton, *The Pulpit of the American Revolution . . .* (Boston and N.Y., 1860), 242–43.

pastor of Boston's First Baptist Church, summed up his private feeling of political compulsion: after the Coercive Acts of 1774, "we have," he wrote Patience Wright, "too great a Sense of the Privileges of Englishmen, too much of the Spirit of Britons, and too great a Conviction of our own Importance, to consent to be Slaves." As a footnote, Stillman asked his correspondent to remember him to that "celebrated female Advocate for the Rights of Mankind, Mrs. Macaulay."[33] The New England clergy's arguments for resistance to English misrule contributed much to colonial unity on the eve of independence.

II

If Mayhew led New England clerical criticism of England, James Otis mounted the first political offensive using the law as justification. A Harvard graduate, Otis was able to study history with the resources of his college library. He developed a taste for reading and wanted to buy books for himself. In a familiar type of student letter, Otis was soon asking his father for more money: "If you Can possibly Spare Some money for to buy me Some Books if it is but ten Pounds-worth for if I live at home next Year in order to follow my Studies I had as good pretend to Run with my legs tyed as to make any Progress with what Books I have."[34] Evidently his father responded obligingly, despite his son's lack of punctuation, for Otis encountered no difficulties in his law studies with the esteemed Jere-

33. Samuel Stillman to Patience Wright, Nov. 13, 1774, "Letters to Josiah Quincy, Jr.," Massachusetts Historical Society, *Proceedings* 50 (1917): 475.

34. James Otis to his father, June 17, 1745, Waterson Manuscripts, Massachusetts Historical Society, quoted by Shipton, *Sibley's Harvard Graduates,* XI, 247–48. In his excellent study of Otis, ibid., 247–87, Shipton describes Otis as being able to see both sides of a question too well, and as a result he "so qualified and explained his original position that he gave aid and comfort to the opposition. Any quotation from his works is likely to be misleading because it does not have its context with it."

miah Gridley, then Attorney General of Massachusetts Bay. Otis was admitted to the Massachusetts bar in 1748, but began his career as a lawyer by spending more time with his books than with clients.[35] He read his Coke with care and studied the works of William Hawkins, whose *Abridgement of the First Part of Lord Coke's Institutes* and *Pleas of the Crown* were as useful as they were popular. Otis studied English common law carefully. The Writs of Assistance case gave him his opportunity to demonstrate his legal acumen.

The writs were a species of search warrant used with vigor against colonial smugglers after 1755. More effective than ordinary search warrants, the writs enabled any customs official in company with a court officer to conduct a general search in any place or habitation where smuggled goods were believed to be. These writs originated during the reign of Charles II and were extended to the American colonies by the Navigation Act of 1696. The only limitation to these broad authorizations for search was that a writ expired six months after the death of a reigning sovereign. Thus upon the death of George II in October 1760, Thomas Lechmere, Surveyor General of the Customs in America, applied to the Massachusetts Superior Court for fresh authority. The Court agreed to hear the opposition of Massachusetts merchants as presented by Oxenbridge Thacher and James Otis; the case for the Crown was made by Attorney General Gridley, Otis' legal mentor.[36]

The actual legality of the writs can hardly be questioned. While, as William Blackstone conceded, a general warrant "is illegal and void for it's certainty,"[37] Parliament had always reserved the right to

35. Shipton, *Sibley's Harvard Graduates,* XI, 248.

36. There is a useful summary of the Writs of Assistance case in Lawrence H. Gipson, *The Coming of the Revolution, 1763–1775* (N.Y., 1954), 34–49; see also Joseph R. Frese, "James Otis and Writs of Assistance," *New England Quarterly* 30 (1957): 496–508.

37. Blackstone, *Commentaries* (London, 1783), IV, 291, quoted in Richard L. Perry, ed., *Sources of Our Liberties . . .* (Chicago, 1959), 304.

make exceptions, and English legal usage indicated that similar writs had long been observed.[38] Consequently when Otis reviewed the question of their legality, he came in conflict with the established authority of Parliament itself, and his blunt denial of Parliament's power captured the imagination of John Adams.

"Otis was a flame of fire," according to this enraptured listener in the Massachusetts Court. "Every man of an immense crowded audience," Adams continued, "appeared to me to go away, as I did, ready to take arms against Writs of Assistance. Then and there, was the first scene of the first act of opposition, to the arbitrary claims of Great Britain." Although some may dispute Adams's conclusion that "then and there, the child Independence was born," there is general agreement that Otis offered a persuasive and eloquent argument.[39]

Otis's approach was that of a lawyer who had investigated the history of common law, which he regarded as the protection of all Englishmen, wherever located. For Otis, the British constitution was essentially a government of law, a law which was superior to both executive and legislature, a law which went back (as Coke claimed) to time immemorial. Otis searched into "the old Saxon laws," he reviewed the affirmations of Magna Charta and "the fifty confirmations of it in Parliament," and like Mayhew he took careful note of past occasions when the fundamental laws of England had been violated. He identified the writs with the kind of power "which in a former period of English history, cost one King of England his head, and another his throne."

Otis now reached the heart of his case: Parliament had no constitutional authority to authorize writs which contradicted the "fundamental rights" of Englishmen. He based his argument on Coke's opinion in Bonham's Case (1606) as cited in Charles Viner's *Gen-*

38. G. W. Wolkins, "Writs of Assistance in England," Massachusetts Historical Society, *Proceedings* 66 (1942): 357–64.

39. William Tudor, *The Life of James Otis . . .* (Boston, 1823), 60. Tudor's compilation of the Adams accounts of the Otis speech may be found on pp. 63–86.

eral Abridgement of Law and Equity,[40] but Otis was probably familiar with Coke's original comment (in his *Reports*) that "it appears in our books, that in many cases, the common law will control acts of parliament, and sometimes adjudge them to be utterly void."[41]

Otis saw in this a historical substantiation for his contention that the writs were indeed against English common law and therefore void. Although he had looked deeply into historical precedents, and sought to support his argument with previous examples, the weight of legal authority in the past was frequently against him. So he relied on more ancient, more fundamental principles. There could be, he declared, "NO PRESCRIPTION old enough to supersede the law of nature." In pleading that an act of Parliament against common law was void, he argued out of the "Proeme" of Coke's *Second Institutes* against the legal precedents cited by Gridley. He insisted that Americans were fully entitled to the rights guaranteed under common law and also the rights beyond it, rights which he believed controlled common law. Englishmen in America, he pleaded, could claim the same privileges "as any inhabitant of London or Bristol, or any part of England."[42] He impressed Chief Justice Hutchinson, a historian himself, but the decision of the Court was in favor of the writs. No one was greatly surprised when Parliament confirmed its belief in its own authority by reenacting the writs in the Townshend Acts of 1767.

Although defeated in this first encounter, Otis did not abandon his concern for colonial rights. Unhappily while he was sufficiently

40. Appendix A, Adams, *Works*, II, 522; see Sir Edward Coke, *Reports*, III, 107–18.

41. Coke was probably too much the Parliament-man to intend to establish common law as the ultimate arbiter of Parliamentary legislation. He based his decision in Dr. Bonham's case on the statutory reinterpretation rather than on an appeal to rights under fundamental law; see S. E. Thorne, "The Constitution and the Courts: A Reexamination of the Famous Case of Dr. Bonham," in Conyers Read, ed., *The Constitution Reconsidered* (N. Y., 1938), 21. See also Edward S. Corwin, "The 'Higher Law' Background of American Constitutional Law," *Harvard Law Review* 42 (1929): 367.

42. Tudor, *Life of Otis*, 71.

positive about what such rights should be, he was far from consistent on the proper course of colonial action to reclaim them. Otis thought of himself as a realist who had clearly in mind the political goals which should be achieved, but his realism fell short of formulating any specific course of action designed to achieve these goals. His historical and legal investigations gave him a clear enough concept of what should be ultimate colonial objectives, but his periodic flirtation with political ambition disconcerted and alienated many of his earlier admirers.

He never gave up his claim for colonial equality with Englishmen in the mother country with respect to constitutional rights, but he was sometimes prepared to suggest this equality meant an equal subjection to Parliament as a result.[43] On the other hand, his initial conclusion about the supremacy of common law acted as a useful brake upon rash conceptions of Parliamentary supremacy in all things. Parliament's authority was subordinate to common law, and since common law could not be abrogated, any Parliamentary effort to tax America must necessarily be illegal. It followed that if Parliament sought to exert an illegal authority, the colonies would be legally correct in resisting.

And yet this seems like a legalistic game that Otis was playing. He had found a convincing justification for but declined to advocate Revolutionary action despite the provocation of the Sugar and Stamp Acts.[44] Clifford K. Shipton has argued that Otis made frequent admission of the power of Parliament (while simultaneously denying the equity of the use of such authority) in the hope that recognition of a de facto situation would propitiate that body and avoid oppression.[45] This seems doubtful: Otis surely had little to hope for from a Parliament which he had already attacked for exceeding

---

43. Otis, *The Rights of the British Colonies Asserted and Proved* (Boston, 1764), 32–33.

44. For one view of the Otis political minuet, see Ellen E. Brennan, "James Otis: Recreant and Patriot," *New England Quarterly* 12 (1939): 691–725.

45. Shipton, *Sibley's Harvard Graduates*, XI, 261–75.

its constitutional role. His reading seems to have convinced him of the decay of this very body whose judgment he now appears ready to accept. Of the House of Lords, he publicly asserted in 1768 that " 'tis notoriously known there are no set of people . . . more venal, more corrupt and debauched in their Principles." He admitted the peers could claim to be educated, but what did they learn at Oxford and Cambridge? "Why—nothing at all but Whoring, Smoking and Drinking." And the Commons were no better: they were "a parcel of Button-makers, Pin-makers, Horse Jockeys, Gamesters, Pensioners, Pimps and Whore Masters."[46] This, it should be remembered, was offered in the same year that Otis also announced "the power of parliament over her colonies was absolute," and if only there were a few Americans in Westminster, then "the power of parliament would be as perfect in America as in England."[47]

Otis seems to have been unable to accept the implication of his original contentions; yet he would not give them up. He signed the Stamp Act Congress Resolutions only with the greatest of reluctance, because "Parliament had a right to tax the colonies, and he was a d—d fool who denied it."[48] Still, he obviously resented Parliamentary interference in colonial affairs. Later he challenged Parliament to repeal the Townshend duties—"or else they [the English] are lost forever!" He was distressed by the continued presence in America of British troops, troops which would obviously remain as long as there was a crisis. History, he recalled, "is full of examples, that armies, stationed as guards over provinces, have seized the prey of their general, and given him a crown at the expense of his master." England should therefore beware lest "another Caesar should arise and usurp the authority of his master." He knew Caesar as "the destroyer of the

46. Ibid., 274–75.
47. Ibid., 273.
48. Diary, Jan. 16, 1766, Adams, *Works,* II, 179.

roman glory and grandeur," and usurpation might well be the way to British imperial disaster.[49]

And so Otis moved from one political posture to another. One moment he could threaten George III with the fate of Charles I; on another occasion he could recommend trust in Parliament's wisdom; and another time he would subordinate Parliament to common law, and remind that body of its obligation to respect the historical and legal right of Britons to be "as free on one side of the atlantic as on the other."[50] His reputation suffered from his apparently erratic conduct. But by first questioning the legal authority of Parliament in his Writs of Assistance case in 1761, and, after his coffeehouse brawl with John Robinson a decade later,[51] by being a living martyr to British brutality, Otis made his most direct contributions to the colonial cause. He may have been a prisoner to a reputation more radical than he sought. But Otis popularized an important historical conclusion: an appeal to "the rights and privileges confirmed and secured . . . by the British Constitution" could be used to deny British authority. These rights were "our best inheritance."[52]

III

Samuel Adams was no lawyer, nor was he particularly learned, yet in contrast to Otis, he was a wonderfully single-minded man. There could be no question of his extreme hostility, or the consistency of his opposition, to British rule. He was willing to employ any means to gain his ends. He was an uncommonly tough-minded politician, a

49. William Gordon, *History of the Rise . . . of the United States . . .* , 4 vols. (London, 1788), I, 228; Otis, *Rights of the British Colonies Asserted and Proved,* 51–52, 15.

50. Otis, *Rights of the British Colonies Asserted and Proved,* 70.

51. For an account of the political martyrdom of Otis, see the *Boston-Gazette* and the *Boston Chronicle,* both of Sept. 18, 1769.

52. Otis, *A Vindication of the British Colonies* (London, 1769), 47.

skillful agitator, who capitalized upon every possible opportunity.[53]

Lacking the broad intellectual interests of his cousin John and the legal training of James Otis, Sam Adams was nevertheless graduated from Harvard, even receiving his master's degree. Presumably he consulted the shelves of the college library, but with no very fruitful results. Though he absorbed the natural rights philosophy of his era, his convictions and passions were determined more by his practical experience and personal prejudices than by scholarship. He sometimes used history less to demonstrate his own thinking, perhaps, than to influence that of others. His interest in his past was essentially subjective; history to Adams was mainly a manner of expressing a political argument. Since he was an exceptionally shrewd judge of political fashion, the use he made of history indicates something of the historical sensitivity of his colonial audience.

Certainly Sam Adams knew enough history to make frequent use of illustrations and similes from ancient as well as modern times. Well aware of the general disrepute of Julius Caesar, Adams pointed to Caesar's similarity to Thomas Hutchinson and Lord Hillsborough. Caesar had been the "public Executioner of his Country's Rights"; Hutchinson in his ambition and lust for power might prove the same for Massachusetts. Caesar "had learning, courage, and great abilities," even as "the Tyrant of Rome." In comparison Hutchinson and Hillsborough were poor things.[54]

Adams was fond of the classical comparison: the unsteady British empire reproducing the disintegration of Rome. Drafting Boston's statement of *The Rights of the Colonists* in 1772, Adams complained that the British treated their colonists "with less decency and regard

---

53. Recent biographers of Samuel Adams have easily survived the common temptation to champion their subject. Both John C. Miller and Clifford K. Shipton have been warmly critical of Sam Adams's political ethics. See John C. Miller, *Sam Adams, Pioneer in Propaganda* (Boston, 1936), and Shipton, *Sibley's Harvard Graduates*, X, 420–64.

54. *Boston-Gazette*, Oct. 14, 1771.

than the Romans shewed even to the Provinces which They had conquered." In the *Boston-Gazette* of October 14, 1771, he had observed "all might be free . . . if all possessed the independent spirit of Brutus, who to his immortal honor, *expelled the proud Tyrant of Rome.*"[55]

The fall of empires was a mighty theme, a frightening one as Adams drew parallels between his Britain, his America, and Rome of long ago. He wrote John Scollay on the eve of Independence " 'The Roman Empire,' says the Historian [William Robertson], '*must* have sunk, though the Goths had not invaded it. Why? Because the Roman Virtue was sunk.' "[56] Other empires had fallen as well. Adams knew Vertot's *History of the Revolutions of Sweden,* with its melancholy tale of the fall of that "free, martial and valiant people." Swedes, once so great, were now debased, Adams wrote, so far lost that they "rejoice at being subject to the caprice and arbitrary power of a Tyrant." Britons, Bostonians, and Americans might suffer a "like Catastrophe."[57]

English history had been the history of freedom. Would it continue to be? Anthony Ellis's recent *Tracts on Liberty* supplied Adams a historical account of the progress of English liberty. Adams learned of the freedom of "the Northern nations, from among whom the Saxons came into England," bringing representative habits of Saxon government with them across the Channel. The foundation of the original English constitution, Adams read in Ellis, was the inability of "the Supreme Power" to "take from any Man any part of his Property without his Consent in Person or by his Representative." This pure, this perfect right against despotic power was fully confirmed

---

55. "The Rights of the Colonists" adopted by the Town of Boston, Nov. 20, 1772, H. A. Cushing, ed., *The Writings of Samuel Adams,* 4 vols. (N.Y., 1904–8), II, 360; *Boston-Gazette,* Oct. 14, 1771.

56. Sam Adams to John Scollay, Apr. 30, 1776, Cushing, ed., *Writings of Samuel Adams,* III, 286; see also Burgh, *Political Disquisitions,* III, 15, who is citing Robertson's *Charles V,* I, 3.

57. A Letter of Correspondence to the Other Towns, Boston, Nov. 20, 1772, Cushing, ed., *Writings of Samuel Adams,* II, 372–73.

in Magna Charta, and Adams thoughtfully published (in the *Boston-Gazette*) Coke's description of the Charter as "declaratory of the principal grounds of the fundamental laws and liberties of England." Less sure of the intricacies of Dr. Bonham's Case, Adams offered his own judgment that "whether Lord Coke has expressed it or not . . . an act of parliament made against Magna Charta in violation of its essential parts, is void."[58]

These aspects of English history fascinated Adams. He reflected his interest in his wording of the Resolutions of the Massachusetts House of Representatives on the Stamp Act, in October 1765: "one of the main pillars of the British Constitution," he declared, was no taxation without representation; this, "together with all other essential rights, liberties, privileges, and immunities of the people of Great Britain, have been fully confirmed to them by Magna Charta." Everyone knew by now that Americans were "entitled to the same extent of liberty with his Majesty's subjects in Britain." In January 1768 it was Adams again who wrote the address of the House to the Earl of Shelburne. "From the reign of Edward the Third," he declared, "the children of his Majesty's natural born subjects, born passing and re-passing the seas, are entitled to all the rights and privileges of his natural subjects within the realm."[59]

Adams shared the whig historians' distaste for feudalism—that Norman imposition—calling it "a state of perpetual war, anarchy, and confusion." Adams discussed this subject in a House address to Governor Hutchinson in March 1773. He quoted an unnamed but "very celebrated writer" who termed feudalism " 'that most iniquitous and absurd form of government, by which human nature was so shamefully degraded.' " Hutchinson had argued that Americans as English

58. Sam Adams to John Smith, 1765, ibid., I, 55; *Boston-Gazette,* Jan. 27, 1772 (writing as "Candidus").

59. Resolutions of the House of Representatives of Massachusetts, Oct. 29, 1765, and the House of Representatives of Massachusetts to the Earl of Shelburne, Jan. 15, 1768, Cushing, ed., *Writings of Samuel Adams,* I, 24, 154.

subjects held their lands "mediately or immediately, of the Crown." Adams denied this with characteristic vehemence. America, unlike Saxon England, had never been conquered, and so feudalism had not been introduced. Adams allowed that "we hold our lands agreeably to the feudal principles of the King," but this was mere form. The original settlers "wisely took care to enter into compact with the King, that power here should also be equally divided, agreeable to the original [non-Norman, nonfeudal] fundamental principles of the English constitution."[60]

There were other more recent English developments which weakened Adams's esteem for the history of the mother country. Ellis, and later Burgh, reminded him of the enduring problems represented by the Stuarts, and he revealed his familiarity with the seventeenth-century struggle for ancient liberties—with "Mr. Hampden's ship money cause" and the noble martyr Algernon Sidney, whose writings Adams knew well.[61] Adams concluded that England had failed to recover her ancient virtue, despite the staunch fight against the Stuart dynasty—"a race of Kings bigotted to the greatest degree to the doctrines of *slavery.*" He agreed that much was accomplished initially in the settlement of 1688, when "the British constitution was again restor'd to its original principles, declared in the bill of rights,"[62] but the gain had been temporary.

Where Parliament had once resisted Stuart tyranny now it seemed bent on behaving just as despotically as that hated dynasty.[63] Pensions, placemen, and standing armies were the new signs of oppression, the badges of tyranny. Adams recalled reading in Hume's *History* "that if James the Second had had the benefit of the riot act and such a

---

60. The House of Representatives of Massachusetts to the Governor, Mar. 2, 1773, ibid., II, 432–35. For Hutchinson's Address of Jan. 6, 1773, see the *Boston-Gazette,* Jan. 11, 1773.

61. *Boston-Gazette,* Sept. 16, 1771.

62. Ibid., Feb. 27, 1769 (writing as "E. A.").

63. The House of Representatives of Massachusetts to the Earl of Shelburne, Jan. 15, 1768, Cushing, ed., *Writings of Samuel Adams,* I, 158.

standing army as has been granted since his time, it would have been impracticable for the nation to have wrought its own delivery."[64] As early as 1768 Adams thought the future for Americans particularly ominous. He noted "the unnecessary increase of Crown Officers" and gloomily predicted that "the time may come, when the united body of pensioners and soldiers may ruin the liberties of America."[65] He was depressed by " 'the Torrent of Vice' " which he found another "celebrated author" describing as a major menace to empire as well as kingdom. The loss of English virtue was the fundamental fact of modern history, Adams thought. By 1776 the message was plain enough: "no State can long preserve its Liberty where Virtue is not supremely honored."[66] The martyred Sidney, noted Adams later, had observed that "there are times when People are not worth saving. Meaning when they have lost their Virtue."[67]

There were times when Adams thought he had moved much too belatedly for American independence—when he feared the English contagion had spread too far, when he feared Americans themselves even after independence would follow the mother country to moral and political bankruptcy. But when he struggled to stir his colleagues to vigorous opposition to British oppression, he was hopeful that America could yet be saved. And throughout his efforts he found his best arguments in the past. He believed in the natural rights of men, in the English common law and the ancient British constitution as mere distillations of "the Laws of Nature and universal Reason."[68] As he told the Governor of Massachusetts in 1769, "no time can be better employed, than in the preservation of the rights derived from the British constitution. . . . No treasure can be better expended,

---

64. Sam Adams to Arthur Lee, July 31, 1771, ibid., II, 189.
65. The House of Representatives of Massachusetts to Denys De Berdt, Jan. 12, 1768, ibid., I, 146.
66. Sam Adams to Benjamin Kent, July 27, 1776, ibid., II, 305.
67. Sam Adams to John Scollay, Dec. 30, 1780, ibid., IV, 238.
68. Sam Adams to Denys De Berdt, Dec. 20, 1765, ibid., I, 64.

than in securing that true old English liberty, which gives a relish to every other enjoyment."[69]

IV

Josiah Quincy, Jr., was as committed to "true old English liberty" as Sam Adams and better read on its history. An untimely death denied Quincy his opportunity to participate in the military events of the Revolution, but his contributions to the literature of the Revolution were substantial. The youngest of three sons, Josiah Quincy, Jr., was born to a family with sufficient wealth to send all three to Harvard for their education. He graduated in 1763 at the age of nineteen, soon secured his master's degree, and then entered the law office of Oxenbridge Thacher, the attorney who directed the merchants' case in the Writs of Assistance suit in 1761.[70]

Quincy first attracted attention by enlisting with John Adams in the defense of the unpopular British troops tried for the "murders" committed in Boston on March 5, 1770. He employed his recent legal training to fine effect and rightfully claimed the privilege of a fair trial for the unhappy Captain Preston and his men. In the process, Quincy also demonstrated the political charms of the system of English jurisprudence which he championed: there is, he observed, "a spirit" which pervades English law, an air which "inspires a freedom of thought, speech and behavior." He suggested that in a sense both the victims and the accused were products of the nature of the "happy constitution" which English law supported. The "very natural effects" of such a constitution were "an impatience of injuries, and a strong resentment of insult." Justice Trowbridge, summing up,

69. The House of Representatives of Massachusetts to the Governor, June 19, 1769, ibid., I, 348.

70. The best source for Josiah Quincy Jr.'s short life is by his son, Josiah Quincy, *Memoir of the Life of Josiah Quincy, Jun., of Massachusetts* (Boston, 1825).

discussed the nature and meaning of homicide in the common law. Paying his respects to Coke's definition of the law as "the general customs or immemorial usage of the English nation," he reminded the Court that "this law is the birth right of every Englishman; the first settlers of this country brought it from England with them."[71]

Josiah Quincy, Sr., was an omnivorous reader of historical literature that praised liberty, and he bequeathed to his son "Algernon Sidney's works,—John Locke's works,—Lord Bacon's works,— Gordon's Tacitus,—and Cato's Letters" as well as the hope that "the spirit of liberty [might] rest upon him."[72] But works such as Gordon's and Sidney's were merely Quincy Jr.'s favorites among histories. He was reasonably familiar with Plutarch, Robertson, Bolingbroke, Francis Sullivan, Burgh, Rapin, Mrs. Macaulay, and Montagu. Such "True *Whigs*" were supplemented by selective reading in Blackstone, Clarendon, and Hume.

As well grounded in Greek and Roman history as in that of his mother country, Quincy found history both useful and enlightening for what it taught about man. He consulted Plutarch for examples of past tyranny, noting how "no beast is more savage than man, when possessed of power equal to his passion." He found in Clarendon the remark that "it is the nature of man, rather to commit two errors, than to retract one." And William Robertson, "that prince of historians," reporting on social and political corruption, supplied the comment that a people never reform themselves, but reformation "is always forced upon them by some foreign hand." When urging his fellow Americans to new heights of patriotism, Quincy told them to "Brutus-like, therefore, dedicate yourselves . . . to the service of your country." He was confident that America had her fair share of "Bruti

---

71. Frederic Kidder, ed., *The History of the Boston Massacre* . . . (Albany, N.Y., 1870), 230, 260.

72. Will, Feb. 28, 1774, Quincy, *Memoir,* 350.

and Cassii—her Hampdens and Sydneys—patriots and heroes, who will form a band of brothers."[73]

But his chief historical lessons concerned the dangers of standing armies—anciently a peril to Rome, recently a threat to England, currently a menace to America. The occasion for Quincy's commentary on standing armies was the enactment of the Boston Port Act of 1774, the Quartering Act, and the appointment of General Gage as governor. He was, of course, familiar enough with the incendiary situation which large bodies of British troops could create—the Boston Massacre four years earlier had been a frightening example—and the new legislation would keep the atmosphere charged. Quincy turned to his Roman history. Dipping often into Gordon's popular translations of Sallust and Tacitus, Quincy recalled that Roman armies had been frequently "more terrible to the Roman colonies than an 'enemy's army'"—just as Americans were discovering that British troops were more threatening than their recent French antagonists.[74] Referring to "the elegant and instructive history, written by the masterly hand of Tacitus," Quincy then discussed with appropriate Roman examples "the spirit, cruelty, and rapine of soldiers quartered in populous cities." Standing armies were the commonest vehicles for tyranny. Roman and English history provided abundant evidence of the political consequences of such military forces—both Caesar and Cromwell had enslaved their countries with armies "stationed in the very bowels of the land." Quincy concluded that "the history of mankind affords no instance of successful and confirmed tyranny, without the aid of military forces." The British were well equipped for tyranny. An English member of Parliament, noted Quincy, had warned his countrymen that a standing army "is a monster, that will devour all your liberties and properties!"[75]

73. Quincy, *Observations on the Act of Parliament Commonly Called the Boston Port-Bill* . . . (Boston, 1774), in ibid., 366–67, 468–69. Quincy quoted from Robertson's *History of Scotland* . . . , 2 vols. (London, 1759), I, 167.

74. Quincy, *Observations*, in Quincy, *Memoir*, 443–44.

75. Ibid., 407 *n*, 405, 411 *n*.

The capstone to Quincy's argument concerned the character of the British forces. From his studies of pre-Norman England he knew his ancestors had once relied upon a people's militia rather than mercenaries. "In ancient time, the militia of England was raised, officered, and conducted, by common consent," observed Quincy with evident nostalgia. The Saxon militia "was the ornament of the realm in peace, and for ages continued the only and sure defence in war. Was the king himself general of an army, it was by consent of his people." His admiration for the sensible arrangements of "our Saxon ancestors" was not limited to praise for their military system, for Quincy admired their virtually elective monarchy as well. But the Saxon militia supported John Milton's claim that an armed people were " 'the truest and most proper strength of a free nation.' " It seemed to Quincy that England's most serious error was in allowing Henry VII—"a character odious for rapacity and fraud"—to establish "a permanent military band in that kingdom." The Stuarts, of course, he viewed in an even worse light, since they maintained armies "not only against law, but against the repeated resolutions of every Parliament." Charles II kept a standing army because "he found that corruption without force could not confirm him a tyrant, and therefore [he] cherished and augmented his troops to the destruction of his people."[76]

Quincy's sorties into political pamphleteering were too brief to allow an extensive historical commentary. Yet his criticisms of past English monarchs were sharp, reflecting his familiarity with Mrs. Macaulay and James Burgh. He had no love for "that odious and execrable race of tyrants, the house of Stewart."[77] He was distressed that the English, after rising "with a divine enthusiasm" against Charles I, should then first submit to Cromwell (with another standing army) and then "with unexampled folly and madness" restore Charles II

76. Ibid., 413–14, 411 *n*, 417, 423. Quincy cites Rapin.
77. Charles Dilly to Josiah Quincy, Mar. 9, 1775, "Journal of Josiah Quincy, Jun., During His Voyage and Residence in England from September 28th, 1774, to March 3d, 1775," Massachusetts Historical Society, *Proceedings* 50 (1917): 491, 451, 453.

to the throne. Quincy's disgust with this Stuart monarch was unrestrained. Where some colonists might blame the Normans for everything, Quincy preferred to condemn Charles II. The corruption afflicting contemporary England originated with Charles II; the oppression of America derived from legislation enacted by Charles II. Charles II appeared so evil that Quincy could compare him only to the Emperor Charles V, who had so fiercely punished Dutch fighters for freedom. And when he read Temple's account of the later Spanish oppression of the Dutch, Quincy was again reminded of the tyranny of Charles II in England. Under Charles II, Quincy concluded, "Britain, then for the first time, saw corruption, like a destroying angel, walking at noonday." Thanks to that fatal Restoration of 1660, "the science of bribery and corruption hath made amazing progress" in England.[78]

For Quincy the past was "the voice of experience." He tried to listen as best he could. He let such authors as Lord Bolingbroke show him how to "search the history of the world," and he learned how to pursue the course of such singular evils as standing armies—concluding with Mrs. Macaulay that a people's militia was "the natural strength and only stable safeguard, of a free country."[79] He noted meaningful historical parallels: the virtuous Dutch; the courageous Hungarians, who when first called rebels, "were called so for no other reason than . . . that they would not be slaves."[80]

Quincy's historical endeavors received an unusual stimulus: in 1774 he met personally with many of the authors he had read in America, when he made a political pilgrimage to London on the eve of the Revolution to present colonial grievances to Lords North and Dartmouth. There he mingled pleasurably with such "true Whigs" as that "most extraordinary woman" Mrs. Macaulay, and "the celebrated Dr. Burgh." He visited several times with the former, includ-

78. Quincy, *Observations*, in Quincy, *Memoir*, 450–51, 407–9, 446–47.
79. Ibid., 411; from Macaulay's *History of England*, II, 165.
80. Quincy, *Memoir*, 407, 386.

ing an afternoon spent in "improving conversation." He subsequently dined "in the family way" with Mrs. Macaulay's publisher, Edward Dilly, and on another occasion supped "in company with Dr. Priestley, Dr. Franklin, Price and others." Indeed, Quincy was so definitely welcome in this charmed circle that he was even allowed an hour's audience with the dying James Burgh, who for the occasion "took a double dose of opium to allay the pains of the stone." Quite possibly the highlight of Quincy's London visit was listening to Camden and Chatham in the House of Lords. Quincy carefully took down Camden's words: "Acts of Parliament have been resisted in all ages. Kings, Lords and Commons may become tyrants as well as others. Tyranny in one or more is the same." But Chatham far outshone Lord Camden—"he seemed like an old Roman Senator," thought Quincy. When Chatham expressed the "hope the Whigs of both countries [England and America] will join and make a common cause," Quincy knew his visit was not wasted.[81]

But neither was Quincy's trip successful. He had come to England—despite an advanced case of tuberculosis—to argue for the colonists' birthrights as Englishmen, but he found his own yearning for the ancient liberties of "our Saxon ancestors" insufficiently shared in England herself. The lessons of "that sagacious politician" Tacitus were poorly studied outside America; eighteenth-century England seemed unable to recapture that "divine enthusiasm" shown against the Stuarts.[82] There were too few Camdens and Chathams in Great Britain, too few Macaulays and Burghs. It was Quincy's tragedy that he died on his voyage home in 1775, his trip undoubtedly accelerating the disease which took his life. Actually, his effort at personal diplomacy was doubly tragic in its outcome, for he left England knowing that Americans would have to fight for their claim to the legal and historical rights of Englishmen.

81. "Journal," Massachusetts Historical Society, *Proceedings* 50 (1917): 451, 467, 452, 455, 456, 467, 459.
82. Quincy, *Memoir*, 452 n.

CHAPTER V

John Adams:
Political Scientist as Historian

For men anxious to pursue a path of legality, for men seeking security for property against British depredations, for men looking for stability at home and abroad, John Adams was a logical and a persuasive leader. Educated at Harvard (class of 1755), trained in law (under James Putnam), Adams earned his reputation as a patriot and Revolutionary in a series of remarkable essays. His *Dissertation on the Canon and Feudal Law,* his *Novanglus* papers, his *Thoughts on Government,* and his *Defence of the Constitutions* are among the most important patriot writings of his generation.[1]

Adams has long been regarded as a New England Thomas Jefferson, more conservative than his Virginia colleague, but possessed of the same intellectual vigor and curiosity. The comparison does little

---

1. Adams's published writings are included in Charles Francis Adams, ed., *The Works of John Adams,* 10 vols. (Boston, 1850–56). Lyman H. Butterfield is editing *The Adams Papers* in eighty to ninety volumes which will embrace the enormously productive descendants of John Adams; because of the necessary limitations of this letterpress edition, a complete microfilm copy of the Adams Papers has been made available to academic institutions. Adams still lacks a first-rate complete biography; Page Smith's *John Adams,* 2 vols. (N.Y., 1963), has virtues but offers little on Adams's intellectual environment. [This is not the case with more-recent books on John Adams: John R. Howe, *The Political Thought of John Adams* (1966); Peter Shaw, *The Character of John Adams* (1976); and Joseph J. Ellis, *Passionate Sage: The Character and Legacy of John Adams* (1994). —T. C., 1997.]

justice to either Adams or Jefferson. They were both unique. They both deserve to be judged as individuals who studied similar problems. Adams may have bought somewhat fewer books than Jefferson, but he read more. Adams was always reading, always taking notes, always referring to his recent reading in his writings. When he found time he scribbled marginal notes of varying length in over a hundred of his books.[2] Adams had an acute sense of intellectual duty and lectured himself repeatedly on his educational obligations: in 1759, reproaching himself for imagined sloth, he had "Virtue" give him the following orders:

> Rise and mount your horse by the morning's dawn, and shake away, amidst the great and beautiful scenes of nature that appear at that time of the day, all the crudities that are left in your stomach, and all the obstructions that are left in your brains. Then return to your studies, and bend your whole soul to the institutes of the law and the reports of cases that have been adjudged by the rules in the institutes; let no trifling diversion, or amusement, or company, decoy you from your book; that is, let no girl, no gun, no cards, no flutes, no violins, no dress, no tobacco, no laziness, decoy you from your books. . . . But keep your law book or some point of law in your mind, at least six hours in a day.

After admitting he was "too minute and lengthy," he concluded his admonition: "aim at an exact knowledge of the nature, end, and means of government; compare the different forms of it with each other, and each of them with their effects on public and private happiness. Study Seneca, Cicero, and all other good moral writers; study Montesquieu, Bolingbroke, . . . and all other good civil writers."[3]

Adams aimed well. He frequently grew wordy—and probably alienated potential biographers in the process—but his scholarship is undeniable. Anxious to seek the law as best he could "in its foun-

2. There is a fine summation on the Adams character in Zoltán Haraszti, *John Adams and the Prophets of Progress* (Cambridge, Mass., 1952), chap. 2. The Boston Athenaeum is the chief repository of the Adams books, most distinguished for the marginalia inscribed by their owner.

3. Diary, Jan. 3, 1759, Adams, *Works,* II, 59.

tains" (the very words of Blackstone's recommendation of the same goal), Adams determined to furnish himself "at any sacrifice with a proper library." With typical modesty he described how by degrees he had procured the best private library of law in Massachusetts.[4] Law led him directly to history, the study of which he soon discovered indispensable. While English history was important to him, numerous volumes on the Greek and Roman past—Thucydides, Herodotus, Tacitus, Sallust, Livy—crowded Adams's bookshelves, leaving little room for less useful literature. Possibly the one exception Adams cared to make was in favor of Scottish and German romances which "show in a clear light the horrors of the feudal aristocracy."[5]

Adams read many of the same legal and historical authorities other Americans read. The real mark of Adams's individuality is found less in his initial selection of reading than in his frequent return to certain books and his highly personal conclusions. When he later reviewed his educational experience, Adams minimized his college years: here was the ordinary routine of classical studies, endured while exploring the more fascinating worlds of mathematics and natural philosophy. When he began his law studies, he found his reading obligations too vast to allow outside interests; the law of nations, civil law, and common law demanded all his time and energies. But he was happy to add in his seventy-fourth year that "classics, history, and philosophy have, however, never been wholly neglected to this day."[6]

The entries in his diary constitute an introductory inventory of Adams's intellectual resources: in February 1756 he "staid at home reading the Independent Whig"; in March he was transcribing Bolingbroke; in April he read Milton, whose genius "was great beyond conception, and his learning beyond bounds"; in 1759 he was reading Sidney's *Discourses* and often dipped into them instead of dutifully

4. Autobiography, Adams, *Works,* II, 50 *n.*

5. John Adams to Benjamin Rush, Dec. 27, 1810, Worthington C. Ford, ed., *Old Family Letters,* 2 vols. (Philadelphia, 1898), I, 269.

6. John Adams to Shelton Jones, Mar. 11, 1809, Adams, *Works,* IX, 613.

reading law briefs; in 1760 he reproached himself for having read "Coke's Commentary on Littleton" only once—"I must get and read over and over again." But he seems to have found Coke as dreary as did Jefferson, and he often preferred to neglect his law books and return to Bolingbroke instead—indeed he later confessed to having read Bolingbroke's *Works* five times.[7] There was no need to return to Coke that often, since a few years after beginning law practice Adams was introduced to William Blackstone's writing. Charmed by this modern review of English law, Adams bought both the *Law Tracts* and the *Commentaries* as soon as they became available.[8] As a useful supplement to Blackstone—for whom Adams later recommended gratitude without adoration—he read the admirable Lord Kames, author of the illuminating *Historical Law Tracts*.[9]

Adams was always a ready critic. He reported reading Clarendon in 1758 and found him an informed but "very partial Writer." Hume was worse. "A conceited Scotchman," was Adams's description. In another exchange with Jefferson, Adams explained his dislike of Hume's "elegant Lies" which "had nearly laughed into contempt Rapin Sydney and even Lock[e]." Rapin and Sidney were among Adams's preferred authors, along with Nathaniel Bacon, Harrington, Roger Acherley, Thomas Gordon and John Trenchard, Burnet, and,

---

7. Diary, Feb. 15, 16, Mar. 1, 6, Apr. 30, 1756, Nov. 26, 1760, Adams, *Works*, II, 5, 7, 14, 104; Adams to Jefferson, Dec. 25, 1813, Cappon, ed., *Adams-Jefferson Papers*, II, 410.

8. John Adams to Richard Rush, Apr. 14, 1811, John H. Powell, ed., "Some Unpublished Correspondence of John Adams and Richard Rush, 1811–22," *Pennsylvania Magazine of History and Biography* 61 (1937): 432. In his Diary, Nov. 14, 1760, Adams wrote, "I wish I had Mr. Blackstone's Analysis, that I might compare, and see what Improvement he has made upon Hale's." By Nov. 20, 1761, he was gratifying his wish. See Adams, *Works*, II, 100–101, and Butterfield et al., eds., *The Adams Papers* (Cambridge, Mass., 1961–), I, 225. Adams was on the list of subscribers to Robert Bell's 3-volume edition of Blackstone's *Commentaries*. See *Catalogue of the Library of John Adams* (Boston, 1917), 113, 28. The bulk of the Adams law books survive in the Boston Public Library.

9. John Adams to Richard Rush, Feb. 16, 1814, Powell, ed., "Adams-Rush Correspondence," *Pennsylvania Magazine of History and Biography* 61 (1937): 40. John Adams's copy of Kames's *Historical Law Tracts* was a gift from the author in 1761 (now in the Boston Public Library); see Diary, Feb. 21, 1765, Adams, *Works*, II, 148.

to a lesser degree, Mrs. Macaulay and James Burgh. Adams was no stranger to what he called the fashionable reading of colonial politicians in the 1760s and 1770s.[10]

By 1774 Adams, deeply involved in the colonial crisis with the ministry, concluded that his seventeenth-century heroes alone—Sidney, Harrington, Milton, Nedham, Burnet—"will convince any candid mind, that there is no good government but what is republican."[11] He also liked the eighteenth-century temper of Mrs. Macaulay, with whom he corresponded. Her *History of England* Adams read at one time "with much admiration." She wrote with the proper perspective, since her plan, which, said Adams, "I have ever wished to see adopted by historians," was "to strip off the gilding and false lustre from worthless princes and nobles, and to bestow the reward of virtue, praise, upon the generous and worthy only."[12] James Burgh sent Adams a copy of his *Political Disquisitions;* it arrived in 1774 as he was writing the *Novanglus* papers. Adams found these volumes every bit as timely as did his associates in the First Continental Congress. "I cannot but think," he wrote Burgh, that "those *Disquisitions* [are] the best service that a citizen could render to his country at this great and dangerous crisis."[13]

Adams studied history more from a sense of critical curiosity than from a desire for substantiation of colonial claims, although his selective reading sifted out whiggish views in support of American

10. John Adams to Benjamin Waterhouse, May 18, 1820, Worthington C. Ford, ed., *Statesman and Friend; Correspondence of John Adams with Benjamin Waterhouse, 1784–1822* (Boston, 1927), 154; Adams to Thomas Jefferson, Dec. 25 and July 15, 1813, Cappon, ed., *Adams-Jefferson Letters,* II, 410, 357; Adams to Richard Rush, Feb. 16, 1814, Powell, ed., "Adams-Rush Correspondence," *Pennsylvania Magazine of History and Biography* 61 (1937): 40; Diary, Feb. 16, 1756, Adams, *Works,* II, 5.

11. *Thoughts on Government* (Philadelphia, 1776), Adams, *Works,* IV, 194.

12. John Adams to Mrs. Macaulay, Aug. 9, 1770, ibid., IX, 332.

13. Adams received presentation copies of the first 2 volumes of Burgh's *Political Disquisitions* early in 1774 (Burgh's inscription is dated Mar. 7, 1774); in 1775 Burgh had his publishers send a complete 3-volume set. All 5 volumes are now in the Boston Public Library. John Adams to James Burgh, Dec. 28, 1774, ibid., IX, 350–51.

doctrines about the historic rights of Englishmen. Essentially pessimistic in his appraisal of man, Adams found little evidence of the human progress discovered by others. History for Adams was at least in part a record of human errors. He arrived at his own conclusions about the causes of political catastrophes in the past; and since he did not anticipate any great change in human nature, he laid plans to compensate for human weakness. The greater part of Adams's historical investigations were devoted to studying governments which had failed, he believed, because of their unbalanced structure. Adams moved from the study of history as it reflected on colonial relations with England to the study of history as it illuminated his political philosophy. He found history, law, and philosophy relevant to an examination of colonial rights, but after independence he shifted the emphasis of his historical studies to other political problems.

I

Like most Americans, Adams was a contented subject of the new king in 1760. After reading Bolingbroke's *Patriot King,* he was particularly impressed with the grand promises of George III — "to patronize religion, virtue, the British name and constitution . . . the subjects' rights, liberty." These, Adams concluded, "are sentiments worthy of a king;—a patriot king."[14] Disillusionment soon set in. The Stamp Act, enacted in 1765, seemed to Adams a clear invasion of colonial rights and an occasion for examining whether or not "protection and allegiance [are] reciprocal." If the King would not protect his American subjects from unconstitutional Parliamentary taxation, "are we not discharged from our allegiance? Is it not an abdication of the throne?"[15] To questions such as these Adams addressed himself in his *Dissertation on the Canon and Feudal Law.*

First discussed in the privacy of Gridley's Sodalitas Club and later

14. Diary, Feb. 9, 1761, ibid., II, 117–18.
15. Diary, Dec. 21, 1765, ibid., 162.

published in the *Boston-Gazette* in 1765, Adams's *Dissertation* was a notable exploration of colonial rights which anticipated many of the political arguments of James Wilson, John Dickinson, and Thomas Jefferson. Yet in the *Dissertation* Adams did not arrive at any strongly defined conclusion. As Charles Francis Adams noted later, it was a searching, analytical sketch, with hints for future inquiries.[16] John Adams was feeling his way, following the lines of thought prompted by growing sensitivity to the political implications of his reading. If there is a fundamental and unifying theme to his essay, it must be Adams's awareness of the importance of political education. At the very outset he referred to ignorance as a principal cause of the ruin of mankind. His mission was to combat ignorance with information. He wanted fellow colonists to know their rights, and he wanted fellow Englishmen to know that the colonists would resist encroachments upon such rights. Education was vital for Englishmen on both sides of the Stamp Act controversy.

The fundamental question of 1765, as Adams saw it, was enveloped in history. In a historical review which he later described as superficial, Adams analyzed Old World tyranny as deriving from two chief sources: canon law and feudal law. The former he identified with the "astonishing constitution of policy . . . framed by the Romish clergy for the aggrandisement of their own order." For illustration he pointed to Robertson's newly published *History of Charles V.* Feudal law was similar, employed "for the same purposes of tyranny, cruelty, and lust." Originally, it was "a code of laws for a vast army in a perpetual encampment," and its corollary was the investment of the monarch with all the lands within his kingdom. All men held their lands of the king, and the common people lived in "a state of servile dependence." While either system was evil enough, history points to a worse calamity, namely the union of the two. Liberty, virtue, and

16. Among Adams's admirers was Mayhew's friend Thomas Hollis. Hollis had the *Dissertation* reprinted in the London *Chronicle,* and called it "one of the finest productions ever seen from North America." Ibid., III, 447.

knowledge "seem to have deserted the earth" until the first glimmer of light came in the form of the Reformation. The English became enlightened and rose against "the execrable race of Stuarts" to break the yoke of feudal and religious tyranny.[17]

This was Adams's description of the historical setting for the colonization of America. His colonial ancestors came not for religious reasons alone, but out of "a love of universal liberty, and a hatred, a dread, a horror, of the infernal confederacy before described." The Puritan leaders succeeded because they were educated, knowledgeable men—"some of them have left libraries that are still in being, consisting chiefly of volumes in which the wisdom of the most enlightened ages and nations is deposited."[18] Being educated men, the Puritans knew the evils of even a diluted religious tyranny as represented by a "diocesan episcopacy," so they took care to found their colony on the solid ground of "the Bible and common sense." They also repudiated feudalism: "They detested all the base services and servile dependencies of the feudal system. They knew that no such unworthy dependencies took place in the ancient seats of liberty." And modern New Englanders, Adams added, should note the writings of Lord Kames ("a Scottish writer of great reputation"), who termed feudal law "a constitution so contradictory to all the principles which govern mankind" that it could be secured only "by foreign conquest or native usurpations." Since Americans were not a conquered people, feudalism had no place in the colonies. Americans, who could claim to hold their lands allodially, had chosen instead to go through the form of holding their lands from the Crown "as their sovereign lord." This, Adams insisted, should be a form only. It was no right of entry for feudal tyranny.[19]

---

17. "Dissertation on the Canon and Feudal Law," Aug. 1765, ibid., III, 449, 450.

18. Ibid., III, 451–52.

19. Ibid., 454. In Adams's view, Kames's opinions were the more remarkable because their author was Scottish: most Scotsmen "have not the most worthy ideas of liberty," explained Adams.

Adams kept returning to his theme that knowledge was the road to freedom. The colonists would maintain their freedom because of "their knowledge of human nature, derived from history and their own experience." They had an obligation to make known their knowledge, and to express resentment of British misrule. England surely would respond when suitably informed of her errors: to say otherwise would be to represent "every member of parliament as renouncing the transactions at Runing Mede." England surely recalled "that the prince of Orange was created King William by the people, on purpose that their rights might be eternal and inviolable." It was true, Adams conceded, that some in England had become "luxurious, effeminate, and unreasonable." But "let us presume," he added, "that the spirit of liberty is as ardent as ever among the body of the nation, though a few individuals may be corrupted." [20]

Americans were under a historical obligation to protest invasions of their rights and to resist any resurrection of canon and feudal tyranny. Adams concluded his essay with a dramatic series of injunctions to his readers: they must persist in their search for political wisdom; they must study history; they must examine the British constitution; they must review the examples of past British defenders of freedom; they must look again at the fortitude of their immediate forefathers, who first settled America; the colonial clergy should make "the pulpit resound with the doctrines and sentiments of religious liberty"; the colonial lawyer should (like Adams) "proclaim 'the laws, the rights, the generous plan of power' delivered down from remote antiquity"; quoting his favorite Bolingbroke (but not identifying his source), Adams reminded fellow lawyers to "let it be known, that British liberties are not the grants of princes or parliaments, but original rights, conditions of original contracts"; and finally, the colleges should "join their harmony in the same delightful concert"; academic orations and essays should dwell upon "the

20. Ibid., 455, 462.

108

beauty of liberty and virtue, and the deformity, turpitude, and malignity, of slavery and vice."[21] All colonial energies should be directed toward creating a universal concern with freedom: the youngest and most tender mind should receive proper political education.

Adams was seeking something more than an informed measure of colonial protest. He wanted a colonial populace suitably sensitized to and properly informed on its rights. He was thinking in terms of historical parallels: the last major occasion for resistance to tyrannical encroachments had been in the seventeenth century, which "by turning the general attention of learned men to government . . . produced the greatest number of consummate statesmen which has ever been seen in any age or nation." Who would ever have heard of a Milton, a Harrington, a Sidney, or a Locke, had it not been for the political circumstances which drew these men from other activities? Perhaps, mused Adams, Americans could match their performance. At least the colonists should not be "driven blindfolded to irretrievable destruction." The plain fact was, "there seems to be a direct and formal design on foot, to enslave all America." The initial step would be the introduction of the canon and feudal law, which "though greatly mutilated in England, are not yet destroyed," and the Stamp Act was a devious effort to begin the process. Since the Stamp Act taxed such avenues to knowledge as newspapers and college diplomas, it could destroy the colonists' opportunity to investigate their actual rights. Americans had better seek wisdom while they might and employ it against this "direct and formal design" of the misguided mother country.[22]

Adams's *Dissertation* was not limited to the tyranny represented by the Stamp Act. He also outlined his reflections on the historical and constitutional questions raised by the measure. He sought to define the origins of the rights to which he laid claim. They were,

21. Ibid., 462–63.
22. Ibid., 463–64.

he said, God-given, "antecedent to all earthly government," and yet supported by the British constitution. This was not, as Randolph G. Adams once contended, "a mere confusion of intellectual and political philosophy, [that] we can profitably dispense with."[23] John Adams was turning his attention to the historic exercise and recognition of man's natural rights. Under the British constitution as Adams came to see it "all men are born equal; and the drift of the British constitution is to preserve as much of this equality as is compatible with the people's security."[24] And the "grand," the "fundamental principle" of the constitution is in Magna Charta: "that no freeman should be subject to any tax to which he has not given his own consent."[25] The Stamp Act was a historic departure from the constitution to which Adams gave allegiance. He and other American colonists had no representation in Parliament. The Stamp Act was invalid, "it not being in any sense our act, having never consented to it."[26]

II

Pursuing the lines of inquiry thus begun, Adams noted the contrast between the England of King John and that of King George III. "The ancient barons who answered with one voice, 'We will not that the laws of England be changed, which of old have been used and approved,'" now "seem to have answered that they are willing those laws should be changed with regard to America in the most tender point and fundamental principle."[27] He looked at the history of England to discover "how many arbitrary reigns do we find since the conquest." Even Queen Elizabeth had tried to infringe Parliamentary

23. Ibid., 449; Randolph G. Adams, *Political Ideas of the American Revolution* . . . , 3d ed. (N.Y., 1958), 113.

24. *Boston-Gazette,* Jan. 27, 1766 (signed "Clarendon").

25. "Dissertation on the Canon and Feudal Law," Adams, *Works,* III, 466.

26. Diary, Dec. 20, 1765, ibid., II, 158.

27. Instructions of the Town of Boston to their Representatives, May 15, 1769, ibid., III, 508.

privilege, only to be rebuffed by a sensitive Commons. The Stuarts, to their shame, failed to digest the lessons of Tudor history and created the need and opportunity for men like Algernon Sidney, "an enlightened friend of mankind, and a martyr to liberty."[28] Sidney fascinated Adams. He represented so many of the qualities Adams would have liked to become known for himself. At the Boston "massacre" trial, where he served as defense attorney for Captain Thomas Preston and the eight British soldiers of the 29th Regiment, Adams proudly cited Sidney's respect for law as "written reason."[29] He shared the general whig distaste for mercenary troops, and portrayed the Boston "massacre" as "the strongest proof of the danger of standing armies."[30]

In his exchange with William Brattle, published in the *Boston-Gazette* in 1773, Adams began an examination of ancient history. He acknowledged his indebtedness to Coke and Blackstone in a review of the history of the British common law he admired so much. The codification of Edward the Confessor he described as "no more than a fresh promulgation of Alfred's code." Common law "is of higher antiquity than memory or history can reach." The rights supported by Alfred "have been used time out of mind." Even the Norman conquest could not crush the rights incorporated in the English common law — "William the Conqueror confirms and proclaims these to be the laws of England . . . and took an oath to keep them inviolable himself" — and Magna Charta "was founded on them."[31]

Unlike many of the historians he studied, Adams did not in-

28. *Boston-Gazette,* Feb. 9 and 16, 1767 (signed "Winthrop"). See Adams, *Works,* III, 489–93.

29. Kidder, *History of the Boston Massacre,* 258–59. Four years later Adams reread Burnet's *History of His Own Time* on past martyrs "to English Liberties," and reflected gloomily on the fate of Hampden, who fell in battle, Sidney who died "on the scaffold, Harrington in jail, etc." As he told James Warren, "This is cold comfort. Politics are an ordeal path among red hot ploughshares." See Adams to James Warren, June 25, 1774, Adams, *Works,* IX, 339; for his comment on reading Burnet, see Adams to Mercy Otis Warren, Jan. 3, 1774, Ford, ed., *Warren-Adams Letters,* I, 21.

30. Diary, Mar. 5, 1773, Adams, *Works,* II, 317–18.

31. "To the Printers of the Boston Gazette," Feb. 1, 1773, in ibid., III, 540–41.

sist on the antiquity of Parliament in the course of his admiration for the antiquity of common law. Parliament was presently oppressing Americans, and Americans should know that its pretension to authority was relatively recent. He praised his Saxon ancestors as "one of those enterprising northern nations," but charged that they "carried with them . . . the customs, maxims, and manners of the feudal system" to England, where they "shook off some part of the feudal fetters, yet they never disengaged themselves from the whole." There had indeed been a "wittenagemote, or assembly of wise men," but the Saxon monarchs only condescended to take its advice "in some few instances." Such "particular examples of royal condescension could form no established rule." The fact was, Adams concluded, the king in Saxon times "was absolute enough" to control the judiciary, and unhappily the King in the 1770s was trying to repeat the accomplishment in America.[32]

Adams had read critically enough to doubt the real meaning of pre-Norman English history. He found evidence to refute Brattle's claim that in Saxon times royal judges received appointments and estates for life, but he had to admit he would not "lay any great stress on the opinions of historians and compilers of antiquities, because it must be confessed that the Saxon constitution is involved in much obscurity." Adams noted how Saxon history had become a political football: "the monarchical and democratic factions in England, by their opposite endeavors to make the Saxon constitutions swear for their respective systems, have much increased the difficulty of determining . . . what that constitution, in many important particulars, was."[33] He was therefore much happier to turn to Rapin, Mrs. Macaulay, and Burgh on recent English history than on the Saxon period, and so in his final reappraisal of the colonial case, Adams dwelt on a past in which he had more confidence.

32. Ibid., 545.
33. Ibid., 543.

The first occasion was an exchange of addresses between Governor Hutchinson and the Massachusetts General Court in 1773. The immediate controversy was over the British decision that crown officials would henceforth receive their salaries from the royal exchequer. Bostonians denounced this as a further step toward complete slavery. Hutchinson in turn attempted to reconcile his fellow colonists with the British concept of the empire and its constitution: it was, he told the Assembly, "the sense of the Kingdom" that when Massachusetts was settled it was "to remain subject to the supreme authority of Parliament." John Adams, charged with drafting the response of the House of Representatives, carefully eschewed the "popular talk" about "democratical principles"; arguments based "on nature and eternal and unchangeable truth" ought to be "well understood and cautiously applied." [34] Instead he concentrated upon "legal and constitutional reasonings," and submitted a documented treatment of American colonization. The colonies, he contended, were never annexed to the English realm; their charters specified an allegiance to the English Crown. The colonies were part of the empire, but not an appendage of the kingdom; Parliament therefore had no legal right to legislate for Massachusetts. The charter was a grant of the King and vested the authority in the legislature to make laws which should be conformable to the principles of the English constitution and the statutes existing when the charter was granted. Adams noted that "no acts of any colony legislature are ever brought into Parliament"—they are laid before the King for his approval. History showed that Charles I had denied Parliament's right to legislate for the colonies, because "the colonies were without the realm and jurisdiction of Parliament." And before that James I had insisted "America was not annexed to the realm and it is not fitting that Parliament should make laws for these countries." Adams was convinced that

---

34. Alden Bradford, ed., *The Speeches of the Governors of Massachusetts from 1765–1775; and the Answers of the House of Representatives to the Same* (Boston, 1818), 339; Autobiography, Adams, *Works,* II, 310; Adams to William Tudor, Mar. 8, 1817, ibid., 313.

"no country by the common law was subject to the laws of Parliament, but the realm of England."[35]

The second opportunity for Adams's historical review of the place of the colonies in the imperial structure came with the patriotic need for a response to Daniel Leonard's "Massachusettensis" letters, a plea for submission to Parliamentary authority. John Adams began his reply—the famous *Novanglus* papers—in the January 23, 1775, issue of the *Boston-Gazette*. What followed was more than a "History of the Dispute with America, from its Origin in 1754 to the Present Time, 1774." It was a careful study of the constitutional history of the British empire and the dominions which comprised that empire. Adams pointed to the relationship between Edward I and Henry VIII: in the thirteenth century Wales had been annexed to the dominions of the English Crown by a royal decree, not an act of Parliament; Wales was unrepresented in Parliament and was not subject to that body until new legislation was enacted under Henry VIII in 1536. Scotland supplied a similar example: for a century after the accession of James I the English Parliament lacked authority in Scotland, until the enactment of the Act of Union in 1707. So too with Ireland: although conquered by Henry II, Ireland was not subject to Parliament until the enactment of Poynings' Law under Henry VII. No such legislation had ever been enacted for America. And if Wales, a conquered country, could know independence from Parliament, so too should an unconquered America. Each of the American colonies was a separate realm of which the King was sovereign.[36]

In establishing from a study of history the colonies' independence of Parliament, Adams did not leave the door open for royal despotism. Delving into Coke's *Institutes*, Adams demonstrated that while the King might "rule the divers nations and kingdoms of his empire" in his political capacity, he had "to govern them by their distinct

35. Bradford, ed., *Speeches*, 355, 354.
36. *Novanglus; or, A History of the Dispute with America, from Its Origin, in 1754, to the Present Time; Written in 1774*, Adams, *Works*, IV, 17–18, 156, 123.

laws." Specifically, the King was subject to the British constitution. "There is no fundamental or other law that makes a king of England absolute anywhere, except in conquered countries."[37] A king who abuses his sovereignty forfeits his title.

Perhaps Adams's most effective point was scored against the contention of "Massachusettensis" that resistance was futile. The colonists, claimed Adams, could not possibly lose in their contest: "If they die, they cannot be said to lose, since death is preferable to slavery." And as they resist they can take heart from history; if Charles I had not been challenged by the Puritans, he "would undoubtedly have established the Romish religion, and a despotism as wild as any in the world." Cromwell's usurpation of power may have been unfortunate, but even so his government was infinitely more glorious and happy than that of his Stuart predecessor. Every effort against tyranny had had beneficial results. "Did not the English gain by resistance to John, when *Magna Charta* was obtained?" Did not the Dutch in their revolt against the Spanish? The Swiss against the Austrians? The Romans against Tarquin? The English against James II? Indeed, Adams added proudly, Americans took part in the Glorious Revolution of 1688 when they rose against the regime of Sir Edmund Andros. And just as the English had contracted with William and Mary to rule in place of James II, so did Americans make a compact acknowledging the new sovereigns. "The oaths of allegiance are established by a law of the Province," further demonstrating that "our allegiance to his majesty is not due by virtue of any act of a British parliament, but by our own charter and province laws."[38]

Adams buttressed his claim to English rights by referring to the well-known *Pleas of the Crown* of William Hawkins. According to the *Novanglus* papers a monarch could forbid his subjects from emigrating; but once permission was given, a colonist carried his rights with him. "Our ancestors were entitled to the common law of En-

37. Ibid., 145, 127.
38. Ibid., 18, 17, 114.

gland when they emigrated, that is, to just so much of it as they pleased to adopt." In reality, "our ancestors, had a clear right to have erected in this wilderness a British constitution . . . or any other form of government they saw fit."[39] Both King and Parliament seemed not only to forget their obligations, but to overlook the basic nature of the government of which they were parts. Adams argued that he was not attacking the British empire because there was no such thing. Citing Aristotle, Livy, and Harrington, he declared "the British constitution is much more like a republic than an empire." A republic was "a government of laws, and not of men." According to this definition, "the British constitution is nothing more or less than a republic, in which the king is first magistrate." But an empire on the other hand "is a despotism . . . a stretch of tyranny beyond absolute monarchy."[40] Rome in her republican (pre-Emperor) stage illustrated Adams's argument. Roman colonies were allowed "the privilege of cities," which gave them Roman rights without Roman subjection. In this respect Adams thought "that sagacious city" of Rome revealed an awareness of difficulties "similar to those under which Great Britain is now laboring. She seems to have been sensible of the impossibility of keeping colonies planted at great distances, under . . . absolute control."[41]

The explanation of England's historical and political blindness lay

39. Ibid., 122.

40. Ibid., 106–7. Rather than tinker with his best phrases and thoughts, Adams, like Jefferson, chose to repeat them frequently and without alteration. In his letter to John Penn early in 1776, John Adams again mentioned his allegiance to Sidney, Harrington, Locke, Milton, and Burnet: he reaffirmed that "the true idea of a republic is an empire of laws, and not men; and therefore, as a republic is the best of governments, so that particular combination of power which is best contrived for a faithful execution of the laws, is the best of republics." Adams concluded that the "only valuable part of the British constitution" is its predominant republicanism. Adams, *Works*, IV, 204. When Adams was later accused of being an Anglophile and monarchist, it was because his partisan critics either did not understand, or did not care to understand that in Adams's logic a man could be both a monarchist and a republican if the monarch maintained his role as a first magistrate in an empire of laws.

41. *Novanglus,* 1774, ibid., IV, 102–3.

with the contemporary condition of the mother country. In his *Novanglus* essays Adams agreed that Americans presently enjoyed "the British constitution in greater purity and perfection than they do in England," and inquired: "Whose fault is this? Not ours." Fresh from reading the second volume of Burgh's *Political Disquisitions,* a book which he proclaimed "ought to be in the hands of every American who has learned to read," Adams declared that modern England "is loaded with debts and taxes, by the folly and iniquity of its ministers." Her virtue was gone. "When luxury, effeminacy, and venality are arrived at such a shocking pitch in England; when both electors and elected are become one mass of corruption; when the nation is oppressed to death with debts and taxes, owing to their own extravagance and want of wisdom, what would be your condition under such an absolute subjection to parliament?" Corruption was now so deeply implanted in England "as to be incurable, and a necessary instrument of government." England needed revenue from America, not because of legitimate expenses incurred in the late war with France, but because of waste and political depravity: "Corruption, like a cancer . . . eats faster and faster every hour. The revenue creates pensioners, and the pensioners urge for more revenue. The people grow less steady, spirited, and virtuous, the seekers more numerous and more corrupt, and every day increases the circles of their dependents and expectants, until virtue, integrity, public spirit, simplicity, and frugality, become the objects of ridicule and scorn, and vanity, luxury, foppery, selfishness, meanness, and downright venality swallowing up the whole society."[42]

These, then, were "the most melancholy truths" of contemporary England. The English people were depraved, the Parliament and government venal and corrupt. Even if Americans were given direct representation in this sort of Parliament, "a deep, treacherous, plausible, corrupt minister would be able to seduce our members to

42. Ibid., 116–17, 21, 37, 28, 54, 43.

betray us as fast as we could send them." The British in their iniquity aimed for the total destruction of colonial charters, and English liberties. The British constitution—in England—had arrived "nearly to that point where the Roman republic was where Jugurtha left it, and pronounced it 'a venal city, ripe for destruction.' "[43]

From reading Harrington, Adams recalled an observation on colonies weaning themselves "when they come of age." Adams felt obliged to conclude his *Novanglus* analysis with an observation that "the colonies are now nearer manhood than ever Harrington foresaw."[44] In fact, maturity was now being thrust upon Americans by their declining mother country.

III

Between 1761 and 1776 Adams traveled a long and difficult road. He had begun with the questions: "Where are the rights of Englishmen! Where is the spirit that once exalted the souls of Britons?"[45] He had examined the history of "English liberties" and concluded that they were "but certain rights of nature, reserved to the citizen by the English constitution, which rights cleaved to our ancestors when they crossed the Atlantic." He had become familiar with the major English writers on contemporary England, and while he could still in 1774 express to Burgh the hope "that in spite of bribery, some alteration in the House of Commons for the better might be made," his reading of Burgh confirmed his belief "that every trick and artifice of sharpers, gamblers, and horse-jockies, is to be played off against the cause of liberty in England and America." In reality "no hopes are to be left for either but in the sword."[46] England was tottering on the

43. Ibid., 54, 139, 78–79, 54–55.
44. Ibid., 104.
45. Diary, Jan. ? 1761, ibid., II, 112.
46. *Novanglus,* 1774, and John Adams to James Burgh, Dec. 28, 1774, ibid., IV, 124; IX, 351.

edge of a precipice, and Adams had no desire to join her in any game of eighteenth-century brinkmanship. As Adams told John Avery less than a year after the Declaration of Independence, there was indeed "abundant evidence of a fixed design to subjugate America." Any reasonable acquaintance with England's recent history demonstrated "how completely their government was corrupted."[47] Separation had been, and was, essential.

But independence was not enough. The American colonies could learn from history not only in substantiating their claims against England but also in ensuring their political survival. Adams saw that independence demanded skilled political craftmanship in erecting a new polity. He knew what he wanted to avoid, and he offered a historical exposition of how best to prevent the sins of the English fathers being visited upon American descendants. Radical in his language against England, he was yet conservative in his domestic political expression. "I dread the Spirit of Innovation," wrote Adams anxiously a few weeks before independence.[48]

In a lengthy letter in 1776 to George Wythe on the importance of constitution making, subsequently published as *Thoughts on Government,* he called for a popularly elected assembly, a council chosen by the legislature, and a governor elected by both bodies; judges were to be named by the governor, and there would be provision for a people's militia, public education, and even sumptuary laws to foster frugality. He was vigorously opposed to a unicameral legislature—Turgot's admiration for one stimulated Adams to pen his extraordinary *Defence of the Constitutions* a decade later—because it made for an unbalanced government. As a convenient and familiar example he cited the Long Parliament of Cromwell's time. It was too easy for an all-powerful assembly to either emerge as an oligarchy itself, or abdi-

47. John Adams to John Avery, Mar. 21, 1777, ibid., IX, 458. John Adams to Abigail Adams, Mar. 19, 1776, Adams, ed., *Familiar Letters,* 146.

48. John Adams to Mr. Hitchbourne, May 29, 1776, Letterbook #2, Adams Papers, Massachusetts Historical Society.

cate its power to a single tyrant like Cromwell.[49] Another safeguard against England's current condition would be rotation of all offices and frequent elections. Obadiah Hulme's *Historical Essay* had identified annual elections as the keystone of Saxon government, and upon its title page ran the slogan: "*Where annual Election ends, there Slavery begins.*"[50] John Adams in his *Thoughts on Government* declared that there was not "in the whole circle of the sciences a maxim more infallible than this, 'where annual elections end, there slavery begins.'" Adams confirmed his attachment to this principle not only in his letter to John Penn of North Carolina in 1776, but also in his 1779 *Report of a Constitution* for Massachusetts, where he called for annual elections of senators, representatives, and the governor.

Whether or not Adams quoted Hulme accurately by accident or had been rereading the first volume of Burgh's *Disquisitions* (where Hulme's maxim was slightly misquoted), he was obviously still familiar with his Saxon history.[51] Well aware of the corruptibility of man, he thought annual elections might discourage it. Sumptuary laws might at least impede the growth of luxury and corruption. Public education would assure dissemination of knowledge, and knowledge, Adams reminded Joseph Hawley in August 1776, "is among the most essential foundations of liberty." Within a year Adams was discussing this theme with his ten-year-old son. Urging a careful study of history on young John Quincy, he suggested a comparison of the American Revolution with others that resembled it: "The whole period of English history, from the accession of James the First to the accession of William the Third will deserve your most critical

49. *Thoughts on Government,* Adams, *Works,* IV, 195.

50. Hulme, *Historical Essay.*

51. *Thoughts on Government,* and *Report of a Constitution,* Sept. 1779, Adams, *Works,* IV, 197, 234-51; see also Burgh, *Political Disquisitions,* I, 83. In his letter to John Penn, Jan. 1776, Adams commented that elections "may be septennial or triennial; but for my own part, I think they ought to be annual; *for there is not in all science a maxim more infallible than this,* where annual elections end, there slavery begins." Adams, *Works,* IV, 205 (Adams's italics).

attention." In addition to England, Adams recommended attention to "the history of the Flemish Confederacy," along with the independence of the Swiss from Austria. He also singled out Sir William Temple's treatment of the United Provinces and the Abbé Vertot's accounts of the revolutions in Portugal, Sweden, and Rome. Clearly, he intended that his young son should acquire some insight into his father's idea of "the most essential foundations of liberty."[52]

As Adams contemplated the problem of maintaining American political integrity, of applying the principles of politics to the reconstruction of popular authority during and after the War for Independence, he turned again to his knowledge of English history and political science, modifying in some respects his high regard for English whig writing but not his opinion that "nine tenths of the [American] people were high whigs."[53] It was one thing to agree to name the first American warship *Alfred* "in honor of the founder of the greatest navy that ever existed,"[54] but it was another to argue — as he believed Burgh and Mrs. Macaulay had — that an omnipotent popular assembly would be a political cure-all. Annual elections might reduce the human proclivity for corruption, but a revival of the so-called Saxon system would, in Adams's view, be unwise. In his continued contacts with the English reformers, Adams expressed his honest doubt about this construction of an ideal constitution. To Richard Price he explained why in 1787 he undertook his *Defence of the Constitutions:* his fellow Americans were "running wild, and into danger, from a too ardent and inconsiderate pursuit of erroneous opinions of government." These dangerous ideas "had been propagated among them by some of their ill informed favorites, and by various writings which were very popular among them . . . particularly Mrs. Macaulay's *History,* Mr. Burgh's *Political Disquisitions,*

---

52. John Adams to Joseph Hawley, Aug. 25, 1776, Adams, *Works,* IX, 434; John Adams to John Quincy Adams, July 27, 1777, Adams, ed., *Familiar Letters,* 284.

53. *Novanglus,* 1774, Adams, *Works,* IV, 73.

54. Autobiography, Nov. 28, 1775, ibid., III, 12.

Mr. Turgot's letters." All were "excellent in some respects," but all were "extremely mistaken in the true construction of a free government."[55] The common mistake was the same one which endangered eighteenth-century England—an unbalanced government. An unrestrained popular assembly would be as dangerous as an unrestrained despot, and any unicameral legislature, virtual or otherwise, contained this basic weakness.

Adams's most sustained analysis of balanced government—*The Defence of the Constitutions of Government of the United States of America*—comprised a three-hundred-duodecimo-page study of the lessons of "the history of Europe, and of England in particular," in which Adams demonstrated his continuing familiarity with the past and his awareness of its value as an instrument of statecraft.[56] The *Defence,* Adams's major work, is a compendium of readings; three-quarters of volume one, nine-tenths of volume two, and the first half of volume three were made up of excerpts from other authors. Here we see Adams as a connoisseur of history as an art and as a science, deeply interested in how history was written and keenly aware of its limitations. And yet, as he frantically copied away from books on republican governments, he seems to have really believed that by piling up such examples of recorded experiences he was showing his countrymen how to frame a foolproof constitution. The constitution-makers, meeting at Philadelphia a few months later in 1787, employed a similar technique, reviewing past constitutions for their flaws and weaknesses in an effort to discern the most stable composition for American national needs.[57]

55. John Adams to Richard Price, May 20, 1789, ibid., IX, 558–59. In Mrs. Macaulay's opinion a more representative House of Commons would have rescued England from the excesses of a Parliament which had become unbalanced in the favor of the aristocracy.

56. *A Defence of the Constitutions of Government of the United States of America* (London, 1787), in ibid., IV, 298.

57. The debates of the Philadelphia convention amply bear this out, as do the efforts of Jay, Madison, and Hamilton to secure the ratification of their Constitution through the *Federalist.* See Raoul S. Naroll, "Clio and the Constitution: The Influence of the

Antedating the new Federal Constitution by a few months, Adams's review took the form of a retort to M. Turgot's praise of unicameral legislatures; it was a legal and historical brief for his political contentions. He combed over the whole range of history to deny the effectiveness of investing a single assembly with all the functions of government. Although he stated flatly that "there can be no free government without a democratical branch in the constitution," he was equally emphatic in his declaration that "a simple and perfect democracy never yet existed," and never would. Many professed democracies—such as the Swiss cantons—were really aristocratic republics; where such a republic enjoyed a careful system of checks and balances between the three branches of government (executive, legislative, and judicial), it succeeded. Throughout history there was a definite trend toward hereditary self-entrenchment in office; human beings, whether English, American, Greek, or Roman, were much the same. If the aristocracy dominated, the balance was destroyed and oligarchy resulted, and this could be prevented only by an alliance of the executive and the popular power. "If there is one certain truth to be collected from the history of all ages," Adams stressed, "it is this; that the peoples' rights and liberties, and the democratical mixture in a constitution, can never be preserved without a strong executive, or, in other words, without separating the executive from the legislative power." Where there was a weak executive—as Adams noted with the Dutch when he served as American minister to the United Provinces—a strong hereditary oligarchy held political power. Frequently a monarch served as an effective balance against the nobility, as in the regal republic of England after 1688; but when the Crown allied with the aristocracy, the corrupted modern English condition would be the result.[58]

Study of History on the Federal Convention of 1787" (Ph.D. diss., University of California at Los Angeles, 1953).

58. *Defence*, Adams, *Works*, IV, 289–90. The best recent reviews of Adams's *Defence* are found in R. R. Palmer's *The Age of the Democratic Revolution: The Challenge* (Princeton, 1959), 271–76; and in Haraszti's *John Adams and the Prophets of Progress*, 26–48. I can-

Ranging far and wide in his historical survey, Adams insisted that Americans should be more conversant with ancient Greece. He used Greek history in one instance as a vehicle to explain the uses of the past:

> The history of Greece [he wrote] should be to our countrymen what is called in many families on the continent a *boudoir,* an octagonal apartment in a house, with a full-length mirror on every side, and another in the ceiling. The use of it is, when any of the young ladies or young gentlemen if you will, are at any time a little out of humor, they may retire to a place, where, in whatever direction they turn their eyes, they see their own faces and figures multiplied without end. By thus beholding their own beautiful persons, and seeing, at the same time, the deformity brought upon them by their anger, they may recover their tempers and their charms together. A few short sketches of the ancient republics will serve to show, not only that the *orders* we defend were common to all of them; but that the prosperity and duration of each was in proportion to the care taken to balance them.[59]

Actually Adams's sketches were neither short nor few, but they handsomely demonstrated his anxiety for balance. The miseries of ancient Greece derived directly from its lack of political balance: the political pendulum "was forever on the swing."[60]

When he moved to Rome, the story was similar; Polybius supported the view that "the best government is that which consists of three forms, *regis, optimatum, et populi imperio.*"[61] So long as Rome balanced "the powers of the consuls, senate, and people," she maintained her greatness.[62] But while in Greece the aristocracy usually toppled

---

not agree with Palmer's view that Adams was excessively doctrinaire, and that Adams refused to admit the corruption of the British constitution. The constitution Adams admired so extravagantly was that of England in 1688—which he believed *ought* to be restored and would be. Adams's model was a constitution which ought to exist in England and did exist in America.

59. *Defence,* Adams, *Works,* IV, 469.
60. Ibid., 285.
61. Ibid., 383; see also 542–49.
62. Ibid., 435.

the state, in Rome "corruption began with the people sooner than in the senate," and in this the Romans enjoyed something in common with "the Teutonic institutions described by Caesar and Tacitus." In Germany there was no fixed balance, but a continual pulling and hauling between hereditary kings and nobles for power; "the people sometimes claimed it, but at last gave it up to the king, as the least evil of the two, in every country except England."[63]

Having resided in London for two years before writing his *Defence*, Adams was prepared to reassess the English situation. He concluded that the British constitution — the pre-1763 whiggish constitution of the Glorious Revolution — for which he had fought so strenuously in the 1770s might yet reemerge in the mother country. It now seemed possible to look for his idealized, and modernized, British constitution in England as well as in America: "The improvements to be made in the English constitution," wrote Adams, "lie entirely in the house of commons." If there were a substantial measure of electoral reform — much along the lines urged by English reformer John Cartwright — and the popular arm of the legislature thus strengthened, "it would be impossible to corrupt the people of England." It was up to the people of England to "take care of the balance, and especially their part of it." The fundamental structure was sound enough. Following De Lolme's imaginative view, Adams described the English constitution as a perfect blend of feudal institutions (he now described Hume's treatment of feudalism as an "admirable" account) and the better features of the Greek and Roman republics. The outcome was "that noble composition which avoids the inconveniences, and retains the advantages of both."[64] The balance of powers between Crown, aristocracy, and people in England made "the English constitution . . . the most stupendous fabric of human invention." Americans had translated its best features to their own needs, and

---

63. *Novanglus,* ibid., IV, 103; *Defence,* ibid., 297–98, 573.

64. Ibid., 468, 298. Adams's respect for De Lolme was enormous: "the ingenious Genevan" offered "a more intelligible explanation" of the English constitution than any Englishman. *Discourses on Davila* (1790), in ibid., VI, 396.

they deserved applause instead of the censure of M. Turgot. In this instance, argued Adams, there was virtue in imitation; the English constitution was "the result of the most mature deliberation on universal history and philosophy." Moreover, the Americans had improved upon the model, initiating in the states annual elections of legislators and governors. "The United States of America," he declared, "have exhibited, perhaps, the first example of governments erected on the simple principles of nature," opening a new era in history. "Thirteen governments thus founded on the natural authority of the people alone, without a pretence of miracle or mystery, and which are destined to spread over the northern part of that whole quarter of the globe, are a great point gained in favor of the rights of mankind." Adams's *Defence* of the American constitutions was thus a defense of human rights as well; it "was really written," he said, "to lay before the public a specimen of that kind of reading and reasoning which produced the American constitutions," readings, as he said in his preface, "collected from the history of all ages."[65]

IV

An ardent, even passionate, advocate of the separation of powers, Adams hammered away throughout the remainder of his life at the necessity in free government for "an effectual control of rivalries," an effective control of power: "Power must be opposed to power, force to force, strength to strength, interest to interest, as well as reason to reason, eloquence to eloquence, passion to passion." Occasionally dispirited by his vicissitudes in politics and by the failure of Americans to study his historical materials and their validity, he sometimes succumbed to pessimism. Perhaps, he told Jefferson in 1812, he should have devoted his energies to the study of science instead of history and politics. The time seemed wasted which he had given to

65. Ibid., IV, 359, 556, 292–93, 290.

Nathaniel Bacon, Roger Acherley, Bolingbroke, De Lolme, Harrington, and Sidney ("with twenty others upon Subjects which Mankind is determined never to Understand"). His favorite writers were not just neglected, but "nearly laughed into contempt," thanks in part to the popularity of historians like David Hume—with his "elegant Lies." Hume's *History*, Adams told Jefferson, "has been the bane of G[reat]. B[ritain]. It has destroyed the best Effects of the Revolution of 1688," and "disgraced all the honest Historians." Writers such as Rapin, Sidney, Burnet, and Coke, in Adams's view, still contained "more honest Truth than Hume and Clarendon and all their disciples and Imitators." Despairingly he asked Jefferson, "Who reads any of them at this day?"[66]

Adams's "honest Historians" retained a wider following than he realized. But their readers reached differing political conclusions. In 1825 Adams, like Jefferson, received an inscribed copy of John Cartwright's last book, *The English Constitution Produced and Illustrated*. Cartwright read and admired Adams's historians but emerged with a plea for a return to a Saxon-styled democracy. Adams conceded Cartwright's "ardent love for liberty," but denied he understood the system necessary to secure it. History did not give Adams any confidence in a constitutional structure in which the popular branch dominated. History showed him that the people never succeeded in maintaining their liberties; only a balanced, aristocratically inclined republic would do that. Cartwright was "one of those ardent spirits whose violent principles defeated all their benevolent purposes."[67]

Despite his pessimistic backsliding on occasion, Adams remained throughout his life an unreconstructed Whig, and his political purpose—from his *Dissertation on Canon and Feudal Law* in 1765, through

66. John Adams to Jefferson, Feb. 3, 1812, July 15, 1813, Dec. 16, 1816, Cappon, ed., *Adams-Jefferson Letters*, II, 294–95, 357, 502.

67. Adams to Jefferson, Feb. 25, 1825, ibid., II, 609–10. For a more substantial discussion of Cartwright, see chap. 8, 180–82, below, which describes the very different response made by Jefferson to *The English Constitution*.

his final letters to Jefferson in the 1820s—was undergirded by his acute reading and writing of history, his accumulation of and commentary on facts about the past. Perhaps the only history in which Adams found real satisfaction in his last years was the history he and his generation had made. A year before his death he wrote to Jefferson and recalled "with rapture" the happier times of the Revolutionary struggle against England. They were "golden days when Virginia and Massachusetts lived and acted together like a band of brothers." He hoped the world would hear no more of crises such as the Sedition Act in 1798 or the Hartford Convention in 1814. He hoped, he concluded, "it will not be long before they may say redeunt saturnia regna."[68] For the future he advocated a careful study of history and a regard for the guides of the past: "Without wishing to damp the ardor of curiosity," he told some young Philadelphians in 1798, "or influence the freedom of inquiry, I will hazard a prediction, that, after the most industrious and impartial researches, the longest liver of you all will find no principles, institutions, or systems of education more fit, in general, to be transmitted to your posterity, than those you received from your ancestors."[69]

68. Adams to Jefferson, Feb. 25, 1825, ibid., II, 609–10.
69. John Adams to the Young Men of the City of Philadelphia, the District of Southwark, and the Northern Liberties, Pennsylvania, May 7, 1798, Adams, *Works,* IX, 188. For a stimulating essay on Adams as a conservative, see Clinton Rossiter, "The Legacy of John Adams," *Yale Review* 46 (1957): 528–50. "His sense of history, the greatest of teachers," writes Rossiter, "was keen; his devotion to tradition, the essence of wisdom, was respectful; his reliance on an unknowable God was a tribute to his ancestors and to his humility."

CHAPTER VI

Three Pennsylvanians:
John Dickinson, James Wilson,
Benjamin Franklin

Pennsylvania made important contributions to the intellectual origins of the American Revolution. The first and second Continental Congresses met in Philadelphia; the famed Library Company served as the first Congressional library; and Pennsylvanians made notable additions to the political literature of the Revolutionary era. The writings of Pennsylvania's chief spokesmen—Benjamin Franklin, John Dickinson, and James Wilson—made frequent and effective use of history. Dickinson and Wilson were both lawyers and approached history from similar vantage points; Franklin, if less deliberate in his investigation of history, was no less enthusiastic about its study or political value.

I

Once hailed as "the penman of the American Revolution,"[1] John Dickinson earned this rare praise by drafting the resolutions of the

1. Moses Coit Tyler, *The Literary History of the American Revolution, 1763–1783*, 2 vols. (N.Y., 1897), II, 24.

Stamp Act Congress in 1765 and writing his *Letters from a Farmer in Pennsylvania* in 1767 and 1768. Always deeply affected by "the Charms of liberty," he believed the American cause "of too much dignity, to be sullied by turbulence and tumult." Patriots, he urged, "should breathe a sedate yet fervent spirit, animating them to actions of prudence, justice, modesty, bravery, humanity, and magnanimity."[2] Dickinson was undoubtedly a reluctant Revolutionary, a politician afflicted with the ability to see both sides of a question. He was, as a recent writer expressed it, "too careful, too refining in thought to see an issue in black and white."[3] Dickinson himself wrote in 1767: "We cannot act with too much caution in our disputes. Anger produces anger; and differences that might be accommodated by kind and respectful behaviour, may, by imprudence, be enlarged to an incurable rage."[4] His reputation as a patriot suffered from his apparent efforts to avoid separation from England at a time when many of his associates pressed for complete independence. But despite all such pleas for prudence Dickinson was firmly committed to contend for the liberty delivered down to him by his ancestors.[5] His caution has been mistaken for fear, his conservatism in political method for conservatism in political belief.

Dickinson's absorption with history and the type of history he favored illuminate the emergence of a patriot whose resolution consistently conquered his instinct for caution. Born to great wealth and raised an aristocrat, Dickinson studied for a legal career, entering John Moland's law office at eighteen and transferring to the Middle

2. Dickinson to Thomas McKean, Mar. 4, 1801, McKean Manuscripts, Historical Society of Pennsylvania; Dickinson, *Letters from a Farmer in Pennsylvania,* Ford, ed., *Writings of Dickinson,* 324.

3. John H. Powell, "John Dickinson and the Constitution," *Pennsylvania Magazine of History and Biography* 60 (1936): 5.

4. Dickinson, *Farmer's Letters,* Ford, ed., *Writings of Dickinson,* 326.

5. This phrase, derived from Sallust, was a particular favorite of Dickinson's. He used it in his May 24, 1764, *Speech* and in concluding his *Farmer's Letters,* ibid., 9, 406.

Temple in London at twenty-one. In England he studied antiquity at first hand, reporting back to his father on wonderful walks along the same paths "frequented by the Antient Sages of the Law." With awe and reverence he contemplated the likelihood that he was studying "in the Chambers where Coke or Plowden had meditated." His awe was not for the more visible signs of the English past, but for the magnificence of the historical associations. Musingly he let himself drift back to the time when "a Hampden, and a Holt opposed encroaching Power, and supported declining Justice."[6]

In these happy circumstances, close to history and to London's bookstores, Dickinson developed his taste for books. "I am wholly taken up with reading," he reported to his father; and even discounting the inevitable exaggerations of youth, Dickinson seems to have acquired steady reading habits. He boasted of his library and his scholarly accomplishments. "I have acquired," he told readers of his *Letters from a Farmer,* "a greater knowledge in history, and the laws and constitution of my country, than is generally attained by men of my class."[7] Even without a catalogue of his library, one can easily determine the sources he drew upon for such historical, legal, and constitutional learning. Sales slips reveal when he bought Blackstone's *Law Tracts* and *Commentaries.* His commonplace books confirm his interest in Bolingbroke and Tacitus. His enthusiasm for reading led to the purchase in 1762 of a share in Franklin's Library Company. As early as 1756, he was citing Rapin's *History of England* in a letter to his mother, and on the eve of the Revolution he became involved in a lively exchange with the English publisher Edward Dilly over Burgh's

6. Dickinson to his father, Samuel Dickinson, Mar. 8, 1754, Colbourn, ed., "Dickinson's London Letters," *Pennsylvania Magazine of History and Biography* 86 (1962): 257.

7. Dickinson to his father, Mar. 29, 1754, ibid., 265; *Farmer's Letters,* Ford, ed., *Writings of Dickinson,* 307. One must necessarily make some allowance for Dickinson's purposeful exaggeration in his public writings; and yet his apparent immodesty concerning his library is quite in keeping with the tone of his surviving private correspondence, and, indeed, reminiscent of the bibliophilic boasting of John Adams.

Political Disquisitions.[8] The intellectual background which Dickinson thus provided for himself affected his political conduct.

Dickinson made his political debut, not in a defense of colonial rights, but on an intracolonial issue involving the Penn family proprietorship. Franklin and Galloway had joined forces to agitate for the overthrow of the privileged Penns and the establishment of a crown-colony status for Pennsylvania. Dickinson opposed the proposed change, and so exposed himself to violent criticism for his apparent conservatism.

Dickinson did not think the proprietary arrangement was without fault. But at least the evils of proprietary government were known evils, and these he preferred to the alternative offered—a closer attachment to the British Crown that might bring unpredictable evils. He feared the anti-Penn faction would only change things for the worse. Drawing upon his recent reading, he recalled previous examples of unwise political haste. He pointed to Robert Molesworth's *Account of Denmark,* which described how "the commons of Denmark, smarting under the tyranny of their nobility, in a fit of vengeful fury *suddenly* surrendered their liberties to their king; and ever since . . . have detested the *mad moment* which slipt upon them the shackles of slavery." He cited Rapin's *History of England* on the precipitate uprising of the Duke of Monmouth against James II, which when compared with the gloriously successful revolution led by William of Orange, proved the wisdom of "a wise delay."[9] Dickin-

---

8. The first edition of Blackstone's *Commentaries* was published in 1765–69, and Dickinson was billed for the third volume on Jan. 26, 1769. See Logan Papers, XXXIV, 54, Historical Society of Pennsylvania. A bill for Blackstone's *Law Tracts* (Oxford, 1762) was sent to Dickinson by David Hall on Sept. 3, 1763, ibid., XXXIV, 11. Dickinson's commonplace books repose in the Historical Society of Pennsylvania; they were sparsely entered. Dickinson to his mother, Mary Cadwalader Dickinson, June 6, 1756, Colbourn, ed., "Dickinson's London Letters," *Pennsylvania Magazine of History and Biography* 86 (1962): 448. The Dilly letters began in Mar. 1774. James Burgh sent Dickinson a set of his *Political Disquisitions* "as a small Token of Respect for His Patriotic Virtue"; the volumes and letters are in the Library Company of Philadelphia.

9. Dickinson, *Speech,* May 24, 1764, Ford, ed., *Writings of Dickinson,* 24.

son was already alert to the question of political timing. History had made him acutely aware of earlier ill-timed efforts at change. He understood the need for as complete preparation for political action as possible.

Just as Dickinson sided with the Penns in 1764 rather than risk the hazards of Pennsylvania's becoming a crown colony, so too did he oppose English legislation in 1765 which would have had equivalent consequences. The Stamp Act seemed to confirm the wisdom of his cautious historical reflections over the proprietary question, and it set the stage for a much more extensive use of the past. Dickinson based his arguments on a total acceptance of God-given natural rights as substantiated in the English constitution.[10] With history as his support, he devoted himself to "the Principles of *English* Liberties," which, with their legal and representative provisions, comprised "the Birthright of Englishmen, and the Safeguard of their Persons and Properties."[11] The colonists, Dickinson stressed, were Englishmen entitled to the privilege of taxing themselves. Consequently, the mother country had no legal or constitutional right to levy stamp duties on the American colonies.

This was a strong position. Dickinson's formulation of the constitutional inheritance of all Englishmen led him to insist that Englishmen carried with them a legal right to self-government wherever they might go, a claim from which he never retreated. The only British legislation to be obeyed was that which Englishmen in America chose to accept. The only connection between the American colonies and the mother country was that of family "affection." He likened the colonists to dutiful children of a beloved but sometimes errant mother country; if they should be punished without cause, Americans would rightfully resent it and might well be

10. Dickinson's Resolutions Adopted by the Assembly of Pennsylvania relative to the Stamp Act, Sept. 21, 1765, ibid., 173–74.

11. Dickinson, A Petition to the King from the Stamp Act Congress, Oct. 19, 1765, ibid., 195.

tempted to sever the fragile ties of ancestral friendship. After all, children had a habit of growing up and maturing. As *Cato's Letters* had urged, the mother country had best remember that only *"by using them well"* could England avoid the complete independence of her colonies.[12] "There can be no friendship between freemen and slaves," warned Dickinson.[13]

Dickinson was not threatening England with American independence, but he made it clear that total separation was to be considered if Parliament should persist in ignoring the English privileges of the colonists. Dickinson was a proud member of the world's greatest empire and said so: "Every drop of blood in my heart is British."[14] He wanted no change in his imperial situation; nor did he want any change in his constitutional condition. He conceived of the British empire as essentially an autonomous association of self-governing provinces linked to the mother country by a common allegiance to the King. He agreed that the colonies had historically accepted Parliamentary legislation directed toward strengthening the empire—he saw most aspects of the navigation system in this light. But Dickinson's basic constitutional principle was the right to be taxed only by one's own representatives. This was the most fundamental of the historical privileges of all Englishmen, and it seemed to Dickinson that the liberal whigs in the mother country should know enough of their own past to appreciate this fact.

Unhappily Parliament did not seem to subscribe to the same constitutional history as Dickinson. The Stamp Act was abandoned solely for reasons of expediency and replaced by the Townshend Acts of 1767. The colonists no longer faced a direct internal tax, but the new import duties were for revenue purposes and the result was still taxa-

---

12. Dickinson, *The Late Regulations Respecting the British Colonies* (Philadelphia, 1765), in ibid., 242–45. See also the *Farmer's Letters,* ibid., 343 *n.*

13. Dickinson, *An Address to the Committee of Correspondence in Barbados* (Philadelphia, 1766), in ibid., 268.

14. Ibid.

tion. His *Letters from a Farmer* offered little new in political argument, but they presented a much more explicit discussion of the historical origins of colonial rights. The popularity of Dickinson's *Letters* was immediate. Nearly every colonial newspaper ran them, and seven different editions were issued in book form by 1769.[15]

He began his *Letters* on a note of historical symbolism, dating the first of the *Letters* November 5, 1767, and taking pains to point out twice that this was the anniversary of the day when William III landed at Torbay to rescue England's constitutional liberties in 1688. He then briefly reviewed British tyranny in America. There was, Dickinson charged, evidence of a consistent Parliamentary program aimed at undermining the constitutional liberties of Englishmen in America. Parliament was practicing a dubious double standard by denying to the American legislatures the rights for which Parliament had fought throughout its history. The Townshend Acts themselves were dismissed: while there was a record of and justification for colonial agreement to trade regulations for the good of all in the imperial family, colonial benevolence would not and could not stretch to the acceptance of duties which were thinly disguised taxes. The Townshend duties were as unconstitutional as the recently repealed Stamp Act. Here then was yet another British encroachment on colonial rights, another "innovation; and a most dangerous innovation" to be strenuously resisted.[16]

But the bulk of the *Letters* was devoted to an account of the vicissitudes of English liberties in England and the lessons to be learned from such trials and tribulations. He looked again at the antiquity of English liberties and the fundamentals of the English constitution.

---

15. John Dickinson, *Letters from a Farmer in Pennsylvania . . .*, ed. R. T. H. Halsey (N.Y., 1903), xix. Dickinson soon earned eager toasts in Boston, where he was linked with Magna Charta, the Bill of Rights, and John Wilkes. See *Boston Evening-Post*, Aug. 22, 1768. He also gained an excellent notice in the London *Monthly Review* 59 (July 1768): 18, where the *Farmer's Letters* were called "a well-connected chain of close and manly reasoning . . . founded upon laudable principles."

16. *Farmer's Letters*, Ford, ed., *Writings of Dickinson*, 312, 348, 316.

He traced the earlier efforts of Parliament to maintain representative government in England, and he praised the English insistence on retaining control of the purse strings. By denying supplies to the Crown, they had ensured the execution of the laws. English history, he said, was substantially one of popular exertion of constitutional authority against kings and ministers who sought to govern despotically. Without their power of the purse, Dickinson concluded, the House of Commons might well have failed to resist royal encroachments upon the people's rights. The House of Commons was to be commended for making "their continual claim of their ancient freedom and birthright."[17] Colonial assemblies should emulate this ancient example.

The English had not been completely successful in their efforts to maintain their liberties. They were afflicted with a standing army, for example, and New York had recently felt the lash of an angry Parliament for failing to vote adequate supplies to a potential vehicle for her own oppression. Here was an example of the smallest beginning bringing "the most extensive consequences." Citing Rapin as his authority, Dickinson related how Henry VII had introduced standing armies into England, beginning with a band of only fifty archers. But by 1684, when Charles II—"in order to make his people *fully sensible of their new slavery*"—mustered his troops, they totaled some four thousand well-armed men. It was highly dangerous to allow any accumulation of encroachments on constitutional rights because the result was either a significant loss of liberty or a bloody upheaval like that in England in the 1640s. Charles I had a head filled "with mistaken notions of his own authority," but his dismal fate was partly brought on by the sheer weight of unremedied popular grievances. The English people concluded that "it would be as dangerous for them to allow the powers which were legally vested in the crown, as those which at any time had been by usurpation exercised by it."

17. Ibid., 364–65, 329 *n*.

Dickinson conceded that this was "putting the gentlest construction on *Charles's* conduct," but his history showed that "the rights
of the subject therefore cannot be *too often* considered, explained, or
asserted." England should recall from her own happier past that "a
people does not reform with moderation."[18]

Dickinson was fascinated by the fate of Charles I, but he was
no less intrigued by events following his execution. Like Algernon Sidney and Catherine Macaulay, Dickinson deplored the role of
Oliver Cromwell, a usurper who based his tyranny on a standing
army. The English people then made the astonishing error of in-
viting the Stuarts back; indeed, observed Dickinson (quoting from
Rapin), the people even allowed Charles II to muster a new army.
Thus had the English "*delivered up* these very rights and privileges
to *Charles* the Second, which they had so passionately, and if I may
say it, *furiously* defended against the designs of *Charles* the *First*," just
"thirty-six years after this last prince had been beheaded."[19] James II
was no improvement either: he was a skillful dissembler, who "when
he *meant* to establish popery, talked of liberty of conscience . . .
and . . . thereby almost deceived the Dissenters into destruction." And
now, in the eighteenth century, there was "a LUST OF POWER in
men of *abilities* and *influence*," a growth of royal influence supported
by increasing opportunities for political patronage which American
taxes would only augment.[20] George III and his ministers seemed as
anxious to tax Englishmen in America without their consent as any
of the tyrannical Stuarts had wished to tax Englishmen in England a
century earlier.

For all the vigor with which Dickinson attacked contemporary

18. Ibid., 308–12, 390–91, 387.
19. Ibid., 393. Dickinson had quoted this same passage from Rapin to his mother
on June 6, 1756; see Colbourn, ed., "Dickinson's London Letters," *Pennsylvania Magazine
of History and Biography* 86 (1962): 448–49. His quotation is from Rapin, *History of England,* II, 733–34. Dickinson's arithmetic was fallible.
20. *Farmer's Letters,* Ford, ed., *Writings of Dickinson,* 346, 379–81.

English politics and government, he was for the present content to remind England of her heritage of liberty and of past efforts for its maintenance. He repeated his call for vigilance and recalled examples of the difficulty of restoring a former freedom once "any ancient law or custom" was broken. It was a comfort to remember that "our wise ancestors were so watchful of their liberty, and so successful in their struggles for it." There was room to hope that England would retain her title to freedom. "The constitutional modes of obtaining relief, are those which I wish to see pursued on the present occasion," concluded Dickinson. Complaint about the Stamp Act had brought a measure of response, and England might still return to "her 'old good humour, and her old good nature,' as Lord Clarendon expresses it." He knew that liberty was generally lost by "the decay *of virtue,*" that " 'SLAVERY IS EVER PRECEDED BY SLEEP,' " but he liked to think that both virtue and vigilance could still be maintained in England and America. The immediate future would decide "what reliance is to be placed in the *temper* of a people, when the prince is possessed of an unconstitutional power."[21] Meanwhile Dickinson had stated his political position for all to see.

Dickinson's use of history in the 1760s was hardly unique; had it been so, he might not have been so effective a spokesman for colonial rights. He was firmly committed to "the Birthright of Englishmen,"[22] and could agree completely with John Adams that American patriots "desire nothing new; they wish only to keep their old privileges."[23] "In FREEDOM we're BORN, and in FREEDOM we'll LIVE," ran the lyrics to the "song for American freedom" Dickinson sent James Otis in the summer of 1768.[24]

21. Ibid., 382, 388, 326–27, 393. Dickinson concluded his *Letters* on a hopeful note, however: he looked to "the strongest probability" that if the colonists expressed their opposition with sufficient vigor, they would have "the same success now, that they had in the time of the *Stamp-Act.*" Ibid., 406.

22. Dickinson, Stamp Act Congress Petition, Oct. 19, 1765, ibid., 195.

23. *Boston-Gazette,* Mar. 13, 1775.

24. Dickinson, "Liberty Song," *Pennsylvania Chronicle* (Philadelphia), July 11, 1768.

The critical years that followed saw no diminution in Dickinson's determination or patriotism; they did see increasing doubt over the recovery of political virtue in the mother country. Continued oppression led Dickinson to conclude that he may well have placed too much reliance upon the temper of the English people, and his correspondence with London publisher Edward Dilly in 1774 helped confirm this view. Dilly wrote at some length about the contemporary decadence of English political life, relating the "Bribery and Corruption . . . [which] engenders Swarms of Placemen and Pensioners . . . [who] like Leeches suck the very vitals of the Constitution." To Dickinson these conditions sounded altogether too familiar. As a young law student he had seen at first hand the degrading spectacle of English Parliamentary elections: "Bribery is so common," he had written his father, "that it is thot there is not a Borough in England where it is not practis'd." This he had then considered "one of the greatest Proofs perhaps of the Corruption of the Age," and now Edward Dilly confirmed the continued decline of England's political virtue.[25] Accompanying Dilly's letters was James Burgh's *Political Disquisitions,* which conveyed the melancholy conclusion that Dickinson's generation was witness to "the subversion of the [English] constitution, and the ruin of the state."[26] Favorably impressed by Burgh's arguments, Dickinson promptly subscribed to Robert Bell's Philadelphia edition of the *Disquisitions.* While reading the edition which Dilly had sent, he formulated an additional argument for resistance to British tyranny: "We should be guilty of treason against our sovereign and the majesty of the people of *England,* if we did not oppose [it]." England's situation seemed so unfavorable to liberty that only Englishmen in America were likely to preserve the ancient rights secured from King John in the thirteenth and from the Stuarts in the seventeenth century. "England," Dickinson now insisted, "must be

25. Edward Dilly to John Dickinson, Mar. 7, 1774, and Dickinson to his father, Jan. 25, 1755, Dickinson Manuscripts, Library Company of Philadelphia.
26. James Burgh, *Political Disquisitions,* I, viii, xxii–xxiii.

saved in *America.*" Eventually "she will *rejoice* that we have *resisted* — and *thank* us for having *offended* her."[27]

Although Dickinson had been very hopeful in the 1760s that the Anglo-American connection would survive and flourish, by the 1770s his doubts and reservations had multiplied. There was an increasing contrast between the English liberties to which he laid claim and actual English political practice. If Americans failed to resist, they might well be degraded to a status which the English people would have reached "had *James* the first and his family succeeded in their scheme of arbitrary power." Dickinson decided that if only one would substitute Parliament for the Stuarts, and Americans for the Britons, the arguments used in the seventeenth-century contests would "apply with inexpressible force and appositeness in maintenance of our cause, and in refutation of the pretensions set up by their too forgetful posterity, over their unhappy colonists."[28] Dickinson, however, was not forgetful. "We are," he had declared firmly in 1773, "*British Subjects,* who are born to Liberty, who know its Worth, and who prize it high."[29]

Dickinson demonstrated just how highly he prized his British liberty. As penman for the First Continental Congress in the fall of 1774 he phrased a petition to George III, appealing for "peace, liberty, and safety." He reminded the King of the colonists' historical correctness: "We wish not a diminution of the prerogative, nor do we solicit the grant of any new right in our favor." But he was already entertaining grave doubts about the outcome of such petitions. England seemed too advanced in perfidy. Peace, he told Arthur Lee, "will come more grateful by being unexpected." It was hard to realize that supposedly intelligent Englishmen would "seriously think of sheathing their swords in bosoms so affectionate to them," or that England would

27. Dickinson, *An Essay on the Constitutional Power of Great-Britain* (Philadelphia, 1774), 62.

28. Ibid., 70–71.

29. Dickinson, *A Letter from the Country . . .* (Philadelphia, 1773), n.p. (Broadside).

be so rash as to embrace a war which would "involve her in immediate ruin." He wondered, in fact, whether there was not a design being prosecuted by the ministry of Lord North "to make his Majesty dethrone himself by the calamities and convulsions his reign is likely to bring on his whole people." Even Samuel Adams was agreeing with Dickinson in 1774: after a pleasant September afternoon in Dickinson's company, Adams awarded him the highest accolade—Dickinson, he told Joseph Warren, was "a true Bostonian." [30]

During the next eighteen months Dickinson apparently lost his appeal in New England. The Coercive Acts remained on the statute books, and in April and June of 1775 came the bloody fighting at Lexington, Concord, and Breed's Hill. Where there had once been a multitude of well-publicized appeals to the King to rid himself of evil ministers and repudiate the acts of a corrupt Parliament, there was now room only for a few last doubtful petitions for harmony and reconciliation. In New England these were rendered obsolete by the recent bloodshed, and John Dickinson was tempted to agree. "What topics of reconciliation are now left for men who think as I do?" he asked dispiritedly. "Will the distinctions between the prince and his ministers wipe out the stain of blood?" [31]

Even so, Dickinson drafted the famous Olive Branch Petition early in July 1775, asking for an end to further bloodshed and urging royal action toward a reconciliation. Dickinson knew that the King would probably reject his Olive Branch; he had offered no concessions to the Crown and demanded "that such statutes as more immediately distress any of your Majesty's colonies may be repealed." But he hoped to strengthen American claims to moderation and to

30. Worthington C. Ford et al., eds., *Journals of the Continental Congress, 1774–1789*, 34 vols. (Washington, D.C., 1904–37), I, 119; Dickinson to Arthur Lee, Aug. 20, 1774, Duane Manuscripts, American Philosophical Society; Samuel Adams to Joseph Warren, Sept. 25, 1774, Cushing, ed., *Writings of Samuel Adams*, III, 158.

31. Dickinson to Arthur Lee, Apr. 29, 1775, in Peter Force, comp., *American Archives . . .*, 9 vols. (Washington, D.C., 1837–53), 4th ser., II, 444–45.

calm those who feared that Congress was moving with rash haste. In effect the Olive Branch gave the King one last opportunity to redress American grievances—actually his first since the debacle at Concord—and it gave an air of injured innocence to the Continental Congress, which sponsored it. As Dickinson told Arthur Lee, "our rights have been already stated, our claims made." Here was Britain's chance to stem the flow of British blood. If Britain ignored the petition, then "the more such treatment will confirm the minds of our countrymen to endure all the misfortunes that may attend the contest."[32]

Dickinson was much more bellicose in his "Declaration of the Causes and Necessity for Taking Up Arms," adopted only a day after the petition to the King. Here Dickinson castigated the blindness and passion for power of Parliament and discussed the menace from "ministerial rapacity" and the "tyranny of irritated ministers." He recalled the freedom inherited "from our gallant Ancestors" and the present generation's obligation to preserve its posterity from the wretched bondage threatened by the mother country. He concluded with the magnificent short statements of colonial condition and intent: "Our Cause is just. Our Union is perfect. Our preparations nearly completed. Our internal Resources are great; and our Assurance of Foreign Aid is certain." Death rather than slavery was now his determination.[33] There was little question of Dickinson's real expectation. Speaking to the New Jersey Assembly in December 1775, he warned that "neither Mercy nor Justice was to be expected from Britain."[34]

32. The Second Petition, July 8, 1775, Ford, ed., *Journals of the Continental Congress*, II, 161; Dickinson to Arthur Lee, July 7, 1775, in Force, comp., *American Archives*, 4th ser., II, 1604.

33. Declaration of the Causes and Necessity for Taking Up Arms, John Dickinson's Composition Draft, in Boyd et al., eds., *Jefferson Papers*, I, 204–12.

34. William A. Whitehead, Frederick W. Ricord, and William Nelson, eds., *Documents Relating to the Colonial History of the State of New Jersey*, 10 vols. (Newark, N.J.,

Unfortunately there were as yet no perfected American union, no nearly completed preparations for war, and no foreign alliance. These were more than aspirations; in Dickinson's eyes they were the prerequisites to independence. When Richard Henry Lee offered his formal call in June 1776 for an end to the Anglo-American connection, Dickinson felt obliged to voice his opposition. He "saw the impossibility that we should ever again be united with Great Britain," but he felt a formal announcement too premature. As John Adams himself noted, Dickinson was not opposed to independence, but to "it's being now declared." Dickinson pleaded earnestly for prudence in timing such a decision; he wanted firmer colonial union, stronger military preparations, and he did not want to be thrown upon the diplomatic mercy of the colonists' ancient enemies, the French. By his final abstention in the vote taken on July 2 he contributed to a form of unanimity. He neither compromised his own convictions nor did he obstruct the majority will.[35]

Dickinson later attempted a vindication of his position. His attachment to the history of the rights of Englishmen in America made him a Revolutionary; but history led him to hesitate over the best way to secure those rights. He had, he related, searched into the past, but could not find in history any instance "of a people, without a battle fought or an ally gained, abrogating forever their connection with a great, rich, warlike, commercial empire, whose wealth or

---

1880–86), X, 691. Dickinson represented the Congress in urging that New Jersey not undertake any fresh petitions of its own to George III; Dickinson referred to French jealousy of England and offered the comforting opinion that "France will not sit still and suffer Britain to conquer." Dickinson apparently did not voice a fear that this could lead to a French rather than an English tyranny in America.

35. Jefferson's Notes of Proceedings in the Continental Congress, June 8, 1776, Boyd et al., eds., *Jefferson Papers*, I, 309, 310. Dickinson's speech against independence has been carefully reconstructed from the original rough notes by John H. Powell; see "Arguments Agt. the Independence of these Colonies—in Congress," *Pennsylvania Magazine of History and Biography* 65 (1941): 468–81.

connections had always procured allies when wanted, and bringing the matter to a prosperous conclusion." [36]

Dickinson never doubted the justness or the constitutionality of the American claim to autonomy. The failure of King and Parliament to accept his interpretation of English and colonial history forced Dickinson into a position he did not seek. His hopes for England's recovery of her ancient virtue, for a realization of the historical justice of the colonial case, did not materialize. Perhaps he suspected this would be so. Twenty years before independence Dickinson had discussed the normal course of tyranny: "When Concessions are made to Princes, tis as ridiculous to think of stopping, as for a Master of a Ship to guess at the Depth of Water in an Ebb Tide. . . . But there is no Flood in Power . . . there is no means in Nature for altering its Course but Violence: I think a moderate Acquaintance with the English History will teach one this Truth." [37]

II

The man who knows history, James Wilson observed in 1768, "already knows mankind in theory, and, for this reason, will be in less danger of being deceived by them in practice." [38] A Presbyterian immigrant from Scotland, Wilson came to America an educated man. He had studied at the Universities of Glasgow and Edinburgh before settling in Pennsylvania in the midst of the Stamp Act crisis. His approach to history was that of a careful lawyer; his approach to colonial politics that of a careful historian. He was always prepared to

36. Dickinson's Vindication, in Charles J. Stillé, *The Life and Times of John Dickinson, 1732–1808* (Philadelphia, 1891), 369; this lengthy *apologia* was first published in the *Freeman's Journal* (Philadelphia), Jan. 1, 1783.

37. Dickinson to his mother, June 6, 1756, Colbourn, ed., "Dickinson's London Letters," *Pennsylvania Magazine of History and Biography* 86 (1962): 449.

38. Quoted by Charles Page Smith, *James Wilson; Founding Father, 1742–1798* (Chapel Hill, 1956), 35. Smith's biography has helped rescue Wilson from an undeserved obscurity; a new and accurate edition of Wilson's papers has helped even more.

demonstrate that his political objectives were pre-established, legal, and historically sound.

Wilson studied his law in John Dickinson's Philadelphia office before beginning his own practice in Reading in 1767. He began with Coke's *Institutes* and Blackstone's *Commentaries* and became familiar with such favorite authors as Rapin, Burgh, and Sidney. He enjoyed the writings of Bolingbroke, Nathaniel Bacon, Francis Sullivan, and Lord Kames.[39] Good lawyers, Wilson concluded, "must pry into the secret recesses of the human heart, and become well acquainted with the whole moral world, that they may discover the abstract reason of all laws: and they must trace the laws of particular states, especially of their own, from the first rough sketches to the more perfect draughts; from the first causes or occasions that produced them, through all the effects, good and bad, that they produced."[40]

Within a year of his move to Reading, Wilson began a careful study of colonial arguments against the British Parliament. Although completed in 1768, his *Considerations on the . . . Legislative Authority of the British Parliament* was not published until 1774, when it attracted attention and respect almost comparable to that accorded Adams's *Novanglus* and Jefferson's *Summary View*. Indeed, Wilson's opening statements that "all men are, by nature, equal and free" and that "the happiness of the society is the *first* law of every government,"[41] show philosophical assumptions common to Wilson and Jefferson. And like Jefferson, Wilson devoted much of his considerable energies to a discussion of the legal and historical rights of Englishmen in the American colonies.

"The Colonists are entitled to all the privileges of Britons," ran

39. Wilson was unusually generous in acknowledging his sources; this partial listing is drawn from his published writings; specific citations follow.

40. "Lectures on Law" (1790), James De Witt Andrews, ed., *The Works of James Wilson . . .* , 2 vols. (Chicago, 1896), I, 38–39.

41. *Considerations on the Nature and Extent of the Legislative Authority of the British Parliament* (Philadelphia, 1774), in Randolph G. Adams, ed., *Selected Political Essays of James Wilson* (N.Y., 1930), 49.

one typical claim. "We have committed no crimes to forfeit [these privileges]. . . . We will leave our posterity as free as our ancestors left us." Fundamental to the British constitution was the right to representative government: Englishmen brought this historical right with them to America; an ocean voyage did not transform freemen into slaves. The right was of extreme antiquity and related directly to "one of the most ancient maxims of the English law," namely "that no freeman can be taxed at pleasure."[42] The American colonies were not conquered provinces; they were settled at private expense under royal charters.

Wilson then turned to an examination of Calvin's Case, as presented by Sir Edward Coke. In 1607 this test case had decided whether a Scot born after James I ascended the English throne was entitled to the rights of English citizenship. The majority of the court held that the subject's allegiance was due solely to the natural person of the King; thus allegiance was personal, not national, and did not require obedience to the laws of any of the King's dominions other than that in which the subject was resident.[43] The subjects of each dominion independently enjoyed their own laws and natural rights. The Irish, too, since they had their own legislature, were connected to England only through the person of the King.[44] This was essentially the connection Wilson had in mind for the American colonies.

As Wilson saw it, the chief difficulty confronting imperial relations was the unconstitutional presumption of Parliament, and he feared that Parliamentary misbehavior was the product of recent

42. Ibid., 50, 59.

43. See Charles H. McIlwain, *The American Revolution: A Constitutional Interpretation* (Ithaca, N.Y., 1958), 92–109. For Wilson's discussion of Calvin's case and its application to Englishmen in America, see *Considerations,* Adams, ed., *Essays of Wilson,* 66–80.

44. Ibid., 67. Wilson was to return to this theme in his Law Lectures where he cited William Robertson's *History of Scotland* in arguing that "Two sovereign states [England and Scotland] may employ the same executive magistrate, or bear allegiance to the same prince, without any dependence on each other; and each may retain all its national rights, free and undiminished." See Andrews, ed., *Works of Wilson,* I, 323.

English history. Since an election was the occasion for popular expression of opinion, the more frequent the election the more real the representative process. History showed that "frequent new parliaments are a part of the British constitution: by them only, the king can know the immediate sense of the nation." It followed that infrequent elections led to a perversion of the British constitution. For example, there was the Long Parliament called by Charles I in 1640. Initially that body proceeded "with vigor and a true patriotic spirit, to rescue the kingdom from the oppression under which it then groaned." In its first flush of recently elected fervor, the Long Parliament worked zealously "to retrieve the liberties of the people" and correct "the tyrannical exercise of prerogative" by the King. But when the King unwisely allowed them to decide their own tenure, Parliament's conduct changed disastrously. Once independent of their electors, the Long Parliament sacrificed both the people and the throne to its love of power. "What an instructive example is this!" Wilson exclaimed. Here was proof of what happened when parliaments forgot their constitutional obligations and lost touch with the true source of political authority, the people. Here was an illustration of the dangers derived from a governing body in which the governed (such as the colonies in 1768) lacked an effective voice. Obviously "Kings are not the only tyrants," concluded Wilson. Indeed, the Long Parliament demonstrated that kings are not even the severest tyrants.[45]

But this was only one "instructive example" from English history. Wilson continued his historical review and turned to the reign of Charles II. With the Restoration, he noted, great care was taken to curb Parliament's propensity to self-aggrandizement. But Parliament now sat at the King's pleasure, and its members again lost contact with the voters after election. A new version of the Long Parliament emerged, a Parliament utterly subservient to royal whim, a Parlia-

---

45. *Considerations,* Adams, ed., *Essays of Wilson,* 55–57.

ment disposed "to surrender those liberties, for which their ancestors had planned and fought, and bled." Here was another ominous illustration of what infrequent elections wrought. "Secure in their seats, while they gratified the crown, the members bartered the liberties of the nation for places and pensions." Not until the Glorious Revolution and the arrival of William and Mary did the situation improve. In 1694 came the Triennial Act, which according to Wilson, was decidedly a step in the right constitutional direction. Unfortunately this measure was replaced in 1716 by the Septennial Act, and so a form of Long Parliament returned. Thus Americans were no more than reasonable in their suspicions of Parliamentary behavior. "Long parliaments," Wilson repeated, "will naturally forget their dependence on the people: when this dependence is forgotten, they will become corrupt." And corruption threatened England's ancient constitution and liberty.[46]

Wilson professed unstinted admiration for the English constitution and "the glorious fabric of Britain's liberty."[47] England's was a magnificent achievement and would continue to be, so long as Parliament did not dominate the Crown nor the Crown dictate to Parliament. His confidence in England's constitutional future would naturally be increased if Parliament were more frequently in communication with the people to whom it was responsible. But in any case Americans did not elect representatives to Parliament. They had their own assemblies, which did not dictate to Westminster; and there was no constitutional reason for the Parliament at Westminster to give orders to the American legislatures.

Wilson's emphasis in 1768 was different from Dickinson's in the *Letters from a Farmer*. Both agreed on the nature of the several colonies as realms in the empire of dominions; and both insisted that they

46. Ibid., 57. Here Wilson cites Montesquieu and Blackstone to buttress his contentions.
47. Ibid., 61.

were self-governing realms with charters (compacts) and allegiance to the King only. But Dickinson had conceded some imperial direction in matters of trade and allowed a regulatory role to Parliament in trade matters which Wilson would deny. Wilson questioned the need for trade regulations in the first place, but in the second assigned this task to the Crown. "If the history of the British constitution, relating to this subject, be carefully traced," he wrote, "we shall discover, that a prerogative in the crown, to regulate trade, is perfectly consistent with the principles of law," provided, of course, that such power be exerted for the public good.[48] The public good remained Wilson's objective. It could not be achieved by any acknowledgment of the superiority of Great Britain over the colonies. His principal message was unequivocal: the "Commons of Great Britain have no dominion over their equals and fellow subjects in America."[49]

When Wilson next made a major address on Anglo-American relations, he was speaking to the Pennsylvania provincial convention of January 1775, called to approve the work of the First Continental Congress. With John Dickinson in his audience, he returned to the historical correctness of the colonial case. Colonial opposition to British encroachments, he said, "stands confessed the lovely offspring of freedom. It breathes the spirit of its parent." Colonial resistance, he continued, was inspired by the same spirit of the British constitution which governed "the convention of the barons at Runnymeade, where the tyranny of John was checked, and magna charta was signed." The spirit which guided the Glorious Revolution of 1688 was now at work in America. Neither Wilson nor the Continental Congress wanted revolution. But they would resist invasions of their established rights. "We know," he declared, "that we have not violated the laws or the constitution." It was the right of British subjects

48. See Wilson's note, ibid., 81–82.
49. Ibid., 75–76.

to resist tyranny: "This right is founded both upon the letter and the spirit of the British constitution."[50]

He reminded his audience that despite the vicissitudes of that constitution, despite its frequent breach, "it has been often renewed: it has been often confirmed: it still subsists in its full force," and as the sagacious Bolingbroke had noted, "'it binds the king as much as the meanest subject.'" Just as the Parliament seemed determined to exceed its constitutional role in the 1760s, now the King himself appeared equally disposed to support Parliament's pretensions in America. If the King and Parliament continued to behave in an unconstitutional fashion, then Americans were constitutionally correct in their opposition to violations of their rights. Wilson concluded by calling again upon Bolingbroke (although this time he failed to cite his source): "The British liberties, sir, and the means and the right of defending them, are not the grants of princes; and of what our princes never granted they surely can never deprive us."[51]

Wilson ended his speech on a softer note. He now made a distinction between royal tyranny and an abuse of royal prerogative. Americans, he contended, were completely loyal to the King. Evil ministers were hiding behind the throne, ministers who "have abused his majesty's confidence, brought discredit upon his government, and derogated from his justice." To be sure, history showed many instances of the king forgetting his constitutional character and conspiring with iniquitous ministers. And George III might do well to recall such "examples in the English history." In the present situation "the distinction between him and his ministers has been lost: but they have not been raised to his situation: he has sunk to theirs." The King should know that "liberty is, by the constitution, of equal antiquity, and of equal authority with [royal] prerogative."[52]

---

50. *An Address Delivered in the Convention of the Province of Pennsylvania*, Jan. 1775, ibid., 91–92.

51. Ibid., 94–96.

52. Ibid., 101, 94.

Within a year, Wilson had been elevated to the Second Continental Congress, where he and his colleagues decided they were ready to fight the just fight for "the virtuous Principles of our Ancestors." In "an address to the inhabitants of the United Colonies" drafted in February 1776, five months before the Declaration of Independence, Wilson argued that "history, we believe, cannot furnish an Example of Trust, higher and more important than that which we have received from your hands. . . . The Calamities which threaten us would be attended with the total Loss of those Constitutions, formed upon the venerable Model of British Liberty, which have long been our Pride and Felicity. To avert those Calamities we are under the disagreeable Necessity of making temporary Deviations from those Constitutions." George III "should be the *Ruler* of a *free* People," and not "be degraded into a *Tyrant* over *Slaves.*" Denying that independence was their goal, Wilson and his fellow congressmen declared "that what we aim at, and what we are entrusting [the people] to pursue, is the *Defence and Re-establishment of the constitutional rights of the Colonies.*"[53]

But the fight to preserve "the constitutional rights of the Colonies" within the empire failed. Even before Wilson's address was drafted, Thomas Paine's *Common Sense* pressed for a more radical solution, and Wilson's address was tabled by Congress. When the vote on the Declaration of Independence came on July 2, Wilson, after painful and reluctant reconsideration, voted for the resolution declaring "the United Colonies FREE and INDEPENDENT STATES."

Having accepted independence, Wilson later sought to elucidate through his law lectures of 1790 the peculiar national characteristics of law in America. In his efforts to enhance the dignity of legal studies he emphasized law as a historical science and suggested its superiority to speculative philosophy. Wilson was not concerned with

---

53. *An Address to the Inhabitants of the Colonies . . . ,* Feb. 13, 1776, ibid., 112–14.

imaginary laws for imaginary commonwealths; he was interested in man, the record of his government and his significance for the independent United States.[54]

From his first lecture—attended by President George Washington and the chief officers of the new Federal Government—Wilson acknowledged the American debt to Anglo-Saxon ancestors. The characteristic of the Anglo-Saxon race was "respect for law, tenacity for liberty." In the lectures that followed, he discussed the original Germanic forefathers of modern Englishmen (and Americans). He turned to Tacitus—among Rome's wisest men—for information on this "free people" who made their own laws. There had been, claimed Wilson, some changes when the ancient Germanic tribes settled in England: "instead of continuing to be hunters, they became husbandmen [and] . . . acquired a permanent and exclusive degree of property in land." In England the Saxons were born free from arbitrary power and were governed by laws "made with their voluntary consent." Citing Nathaniel Bacon's *Discourse of the Uniformity of the Government of England,* Wilson described the chief features of Saxon government. All freemen voted for the Saxon witenagemot, and their monarch's power rested firmly upon the judgment of the freemen.[55] Alfred he singled out as "immortal," an illustration of the view of the legal scholar John Selden that the Saxon King was " 'the choicest of the chosen.' "[56]

The Saxon system was a historical illustration of Wilson's belief in the people as the source of political authority. Wilson could hardly muster much enthusiasm for the Normans. They overthrew the Saxon allodial land tenure and introduced feudalism. William the Conqueror was "averse to the Saxon law of liberty," which he

---

54. "Lectures on Law," in Andrews, ed., *Works of Wilson,* I, 3.

55. Ibid., 1 *n,* 3 *n,* 372, 350; II, 176, 492–93, 61.

56. Ibid., II, 104; I, 70. Wilson also cited Francis Sullivan, whom he termed "a very accurate inquirer," ibid., 62; Wilson and Sullivan agreed on the elective character of the Saxon monarchy.

artfully and successfully undermined gradually. Wilson agreed with
those whig historians who believed the Saxon system too fine to be
destroyed in a fair fight. Post-Conquest English history saw frequent
efforts to restore the Saxon polity. Wilson accepted Coke's judgment
on the role of Magna Charta as merely "declaratory of the principal
grounds of the fundamental laws of England," and he praised subsequent English efforts to reclaim their pre-Norman common law.[57]

Wilson was interested in English common law because it was
transferred to the American colonies. "The common law, as now received in America," Wilson pointed out, "bears in its principles, and
in many of its more minute particulars, a stronger and a fairer resemblance to the common law as it was improved under the Saxons
than to that law as it was disfigured under the Norman government."
He studied the governmental operations of his Saxon ancestors because Americans in their wisdom had restored ancient Saxon customs
to modern constitutional practice. Wilson remarked, "how conge-
nial . . . the principles of the constitution of Pennsylvania are to
those adopted by the government of the Saxons." After all, the Saxon
freemen had a voice in lawmaking; and "the freemen of Pennsylvania, as we now see, enjoy the rights of electors." And, added Wilson,
"this is far from the only instance in which we shall have the pleasure of finding the old Saxon maxims of government renewed in the
American constitutions."[58]

Americans in their wisdom had realized that "great innovations
should not be made: a wise and well tempered system must owe
much to experience." Thus the ancient Saxons had held regular
and fixed sessions of their witenagemot, a practice which had been
wrecked by the Normans. And now the Congress of the United

---

57. Ibid., I, 451–52; II, 155, 255. Coke's *Institutes,* observed Wilson, "are a cabinet
richly stored with jewels of law: but are not those jewels strewed about in endless and
bewildering confusion?"

58. Ibid., I, 445; II, 18.

States had a regular schedule of sessions which could not be disrupted at the pleasure of the executive, as was the case in England.[59]

Wilson was particularly interested in the new federal executive. The ancient Saxons had definitely elected their monarchs, no matter what William Blackstone said to the contrary. The American presidency, Wilson went on, was "a renewal, in this particular, of the ancient English constitution." And a sidelight to this renewal was the power *not* given the presidency. The executive was denied the authority to declare war; instead this decision was assigned to the Congress. To Wilson this was evidence of American good sense in following an ancestral example. The power of making peace and war in Saxon England "was invariably possessed by the witenagemote," and "on this very interesting power, the constitution of the United States renews the principle of government known in England before the conquest." In Wilson's view this was logical since the Saxons and their American descendants had much in common. "We have found, and we shall find, that our national government is recommended by the antiquity, as well as by the excellence, of some of its leading principles."[60] Wilson believed an essential virtue of the new United States lay in its acceptance of Saxon antecedents. "Let us ransack the Records of History," was a typically Wilsonian remark.[61] It was advice he himself followed.

III

When Benjamin Franklin wrote his will in 1788 he began: "I, Benjamin Franklin, printer."[62] This was his trade, his vehicle to success, his opportunity for self-education. He influenced the reading of others

59. Ibid., II, 144, 36–37.
60. Ibid., 61, 57; I, 382–91; II, 58.
61. Wilson Manuscripts, Historical Society of Pennsylvania; see Smith, *James Wilson,* 301.
62. Smyth, ed., *Writings of Franklin,* X, 493.

by his selective publishing and his role in founding and guiding the acquisitions of the Library Company of Philadelphia. Far from a systematic scholar, Franklin was no equal of John Adams or Thomas Jefferson as an omnivorous student of history. But he printed, collected, read, and admired history. "As nothing *teaches*," Franklin quoted from Locke, "so nothing *delights* more than HISTORY." History was the repository of "almost all Kinds of useful Knowledge."[63] When agitating for an academy in Philadelphia he recommended that Pennsylvania's youth read such "classicks" as *Cato's Letters*, Addison, Sidney, and "the best modern Histories, particularly of our Mother Country."[64]

His Library was particularly well stocked with such modern histories. During his 1757–62 sojourn in London he made good use of his book-buying opportunities, purchasing volumes by James Tyrrell, Verstegan, Mascou, Sidney, and James Ralph. The purchase of the Ralph book, *Of the Use and Abuse of Parliaments*, was partly a sentimental gesture. Franklin and Ralph had sailed to England together in 1724, and Ralph stayed on to make an unsteady living as a political hack.[65] But Ralph's two-volume study agreed with many of Franklin's own historical ideas. Ralph had accepted the whole fabric of whig history, starting with the original Saxon transplant of representative government and concluding with a savage indictment of the English constitutional condition of the 1740s. "It is manifest," read Franklin, "that the Constitution is everywhere undermin'd; at the first Sound of the Trumpet, like the walls of *Jericho*, it will sink at once, into a Heap of Ruins." Ralph's recent observations of the English scene were also discouraging: "So great is the Influence of the Crown become,

63. Franklin, *Proposals Relating to the Education of Youth* (Philadelphia, 1749), in Labaree and Bell, eds., *Franklin Papers*, III, 410, 411–12.

64. Ibid., 405–6, 415.

65. John G. Shipley, "Franklin Attends a Book Auction," *Pennsylvania Magazine of History and Biography* 80 (1956): 37–45; Robert W. Kenny, "James Ralph: An Eighteenth-Century Philadelphian in Grub Street," *Pennsylvania Magazine of History and Biography* 64 (1940), 218–42.

so servile the Spirit of our Grandees, and so deprav'd the Hearts of the People, that Hope itself begins to Sicken." The English Parliaments, even before the American revenue legislation of the 1760s, had found "that the grand Secret of G[overnmen]t is to fleece with one Hand, and corrupt with the other."[66]

After reading books such as Ralph's, Franklin could feel at ease in the company of James Burgh and Catherine Macaulay. Like Benjamin Rush, Franklin used his visits to England as opportunities to extend his circle of literary acquaintance. He admired Mrs. Macaulay's *History* and her personal society; he took pleasure in publishing Burgh's angry *Britain's Remembrancer* and in helping Burgh write the second volume of the *Political Disquisitions;* he enjoyed Lord Kames's *British Antiquities* and his Scottish hospitality.[67] Franklin knew his way in the scholar's world. He was familiar with Molesworth's edition of *Franco-Gallia,* Bishop Burnet's *History of His Own Time,* Bolingbroke's works, and the writings of Buchanan, Trenchard, and Cartwright; his second copy of Sidney's *Discourses* came as a gift from Thomas Hollis.[68] Franklin's idea of "that *rara Avis,* a true History," was the work of a Rapin, a Robertson, or a Macaulay.[69] One of the treasured eighteenth-century colonial imprints was the edition of Henry Care's *English Liberties* issued in Boston by James and Benjamin Franklin.[70] These were volumes which helped crowd the shelves of his impressively large library room. When in 1787 Manasseh Cutler gazed upon Franklin's four thousand volumes, he could be pardoned for presum-

66. Ralph, *Of the Use and Abuse of Parliaments,* I, 13, 79; II, 716–17.

67. Verner W. Crane, ed., *Benjamin Franklin's Letters to the Press, 1758–1775* (Chapel Hill, 1950), 90–91, 286–287. Franklin published Burgh's *Britain's Remembrancer* in Philadelphia, 1748.

68. Benjamin Franklin to Thomas Brand Hollis, Oct. 5, 1783, Smyth, ed., *Writings of Franklin,* IX, 104.

69. Franklin to the Printer of the *Public Advertiser* (London), May 20, 1765, ibid., IV, 370.

70. Henry Care, *English Liberties* (Boston, 1721).

ing that they constituted "the largest, and by far the best, private library in America."[71]

Franklin's reading in history illuminated for him in a special way the colonies' relation with England. Well aware of the German origin of the English Saxons, he used this as a point of departure for his satirical "Edict By the King of Prussia." Referring to the "first German settlements made in the Island of Britain" by Hengist and Horsa, he suggested that by the logic of England's claim to rule America, Prussia could claim to rule England. Surely, argued Franklin, England should pay tribute and taxes to the Prussian monarch. Surely Prussia had the right, as the source of original migration to England, to dispatch unwanted Prussian convicts as bondservants to the German settlements in England. In the name of historical consistency, continued Franklin, England should be subjected to Prussian Navigation Acts, to Prussian Wool, Hat, and Iron Acts. "Britain was formerly the America of the Germans," he declared. Like the Saxons from ancient Germany, the Saxons from modern England had migrated at their own expense. They had come to America at their own risk, and "therefore supposed that when they had secured the new Country, they held it of themselves, and of no other People under Heaven."[72] In the margin of one of his books, Franklin scribbled in the question: "Have not all Mankind in all Ages had the Right of deserting their Native Country when made uneasy in it? Did not the Saxons desert their Native Country when they came to Britain?"[73]

His version of Saxon history gave Franklin a political argument he loved to pursue. He was unswerving in his devotion to the principle

71. Quoted by George Simpson Eddy, "Dr. Benjamin Franklin's Library," American Antiquarian Society, *Proceedings* 34 (1924): 206.

72. "Edict by the King of Prussia," Sept. 5, 1773, in Smyth, ed., *Writings of Franklin*, VI, 118–24. This was first published in the *Gentleman's Magazine* of Oct. 1773.

73. Franklin to the Printer of the *Public Advertiser* (London), Mar. 16, 1773, Crane, ed., *Franklin's Letters to the Press*, 226–29; and Franklin's marginal comment in his copy of Allan Ramsay's *Thoughts on the Origin and Nature of Government . . .* (London, 1766), 51. Franklin's copy is in the Rare Book Room, Library of Congress.

of freedom to emigrate. When the ancient Saxons left Europe for England, they not only achieved an independent English settlement but brought with them their habits of representative government and established that government in their new land. It followed that "British subjects, by removing into *America*, do not thereby lose their native rights."[74] Like their ancestors, Englishmen in America had brought with them their habits of self-government, which included "the undoubted right of Englishmen, not to be taxed but by their own consent." To deny the colonists' rights as Englishmen would be to treat them "as a conquered people, and not as true British subjects."[75] In no way could America be identified with either Ireland or Wales, which Franklin and many constitutional historians regarded as conquered provinces; and yet both were better treated by the mother country than were the American colonies, to whom England was "incomparably more obliged."[76]

Recent English history gave Franklin little satisfaction. The English tradition of freedom, he knew, demanded "*an actual share in the appointment of those who frame the laws.*" But, "*a very* great majority of the commonalty of this realm [England] are denied the privilege of voting for representatives in Parliament; and consequently, they are enslaved to a *small number,* who do now enjoy the privilege exclusively to themselves." If this situation continued, it must "speedily cause *the certain overthrow of our happy constitution, and* enslave us *all.*" Insufficient attention was paid to "the ancient and sacred laws of the land"; elections were no longer annual on the original Saxon pattern; Parliament had become too oligarchic and unrepresentative for Franklin's peace of mind.[77]

74. Franklin, "A Dialogue . . . concerning the present state of affairs in Pennsylvania," *Pennsylvania Gazette* (Philadelphia), Dec. 18, 1755.

75. Franklin to Governor Shirley, Dec. 18, 1754, Smyth, ed., *Writings of Franklin,* III, 233–34.

76. Franklin to the *Public Advertiser* (London), Jan. 8, 1770, Crane, ed., *Franklin's Letters to the Press,* 121.

77. "Some Good Whig Principles," was Franklin's comment on these views; see Smyth, ed., *Writings of Franklin,* X, 130–31.

As early as 1755 he had reported on the growing "Corruption and Degeneracy of the People" and questioned the future of English liberties. "I know," he told Richard Jackson, "you have a great deal of Virtue still subsisting among you; and I hope the Constitution is not so near a Dissolution, as some seem to apprehend."[78] But corruption did not subside. Twenty years later, he reviewed English conditions from his London vantage point: there was, he told Joseph Galloway, an "extream Corruption prevalent among all Orders of Men in this old rotten State." Only mischief could come from a closer colonial union with such a decadent mother country.

Franklin now argued that a continued connection with England would inevitably destroy the luster of "the glorious publick Virtue so predominant in our rising Country." England would surely drag America with her into "the plundering Wars, which their desperate Circumstances, Injustice, and Rapacity, may prompt them to undertake." As for these desperate circumstances, Franklin was quite explicit: "Here Numberless and needless Places, enormous Salaries, Pensions, Perquisites, groundless Quarrels, foolish Expeditions, false Accounts or no Accounts, Contracts and Jobbs, devour all Revenue, and produce continual Necessity in the Midst of natural Plenty." Franklin agreed with Burgh that less luxury and corruption and more economy would reduce the need to tax the American colonies. And any American compliance with English revenue requests would only add to England's self-made moral and political disintegration. For the virtuous colonies to maintain any union with their unvirtuous mother country could only "corrupt and poison us also."[79] In fact, Americans were already acquiring an unhealthy taste for luxury, and Franklin's barbed pen once suggested that if only the American colonists would save for two or three years the money now spent on "Fineries and Fopperies," they would have enough to bribe the entire British government.[80]

78. Franklin to Richard Jackson, May 5, 1753, ibid., III, 141.
79. Franklin to Joseph Galloway, Feb. 25, 1775, ibid., VI, 311–12.
80. Franklin to Thomas Cushing, Oct. 10, 1774, ibid., 251–52.

As Franklin saw it, seventeenth-century English Whiggism had miscarried. The political Whigs now in office were successors only in name to the Whigs of the 1680s; he agreed with the observation made in *Cato's Letters* that Whigs in power behaved like their Tory predecessors. Englishmen in America were the Real Whigs in the seventeenth-century tradition, determined that "whenever the Crown assumes Prerogatives it has not, or makes an unwarrantable Use of those it has, they will oppose as far as they are able."[81]

He was not only disturbed over the failure of Parliament to restrain royal prerogative; he was also alarmed at the political pretensions of Parliament. It sought to govern the King's dominions as though they were part of the realm of England, a form of tyranny comparable to that attempted by the Stuarts within the mother country. Franklin agreed with the English pamphleteer who inquired, "Is it not . . . most egregious folly, so loudly to condemn the Stuart family, who would have governed England without a parliament, when at the same time, we would, almost all of us, govern America, upon principles not at all more justified?"[82] Efforts at Parliamentary tyranny were the more frightening to Franklin because he knew "a single Man may be afraid or sham'd of doing Injustice. A Body is never either one or the other, if it is strong enough." A body of men, Franklin explained, "cannot apprehend Assassination; and by dividing the shame among them, it is in so little apiece, that no one minds it."[83]

So long as Franklin could confine his political criticisms to Parliament, he could protest his devotion to his monarch. "All the Difficulties," he once noted, "have arisen from the British Parliament's

81. Franklin to a friend of Lord Hillsborough, Sept. 1772, Crane, ed., *Franklin's Letters to the Press*, 224.

82. *An Inquiry into the Nature and Causes of the Present Disputes* (London, 1769), 26. Franklin inscribed much marginalia on this page; his copy is in the New York Public Library. Franklin's remarks here indicate he was once far from hostile to the idea of American representation in Westminster; see ibid., 23.

83. Franklin's marginal commentary, ibid., 26.

Attempting to deprive [the colonists of] their just rights."[84] He had no reason to think of himself as an imperial secessionist, as some of his political enemies charged. He could hardly dismember what had never been legitimately united. The colonies were self-governing dominions of George III, and Franklin hoped they would always be. His abiding affection for England and his numerous friends in the mother country meant that Franklin's final decision for total separation was reached reluctantly. But in his view historical obligations made independence imperative in the face of British oppression by Parliament and King. If Franklin's monarch was "the Sovereign of all," he was also a king who should not misuse his prerogative. Franklin concluded that George III was at least condoning the persistent encroachments of Parliament. If it was easy to "throw Dust in the eyes of a good King," it was apparently not so easy to get it out again.[85]

IV

It is ironic that these three from Pennsylvania should contribute so much to a revolution they did not want. Franklin, Wilson, and Dickinson did not see themselves as radicals, as theoreticians of rebellion. Franklin spoke for his colleagues when expressing his distaste for "metaphysical reasonings"—"I quitted that kind of reading and study for others more satisfactory."[86] They assumed the happiness and security of mankind as the object of political society, and they turned to law and history to illustrate that assumption. The British constitution was a historical reality for all three men. The rights to which they laid claim inhered in a constitution which was theirs by

84. Franklin's marginal commentary, ibid., 21, 24.
85. Franklin to a friend of Lord Hillsborough, Sept. 1772, Crane, ed., *Franklin's Letters to the Press*, 224.
86. Franklin to Benjamin Vaughan, Nov. 9, 1779, Smyth, ed., *Writings of Franklin*, VII, 412.

descent; they argued for rights affirmed by common law ("founded on long and general custom") and restated in such liberty documents as Magna Charta and the Bill of Rights. Fundamental was the "right to resist force employed to destroy the very existence of law and of liberty." They subscribed to what Wilson called the indisputable "Maxims of the *English* Constitution," and with reluctance took up arms to preserve "the virtuous Principles" of their ancestors.[87] If their premises were wrong, then, Franklin drily reminded England, " 'tis their misfortune, not their fault. Your most celebrated writers on the constitution, your *Seldens,* your *Lockes,* and your *Sidneys,* have reasoned them into this mistake."[88]

87. Wilson, *Address,* Jan. 1775, Adams, ed., *Essays of Wilson,* 96, 112.
88. Franklin, "Rejoinder to Tom Hint," *Gazetteer* (London), Dec. 27, 1765, reprinted in Crane, ed., *Franklin's Letters to the Press,* 41.

CHAPTER VII

The Historical Mind of the South

The intellectual history of the American Revolution was largely a history of political ideas, English history invoked against each new policy inaugurated by a British ministry. After 1765, colonial reactions to imperial regulations varied little from New Hampshire to Georgia. The rights of Englishmen applied to all colonists, whether they resided in northern, middle, or southern colonies; the colonial argument against "ministerial injustice" was all pervasive.

Born to power and position, the planter aristocrats of the southern colonies, like the leaders in the other colonies, were determined to maintain their rights and privileges. As political leaders they developed a familiarity with the history of the rights they sought to maintain. As landed litigants they necessarily developed an intimate knowledge of the law. Conflict with the mother country was far from a new experience, and long-standing disputes with their governors prepared them well for the political battles of the 1760s and 1770s.

I

In 1728 Daniel Dulany the elder used arguments against the proprietary government of Maryland that were strikingly similar to those employed by the Revolutionaries four decades later. When Governor Benedict Leonard Calvert vetoed the legislature's third attempt to apply English statutes to Maryland, Dulany insisted upon the right of Marylanders to "the Enjoyment of English liberties; and the Benefit of the English Laws."[1] A Maryland gentleman of taste and wealth, the elder Dulany had studied law in England at Gray's Inn, and in his political disputes in Maryland he earned a reputation as one of "the ablest lawyers of his generation."[2]

Like so many of his political successors, Dulany attacked from a firm legal and historical base. His library included such whig works as Rapin's *History,* Gordon's translation of Tacitus, and Molesworth's *Account of Denmark.*[3] His own pamphlet, *The Rights of the Inhabitants of Maryland to the Benefit of the English Laws,* referred frequently to "the great Oracle of the Law" Sir Edward Coke, *Cato's Letters,* Rushworth's *Historical Collections,* and Henry Care's *English Liberties.* "What I contend for," he asserted, "is, that we derive our Right to British Liberties, and Privileges, as we are British Subjects." His rights came from English common law, "the best and most Common Birth-Right, that the Subject hath." Under common law "every Subject has a Right to the Enjoyment of his Liberty and Property," and when that right was threatened, "recourse must be had to the Law for a Remedy."[4]

For Dulany one of the many attractions of Coke's *First Institutes* lay in its claim that "a British Subject, may with Courage and Freedom, tell the most daring, and powerful Oppressor, that He must not injure him, with Impunity." He knew his English history, and he knew there had been many attacks on the rights and liberties of Englishmen. He looked to Magna Charta as merely "a Declaration of

---

1. Daniel Dulany, *The Right of the Inhabitants of Maryland to the Benefit of the English Laws* (Annapolis, 1728), 2; conveniently reproduced in St. George Sioussat, *The English Statutes in Maryland* (Baltimore, 1903). For the background of the Dulanys, see the excellent biographical study by Aubrey C. Land, *The Dulanys of Maryland . . .* (Baltimore, 1955).

2. Sioussat, *English Statutes in Maryland,* 62, 65.

3. Joseph T. Wheeler, "Reading and Other Recreations of Marylanders, 1700–1776," *Maryland Historical Magazine* 38 (1943): 52–53.

4. Dulany, *Right of the Inhabitants,* 23, 19, 21, 12, 8.

the Common Law" and Parliament's many confirmations of Magna Charta as substantiation of the need for vigilance. Quoting the "ingenious" *Cato's Letters,* he asked "if Men . . . will be great Knaves, in spight of Opposition; how much greater would they be if there were none?"[5] Dulany argued for a historical title to English liberties and urged resistance to encroachments. Readers of his *Rights of the Inhabitants of Maryland* were fully informed of their historical rights.

Dulany's son, Daniel Dulany the younger, brilliantly adapted such arguments to the new imperial problems of the 1760s. Also an outstanding lawyer, the younger Dulany attended Eton, Cambridge, and then the Inns of Court, where he studied at the Middle Temple in company with William Blackstone. Aided by his father's fine library, the younger Dulany was well equipped for his chosen role as critic of the Stamp Act in 1765.

Along with many colonists Dulany was angered not only by the taxation imposed by the Stamp Act, but also by the constitutional assumptions made by its proponents. He was particularly aroused by the ministerial claim "that the colonies were all virtually represented in Parliament, in the same manner as those of the subjects in Great Britain, who did not vote for representatives."[6] Dulany's most successful pamphlet, *Considerations on the Propriety of Imposing Taxes in the British Colonies,*[7] made a frontal assault upon this argument: "It is alledged," complained Dulany, "that there is a *Virtual,* or *implied Representation* of the Colonies springing out of the Constitution of the *British* Government." Indeed, he observed, it must be virtual, "or it doth not exist at all." The fundamental and historical right of all Englishmen was the guarantee that no part of their property could be taken without their consent; thus if the House of Commons did

5. Ibid., 4, 14, 25, 19.

6. See Land, *Dulanys of Maryland,* 168, 190.

7. Dulany Jr., *Considerations on the Propriety of Imposing Taxes in the British Colonies, for the Purpose of Raising a Revenue, by Act of Parliament* (London, 1766).

not virtually represent the colonies, there was no constitutional basis for the Stamp Act.

Dulany's fame rests largely upon the thoroughness with which he demolished British contentions for virtual representation. He noted, for example, that a nonelector was safe from oppression only when such oppression would also fall upon the electors and their representatives; Americans enjoyed no such safeguard. Thanks to county representation, all of England had some measure of real representation in the House of Commons; Americans enjoyed no such security.[8] But Dulany's pamphlet went beyond the issue of virtual representation. He was concerned with the larger question of the constitutional rights of Americans. He looked to the common law as the inheritance of Englishmen on both sides of the Atlantic. He looked to colonial charters as formal acknowledgment *"that their Privileges as English Subjects should be effectually secured to Themselves, and transmitted to their Posterity."* Charters not only confirmed colonial rights under the English constitution, but did so with a precision absent in England, where theory had to reckon with "the veil of Antiquity." Dulany was well aware that once he left the common law, he entered an area of historical uncertainty. He noted that the ancient English constitution "is differently traced by different Men; but of the Colonies the Evidence of it is clear and unequivocal." The best affirmations of English rights were in Magna Charta and the Bill of Rights; in both was the guarantee that *"no Part of their Property shall be drawn from British Subjects without their Consent."* This, Dulany repeatedly insisted, "was an essential principle of the *English* Constitution."[9]

This essential principle could only be maintained by the sort of energy which secured Magna Charta. He reported that in his father's copy of Molesworth's *Account of Denmark* there was a grim enough warning of "an Instance of the excessive Temerity of political ani-

8. Ibid., 2–6.
9. Ibid., 39–42, 5.

mosity." Everyone knew how an apathetic Danish assembly had allowed its powers to be seized by a tyrannical aristocracy; unless Americans stood firmly for their "constitutional *Magna Charta* privileges," they would deserve a similar fate.[10]

In 1765 Dulany achieved a reputation for patriotism, but it was soon dissipated. As the colonial crisis with England worsened, Dulany became more disturbed over the dangers of drastic domestic change than over the constitutional dangers emanating from London. He finally found it necessary to retire from political strife, a decision hastened by his famous debate with a fellow Maryland aristocrat, Charles Carroll of Carrollton. Since Carroll had spent much of his youth in France before visiting London to read some English law, he was less English than Dulany in his educational background. He returned home to a well-stocked paternal library, read widely, and became familiar with Rapin, Blackstone, Robertson, Hume, Gordon's *Tacitus,* and Petyt's *Ius Parliamentum.*[11] With this preparation he criticized the Stamp Act with much the same kind of vigor and language used by the Dulanys, appealing to English common law as the foundation of colonial rights: "By that Law, the most favourable to liberty, we claim the invaluable privilege, that distinguishing Characteristick of the English constitution of being taxed by our own representatives." To Carroll as to Daniel Dulany the younger, British claims of "virtual" representation were cruel mockery. Colonial acceptance of the Stamp Act would subject Americans to the sweeping powers implicit in that legislation and place the colonies at the whim of Parliament. "Are we to trust to the moderation of a British Parliament?" he asked. What manner of men made up the contemporary

10. Ibid., 67 *n.* Dulany's pamphlet is best known—and properly so—as a criticism of the British claim for the colonists' "virtual" representation in Parliament. But one reason for Dulany's emphasis on this point is his concern with real representation as a historical and constitutional right belonging to all Englishmen.

11. Barker, *Background of the Revolution in Maryland,* 67; see also, Ellen Hart Smith, *Charles Carroll of Carrollton* (Cambridge, Mass., 1945).

House of Commons? Men who had been so openhanded with their constitutents' money surely would not be considerate of colonial feelings. Recent Parliamentary behavior, Carroll warned, appeared to carry the strongest marks of despotism.[12]

In 1765 Carroll claimed a colonial right to representative government, denying the constitutionality of the Stamp Act and charging Parliament with being reliable only for its corruption. Unlike the younger Dulany, Carroll did not soften his views. He increased his reading and his book purchasing so that he could be better informed on colonial claims. "Money cannot be laid out better," he told William Graves in 1772, "than in the purchase of valuable books,"[13] and he proceeded to acquire such volumes as Robertson's *Charles V,* Lyttleton's *History of Henry II,* and Dalrymple's *Feudal Property.*[14] As the imperial crisis deepened, he saw less and less cause for hope. Convinced that England's government had declined too far from its former balance and virtue, he was sure that England was ruled by the worst of all governments, "a corrupt aristocracy . . . the least of all others fitted to extensive empire." In a private letter written in 1771, Carroll concluded that the present House of Commons, "which ought to be the representative of the People, has become the instrument of the Ministry, to raise money from the subject." The ministry, he observed, "is commonly composed of rich noblemen, and of some rich commoners, connected together by the ties of kindred or of interest." The Crown had developed "vast influence," and the common people were now utterly corrupted.[15]

The clash between Carroll and the younger Dulany arose over

12. Charles Carroll to William Graves, Sept. 15, 1765, Thomas M. Field, ed., *Unpublished Letters of Charles Carroll of Carrollton, and His Father, Charles Carroll of Doughoregan* (N.Y., 1902), 88–91.

13. Charles Carroll to William Graves, Aug. 14, 1772, J. G. D. Paul, ed., "A Lost Copy-Book of Charles Carroll of Carrollton," *Maryland Historical Magazine* 32 (1937): 215.

14. Charles Carroll to Edmund Jennings, Aug. 9, 1771, to William Graves, Sept. 7, 1773, and Aug. 15, 1774, ibid., 198–99, 220, 223.

15. Charles Carroll to Edmund Jennings, Aug. 9, 1771, ibid., 198–99.

an internal issue, provoking a newspaper debate which called upon history to an extraordinary degree. Early in 1773, Governor Robert Eden claimed the right of setting Crown officers' fees; but the Maryland Assembly insisted that this was their privilege. Dulany, a councilor and a recipient of such fees, sided with the Governor; Carroll with the Assembly. Carroll claimed that the fees were a form of taxation, and that no Englishman should pay taxes to which he had not consented. Eventually, Eden gave up his claim, but the bitter argument which he had started remained a lively political issue. The "Antilon—First Citizen" dispute,[16] an important chapter in the history of the Revolution in Maryland, was carried on in almost exclusively historical terms. For the Revolutionary generation nothing could be more impressive, nothing could be more persuasive than a political view couched in phrases of legal precedent and historical simile.

In his attack on the Governor, Carroll likened Eden's assertion of the right to set fees to Charles I's policy in Hampden's ship money case, and he attacked Dulany as an evil adviser to the Governor. Authority had corrupted the Governor's councilors, Carroll declared; history was full of examples proving that "power is apt to pervert the best of natures." After citing illustrations of Court lawyers betraying the cause of the people, he warned the Governor of the mischief misguided ministers had caused the unfortunate Charles I. Carroll's first letter was warmly applauded by admirers who signed themselves "Independent Whigs."[17]

Dulany's response was weak and injudicious. He conceded Carroll's charges against Charles I: the King's extortion of ship money was "against the fundamental principles of a free constitution" and contrary to the Petition of Right. The best Dulany could offer was a distinction between fees, a proper function of the royal prerogative,

16. This exchange has been edited by Elihu S. Riley, *Correspondence of "First Citizen"—Charles Carroll of Carrollton, and "Antilon"—Daniel Dulany, Jr., 1773* . . . (Baltimore, 1902).
17. *Maryland Gazette* (Annapolis), Feb. 4, Feb. 11, 1773.

and taxes, which were not.[18] Dulany contended that the Crown set and paid the fees of court officers in Westminster Hall, that there was constitutional precedent for the similar action by Governor Robert Eden in Maryland.[19] Carroll denied this, citing Coke and Hawkins as support; but seemingly uncertain of his case, he went on to argue that even if Dulany's facts were correct, an English aberration was hardly justification for similar error in America. Dulany's examples of royal fee-setting were met by Carroll's assertions that such precedents were meaningless out of context. The English constitution, Carroll claimed, was an evolving, changing political structure; English history revealed frequent tyranny, but even more frequent effort to set it aside.[20]

Dulany thus afforded Carroll an excuse for reviewing English constitutional history. He depicted at the outset a happy state of liberty among the ancient Saxons in England; but their freedom was "wrested from them by the Norman conqueror," who "entirely changed the ancient constitution." Carroll's concept of post-Conquest history was not that of the usual whig writer: after 1066 he saw "struggles between monarchy, and aristocracy, not between liberty, and prerogative." The common people were but pawns in the game of politics, remaining oppressed and "a prey to both parties." Only at the end of Henry III's reign did Carroll discover evidence of a House of Commons, which from obscure beginnings, rose to become "the most powerful branch of our national assemblies, which gradually rescued the people from aristocratical, as well as from regal tyranny." Medieval times Carroll described as "that rude and unlettered age," when a barbarous monarchy, unregulated by any "fixed maxims, nor bounded by any certain rights," imperfectly understood the meaning of "publick liberty." He drew often from David Hume in his descriptions of Richard II and Edward III, citing him again when

18. Ibid., Feb. 18, 1773.
19. Ibid., Apr. 8, 1773.
20. Ibid., May 6, 1773.

writing of Henry VII's reign as "one continued scene of rapine and oppression on his part, and of servile submission on that of parliament." Henry VIII was no improvement: he "governed with absolute sway"; under the Tudors Parliaments generally acted "more like the instruments of power than the guardians of liberty." Carroll found time to agree that his readers, searching for more comment on the constitutionality of Governor Eden's fees, might wonder at the relevance of his historical excursion; but his main point was that during this evolution of the government such constitutional questions went unnoticed. "*Silent leges inter arma,*" he commented.

But this observation was substantially appropriate for later history too. Up to 1688, Parliaments were either embroiled in contests with the Crown, or seeking to heal "the bleeding wounds of the nation." He admired the Revolution of 1688, ranking it "among the most glorious deeds, that have done honor to the character of Englishmen"; James II, "by endeavouring to introduce arbitrary power, and to subvert the established church, justly deserved to be deposed and banished." But the eviction of the Stuarts had not been sufficient to secure the ancient English constitution: Parliaments, noted Carroll with regret, "have relaxed much of their antient severity and discipline." Overwhelmed by gratitude to William III, "their great deliverer," and later anxious to prove their trust in the Hanoverian dynasty, Parliaments forgot their proper suspicion of the Crown. In the eighteenth century, continued Carroll, "a liberality bordering on profuseness has taken place of a rigid and austere economy; complacence and compliment have succeeded to distrust and to Parliamentary inquiries, into the conduct and to impeachment of *ruling ministers.*" Carroll knew recent writers in England who complained of "the vast increase of officers, placemen, and pensioners, and to that increase have principally ascribed an irresistible influence in the Crown over those national councils." No one familiar with the House of Commons debates could ignore charges such as those leveled by Edward Southwell in 1744, charges with an immediate pertinence to

Carroll's debate in 1773: "Not only large salaries have been annexed to every place or office under government, but many of the officers have been allowed to *oppress the subject by the sale of places under them, and by exacting extravagant and unreasonable fees,* which have been *so long suffered* that they are now looked upon as the *legal perquisites* of the office, nay, in many offices they seem to have got a *customary right* to defraud the public." Here was an object lesson on the dangers of granting either a colonial governor or an English monarch broad authority over judicial offices.

There was, however, an important difference between England and Maryland: in Carroll's colony, the proprietary government did not, thanks to quitrents, derive its income substantially from taxes voted by the Assembly. If further power were allowed the executive, then the Assembly of Maryland would become a meaningless appendage. In England, on the other hand, the financial necessities of the Crown forced it to make frequent recourse to Parliamentary grants, and thus the House of Commons had emerged in the seventeenth century as a bulwark of the subject's liberty. Only by "the unanimous, steady, and spirited conduct of the people" was liberty achieved. Magna Charta and its confirmations, the Petition of Right of 1628 and the Bill of Rights of 1688, all were "the happy effects of *force* and *necessity.*" Carroll was anxious to maintain an executive dependency upon the people in Maryland. He was only too aware that this essential ingredient to liberty was disappearing in England: "Let us, my countrymen, profit by the errors and vices of the mother country; let us shun the rocks, on which there is reason to fear her constitution will be split."[21]

Carroll dominated the "Antilon—First Citizen" duel. His shafts struck home at Dulany, who responded with intemperate *ad hominem* criticisms of his tormenter. Dulany, even more than Carroll, lost sight of the original issue of fees; he wandered into unfortunate

21. Ibid., July 1, 1773.

byways, attacking Carroll's sources and his Roman Catholic faith. Hume's *History,* declared Dulany, was "a studied apology for the Stuarts"; reliance upon so partisan a writer, Dulany insinuated, was logical for the Roman Catholic Carroll seeking sympathy for his coreligionists. Carroll retorted that Dulany was judging the seventeenth century by the constitutional expectations of the eighteenth; the English constitution "was not so well improved and so well settled in Charles' time as at present."[22]

But if the constitution was better "settled" in Carroll's day, its execution was not. If the fee controversy distressed Carroll in 1773, the consequences of the Boston Tea Party seriously alarmed him in 1774. Now he saw "insatiable avarice," the "ambition of corrupt ministers intent on spreading that corruption thro' America, by which they govern absolutely in G[reat] B[ritain]."[23] Resistance was Carroll's choice. It was not Dulany's. Dulany had always been more concerned with the proper limits of sovereignty than its popular origins. In 1765 he had denied Parliament's propriety in enacting the Stamp Act; he had questioned the constitutionality of Parliamentary taxation of Americans; but he had not doubted the supremacy of Parliament and could not countenance turbulence, disorder, or disobedience to law. And so, a decade later, Dulany declined to join Carroll in resisting British tyranny, despite substantial agreement on the essential constitutional rights at stake. Dulany could criticize tyranny and employ history to identify it; but his respect for law, for authority, was such that he could not offer overt resistance. And so, unlike Carroll, Dulany was not a signer of the Declaration of Independence; nor, like several of his close relatives, was Dulany a loyalist. An uneasy

---

22. Ibid., Apr. 8, 1773. Carroll defended Hume, asserting that the historian did not suppress facts but merely gave "an artificial coloring to some, softened others, and suggested plausible motives for the conduct of Charles." Though "not *entirely impartial,*" Hume was substantially accurate. See ibid., May 6, 1773.

23. Carroll to William Graves, Aug. 15, 1774, Paul, ed., "Lost Copy-Book of Charles Carroll," *Maryland Historical Magazine* 32 (1937): 225.

neutral, Dulany had spent his political force; his unwitting contribution to the Revolution had long since been made.[24]

II

If Maryland achieved a priority in her appeal to certain historical rights, her Virginia neighbors could point to an earlier resistance to British impositions in the 1760s. A leader in such resistance was Richard Bland, a Virginia aristocrat and one of the most active members of the House of Burgesses. Like many a planter's son, Bland studied with a series of itinerant tutors and secured enough of a classical education to enter the College of William and Mary. After graduation he continued an informal course of self-education, relying on a disciplined program of private reading. A self-taught lawyer and historian, he impressed John Adams as "a learned, bookish man."[25] Much of his fine library was later bought by Thomas Jefferson, only to be lost in the Library of Congress fire of 1851, but it is possible to piece together something of the reading interests of this learned gentleman and discover the use to which they were put.

Richard Bland's life was one of continuous public service. For more than thirty years, he served in the Virginia House of Burgesses, where he was said to be a very John Selden in his advocacy of liberty.[26] Bland admired Selden; he would have savored the comparison. When Governor Dinwiddie tried to impose and collect a land-patenting fee—the pistole fee—in 1753, Bland led the opposition to "an Infringement of the Rights of the People," a subversion of "the Laws and Constitution."[27]

Three years later the Virginia Assembly passed, and Governor Fau-

24. See Land, *Dulanys of Maryland*, 308–19.

25. John Adams, Diary, Sept. 2, 1774, Adams, *Works*, II, 362.

26. H. B. Grigsby, *The Virginia Convention of 1776* . . . (Richmond, 1855), 57–58, quoted by Clinton Rossiter, *Seedtime of the Republic* (N.Y., 1953), 252.

27. H. R. McIlwaine, ed., *Journals of the House of Burgesses of Virginia, 1752–58* (Richmond, 1909), 143, 154.

quier approved, the Two-Penny Act, a temporary wartime antiinfla-
tionary measure which allowed contracts, rent, salaries, debts, and
fees usually payable in tobacco to be paid at the rate of sixteen shil-
lings and eight pence per hundred pounds of tobacco, or two pence
per pound. The regulation was dictated by the rapid rise in the price
of tobacco, which had climbed to six pence per pound, three times
its pre-war value. Although the act applied to all transactions involving tobacco as currency, it was the clergy rather than the merchants
who complained. Their annual pay had been set in 1696 at 16,000
pounds of tobacco and confirmed as recently as 1748. For the clergy
the Two-Penny Act meant a cut of two-thirds of their real income,
at least for the year's duration of the act, while their living costs
mounted during wartime inflation. They memorialized the Board of
Trade, praying for a royal disallowance of the Two-Penny Act on the
constitutional ground that it lacked the usual suspending clause; it
had gone into effect before receiving royal examination. The Reverend John Camm represented the clergy in England, and the Privy
Council disallowed the act. The clergy then brought suit for recovery
of their unpaid salaries, and the case of the Reverend James Maury,
Jefferson's teacher, gave Patrick Henry his chance to contest the constitutionality of royal disallowance. Since there were no statutory
grounds for denying Maury's recovery, Henry argued that the original compact between the King and the people had been breached;
"a King," he declared, "by annulling or disallowing Acts of so salutary a nature [as the Two-Penny Act], from being the Father of his
people degenerate into a Tyrant, and forfeits all right to his subjects'
Obedience." [28] Henry denied the right of the King to refuse Virginians the privilege of enacting their own legislation. The jury awarded

28. This rather complex story is told in Gipson, *Coming of the Revolution*, 46–54, and
Richard L. Morton, *Colonial Virginia*, 2 vols. (Chapel Hill, 1960), II, chap. 30. Patrick
Henry's speech was reported by James Maury to John Camm, Dec. 12, 1763, John Pendleton Kennedy, ed., *Journals of the House of Burgesses of Virginia, 1761-1765* (Richmond,
1907), lii–liii.

damages of one penny to the Reverend Mr. Maury, and the clergy's case for full compensation collapsed.

Bland, more thoughtful than Henry, addressed himself to the history of the constitutional power of the King to disallow laws of the Virginia Assembly. His essay, *The Colonel Dismounted* (1763), was a landmark in the evolving colonial argument for self government, outlining in bold strokes what later became the familiar argument of an independent dominion: Virginia had not been created by the King or by Parliament. It was not, therefore, part of the British realm. The English emigrants to America had settled at their own expense in blood and treasure; they owed no economic obligations to the mother country, nor were they under any obligations except that of allegiance to the King. Colonial charters, as Coke had ruled, were compacts by which the King had granted colonists "the Laws of *England,* or a power to make Laws for themselves." Compacts are binding: neither the grantor nor his successors "can alter or abrogate the same."[29]

As "descendants of *Englishmen,*" Virginians were entitled to "the native Privileges our Progenitors enjoyed," privileges which "could not be forfeited by their Migration to *America.*" In England "all Men are born free, are only subject to Laws made with their own Consent, and cannot be deprived of the Benefit of these Laws without a transgression of them." So, too, were the King's subjects in Virginia born free, under the rule of law. Clearly implying that the colonial legislature had exclusive jurisdiction over internal polity, Bland declared that royal instructions about the suspending clause, however much they might serve as "Guides and Directions for the Conduct of Governors," could not "consistently with the Principles of the *British* Constitution . . . have the Force and Power of Laws upon the People." Only the "Legislature of the Colony," he concluded, "have a Right

29. Richard Bland, *The Colonel Dismounted* (Williamsburg, 1763), in the *William and Mary College Quarterly,* 1st ser., 19 (1910): 32–33. There is an excellent essay on Bland in Rossiter, *Seedtime of the Republic,* 248–80.

to enact ANY Law they shall think necessary for their INTERNAL Government."[30]

Bland's position was bold and original, grounded in history and foreshadowing his most important literary and historical effort, his *Inquiry into the Rights of the British Colonies* (1766). Bland's work, the most important publication in Virginia during the Stamp Act crisis, was in Jefferson's opinion "the first pamphlet on the nature of the connection with Great Britain which had any pretension to accuracy of view on that subject."[31] Jefferson's initial excitement is easy to understand.

Bland had been busy reading. He knew the works of William Petyt, Robert Brady, Rapin, Tacitus, and Temple. He seems to have become familiar with Samuel Squire's *Enquiry into the Foundations of the English Constitution* (1753), which proclaimed itself "an Historical Essay upon the Anglo-Saxon Government both in Germany and England." Squire described England's Saxon forefathers as manifesting an "invincible love of liberty": they "were born free, lived under a free government in their first settlements, brought freedom with them into Britain, and handed it down to us inviolate."[32] Following Squire, Bland opened his *Inquiry* with an assertion of the English birthright: it was "as certain as History can make it that the present civil Constitution of *England* derives its Original from the Saxons, who, coming over to the Assistance of the *Britons* . . . established a Form of Government . . . similar to that they had been accustomed

30. Bland, *Colonel Dismounted,* 33, 23, 26.

31. Jefferson to William Wirt, Aug. 5, 1815, Lipscomb and Bergh, eds., *Writings of Jefferson,* XIV, 338.

32. Samuel Squire, *An Enquiry into the Foundations of the English Constitution: or, an Historical Essay upon the Anglo-Saxon Government both in Germany and England,* new ed. (London, 1753), 9, 11, 84. Professor Clyde Henson of Michigan State University has for many years investigated the contents of the Bland library; the Bland copy of Squire, signed "R. Bland" and heavily underlined, was last located in the library of the late Dr. Magnus Martin. I am in Dr. Henson's debt for information on the Bland library in general and for confirming my estimate of the importance of Squire's *Enquiry* in particular.

to live under in their native Country." The original Saxon constitution was "founded upon Principles of the most perfect Liberty." Landholding was allodial (as Squire also insisted), and "every Freeman, that is, every Freeholder, was a Member of their Wittinagemot, or Parliament," until it proved impossible for all freemen to attend in person, when a representative system developed. Under this, all freemen "had a Right to vote at the Election of Members of Parliament."[33] The source of rights and duties, therefore, far from being in "utopian constitutions . . . [which] perhaps never actually existed but in the imagination of speculative men,"[34] or being found in theories of a natural law and divine prescription, was actually to be found in recorded Saxon history.

Saxon history showed a people exerting their "natural Right to relinquish their Country, and by retiring from it, and associating together, to form a new political Society and independent State." Bland drew a parallel with the Englishmen who crossed the Atlantic to America: they had exerted a similar natural right. The natural right of migration was a critical factor in Bland's case for the colonists' "natural rights of *British* Subjects." "When Subjects are deprived of their civil Rights," his *Inquiry* explained,

> or are dissatisfied with the Place they hold in the Community, they have a natural Right to quit the Society of which they are Members, and to retire into another Country. Now when Men exercise this Right, and withdraw themselves from their Country, they recover their natural Freedom and Independence: The Jurisdiction and Sovereignty of the State they have quitted ceases; and if they unite, and by common Consent take Possession of a new Country, and form themselves into a political Society, they become a sovereign State, independent of the State from which they separated. If then the subjects of *England* have a natural Right to relinquish their Country, and

33. Richard Bland, *An Inquiry into the Rights of the British Colonies* (Williamsburg, 1766), reprinted, ed. E. G. Swem (Richmond, 1922), 7.
34. Squire, *Enquiry,* 84.

by retiring from it, and associating together, to form a new political Society and independent State, they must have a Right, by Compact with the Sovereign of the Nation, to remove into a new Country, and to form a civil Establishment upon the Terms of the Compact. In such a Case, the Terms of the Compact must be obligatory and binding upon the Parties; they must be the Magna Charta, the fundamental Principles of Government, to this new Society; and every Infringement of them must be wrong, and may be opposed.[35]

The right to a social compact was inherent in the human being. Bland discussed Magna Charta as a contract; it led him immediately back to the historical rights of Englishmen in America. When Virginians contended for "the natural Rights of *British* Subjects," or the "Blessings of a *British* Constitution," they meant the specific constitutional rights inherited from their Saxon ancestors and transferred in their ancient purity to American shores.[36] Between the ancient Saxon representative system and the Parliament existing in England in 1765, a vast difference existed. Parliament was now unrepresentative; so far had the constitution departed "from its original Purity." Bland estimated that 90 per cent of English citizens were denied the right to vote, and he denounced the idea of a "virtual" representation, as had the younger Dulany. No restoration of England's constitution in "pristine perfection" seemed likely; Bland feared "the Gangrene has taken too deep Hold to be eradicated in these Days of Venality."[37] Only in America did he believe that the ancient constitution had a chance of survival, but if measures like the Stamp Act were tolerated, the prospect for freedom in America would be as dim as in England.

Colonists had "as natural a Right to the Liberties and Privileges of *Englishmen,* as if they were actually resident within the Kingdom." "Under an English Government all men are born free, are only sub-

35. Bland, *Inquiry,* 14–15.
36. John Pendleton Kennedy, ed., *Journals of the House of Burgesses of Virginia, 1766–1769* (Richmond, 1906), 165–66.
37. Bland, *Inquiry,* 11–12.

ject to Laws made with their own Consent, and cannot be deprived of the Benefit of these Laws without a transgression of them." "An essential Part of *British* Freedom," he argued, was that taxes could be levied only by elected representatives.[38] But Bland not only stressed the unconstitutionality of taxation without representation; he also denied the propriety of internal legislation without representation. "If then the People of this Colony are free born," he continued, "and have the Right to the Liberties and Privileges of *English* Subjects, they must necessarily have a legal Constitution, that is, a Legislature, composed, in Part, of the Representatives of the People, who may enact Laws for the INTERNAL Government of the Colony, and suitable to its various Circumstances and Occasions; and without such a Representative, I am bold enough to say, no law can be made."[39] Bland claimed for Virginians the "Right . . . of directing their *internal* Government by Laws made with their own Consent." Indeed, Bland went further than most colonial spokesmen when he wrote that the colonists were "distinct People from the Inhabitants of *Britain*," "independent, as to their *internal* Government, of the original Kingdom, but united with her, as to their *external* Polity, in the closest and most intimate LEAGUE AND AMITY, under the same Allegiance."[40] Thus far had Bland's use of whig history led him by 1766.

Jefferson, who years later thought Bland's *Inquiry* superior to Dickinson's *Letters from a Farmer*, appraised Bland's methodology with some perception. "He would set out on sound principles, pursue them logically till he found them leading to the precipice which he had to leap, start back alarmed, then resume his ground, go over it in another direction, be led again . . . to the same place, and again back about."[41] But Bland wrote his *Inquiry* nine years before Jefferson ad-

38. Ibid., 26, 21.
39. Bland, *Colonel Dismounted*, 33.
40. Bland, *Inquiry*, 19–21.
41. Jefferson to William Wirt, Aug. 5, 1815, Lipscomb and Bergh, eds., *Writings of Jefferson*, XIV, 338. Jefferson's critique of Bland's *Inquiry* was not inappropriate: as we

dressed the same problem more directly in his *Summary View*. Bland's Revolutionary role was that of a political scout, reconnoitering the future battleground but avoiding a pitched battle. Defending the Virginia Assembly in the Parson's Cause—two years before the Stamp Act and nearly five years before the publication of the *Letters from a Farmer*—Bland insisted that "any Tax respecting our INTERNAL Polity, which may hereafter be imposed on us by Act of Parliament, is arbitrary, as depriving us of our Rights, and may be opposed." [42] He undertook to remind his fellow colonists what their rights were and just how substantial were their historical foundations, then boldly stated an important corollary, "Rights imply Equality." [43] He left to Jefferson's generation the final decision on how best to maintain its constitutional inheritance.

When Richard Bland and the Virginia delegation took their seats in the Continental Congress in 1774, Joseph Reed of Pennsylvania was among the many who were impressed. "There are some fine fellows come from Virginia," he wrote, "but they are very high. . . . We understand they are the capital men of the colony, both in fortune and understanding." [44] Reed's appraisal was substantially correct. Among those in Bland's party were Patrick Henry, Richard Henry Lee, and George Washington.

Like Bland, Patrick Henry had been an eloquent opponent of the

---

have seen, Bland did open with an appeal to "the fundamental principles of the English constitution," did then appeal to a record that was "as certain as history can make it" to show how the present English constitutional practice had "departed . . . from its original purity." Bland then drew back, remarked that "we can receive no light from the laws of the kingdom or from ancient history," and appealed to "the law of nature, and those rights of mankind which flow from it." But this in turn led him to an immediate review of the charter history of Virginia, from the reign of Elizabeth I to that of George III, where he found proof that "*Virginia* shall be free from all taxes, customs, and impositions whatsoever." After all, added Bland, the constitution of the colonies was "established on the principles of *British* liberty."

42. Bland, *Colonel Dismounted*, 34.
43. Bland, *Inquiry*, 25.
44. Quoted in Rowland, *George Mason*, I, 179.

Two-Penny Act, and his fiery courtroom oratory in the Reverend James Maury's case had defeated the clergy's opposition to the Assembly's regulation. Henry's preparation for politics was better than reputed. Although he did not have a college education, his father, Colonel John Henry (whose idea of a diversion was reading a Latin dictionary), had spent four years at King's College, Aberdeen, and for five years he served as his son's tutor, imparting a knowledge of Latin and a smattering of Greek. Patrick considered himself "well versed in both ancient and modern History" and acquired a modest library in which law, politics, and history were well represented. When Patrick Henry presented himself for admission to the Virginia bar his examiners found him extraordinarily strong on the laws of nature and nations, on the history of law, and on feudal history.[45]

If Henry attracted the attention of Virginians by his performance in the Parson's Cause in 1762, he achieved national recognition by his response to the Stamp Act in 1765. The House of Burgesses had completed much of the routine business of its May session and many had left Williamsburg when Henry rose to unleash his "torrents of sublime eloquence" against the Stamp Act.[46] He drew heavily on his legal and historical learning in challenging Parliament's right to tax the colonies. The rights which Henry claimed for the colonists were "all the Priviledges, Franchises and Immunities that have at any Time been held, enjoyed, and possessed by the People of Great Britain." He reviewed the royal charters granted Virginia, with their guarantee of the same rights for Virginians "as if they had been abiding and born within the Realm of England." Taxation by and with the consent of the people's representatives was "the distinguishing Characterick of

---

45. George Morgan, *The True Patrick Henry* (Philadelphia, 1907), 431, 464–68. Henry's copy of Blackstone's *Commentaries* survives in the Lilly Library of Indiana University. William Wirt, *Sketches of the Life and Character of Patrick Henry* (Philadelphia, 1817), 29–30.

46. The best account of the debate of the Virginia House of Burgesses—and an evaluation of its impact and importance—is supplied in Edmund S. and Helen M. Morgan, *The Stamp Act Crisis, Prologue to Revolution* (Chapel Hill, 1953), 88–97. See also Robert D. Meade, *Patrick Henry: Patriot in the Making* (Philadelphia, 1957), 170–71.

British Freedom and without which the ancient Constitution cannot subsist." Any British action contrary to such constitutional rights would have "a manifest Tendency to destroy British as well as American Freedom." [47]

In the "most bloody debate" that followed his Stamp Act resolutions, Henry uttered his celebrated and yet far from unique warning to George III: "Tarquin and Caesar had each his Brutus," he cried, "Charles the First his Cromwell." [48] But these were now clichés of history, decorating political arguments widely familiar — historical lessons from which Americans, if not George III, could learn.

George Mason was another Virginian who claimed for Americans all the rights of Englishmen. His contributions to the Virginia Declaration of Rights and the first Virginia constitution are well known; his intellectual background is not. Only ten years old when his father died, George Mason was educated by his learned uncle, John Mercer of "Marlborough," whose large library had over five hundred volumes dealing with law and history. By the 1750s, when he attained his majority, Mason emerged as a scholar who enjoyed "a modest but independent fortune," "the blessings of a private station," and a warm attachment to his native colony and the mother country. [49] He declared that Americans had "sucked in with our mother's milk" the principles of English freedom. Americans were but transplanted Britishers. "We are still the same people with them in every respect" — every respect save one: Americans were "not yet debauched by wealth, luxury, venality and corruption." He insisted on his devotion to the English Crown. As he put it, he was "an Englishman in his principles, a zealous assertor of the Act of Settlement, firmly attached to the present royal family upon the throne." For those who identified criticism of George III with Jacobitism, Mason affirmed

47. Morgan, *Stamp Act Crisis*, 91–95.
48. Meade, *Henry*, 171–73; see also Morgan, *Stamp Act Crisis*, 90–91.
49. Rowland, *George Mason*, I, 52–53; II, 368; I, 388.

his loyalty to the Hanoverians, denouncing Jacobitism as "the most absurd infatuation, the wildest chimera that ever entered into the head of man." He was, Mason repeated, a man "who adores the wisdom and happiness of the British constitution."[50] It was to their British inheritance that Americans appealed: "We claim nothing but the liberty and privileges of Englishmen, in the same degree, as if we had still continued among our brethren in Great Britain." "We cannot be deprived of . . . [our rights], without our consent," Mason warned. He also issued other warnings: a warning that "another experiment [such] as the stamp act would produce a general revolt in America"; that the colonists would not fight alone, but would surely secure outside support from England's enemies—as had the Dutch in their revolt against Spain, from Spanish enemies; that "the same causes will generally produce the same effects . . . what has happened may happen again"; that George Grenville would lead England to disaster—Grenville, who "dared to act the part that Pericles did, when he engaged his country in the Peloponnesian War, which . . . ended in the ruin of all Greece." England must recall "the vigor and spirit of her own free and happy constitution," if she would preserve her empire. In Mason's mind there was a direct relationship between England's political health and England's respect for colonial rights.[51]

In 1773 Mason undertook a review of Virginia's constitutional connection with England. There had been no historical precedent for American colonization; "to the people of Great Britain the scene then opening was entirely new." Although English immigrants to America would "by the laws of Nature and Nations" have carried with them the constitution of the country they came from, entitled to all its advantages, they did not trust themselves completely "to general principles applied to a new subject." To be absolutely secure in their title to "the rights and privileges of their beloved laws and

50. George Mason to the Committee of Merchants in London, June 6, 1766, ibid., I, 381–89.

51. George Mason to a young relative, Dec. 6, 1770, ibid., 150.

Constitution," they made a firm compact with the Crown in their colonial charters. Charters emanated from sovereignty, Mason observed. To the Crown belonged the constitutional power to dispose of newly acquired territory; to the people belonged the power of limiting their rights. "The American Charters, therefore, are legal *ab origine*" compacts in actuality and in theory—American colonies were not like Wales or Ireland, conquered lands. England had no right to govern her colonies as conquered provinces. "We are the Descendants, not of the Conquered, but of the Conquerors." [52]

To Mason, "general principles" of "the laws of Nature and Nations" were less tangible bases for rights than specific provisions of the constitution as it had developed historically. By clear and repeated decision, enactment, and charter, English subjects could be governed only by laws to which they had given their consent through representatives freely chosen by themselves. It was this specific constitutional provision the English ministry was violating: "There is," Mason declared, "a premeditated design and system, formed and pursued by the British ministry, to introduce an arbitrary government into his Majesty's dominions." They were the King's dominions, no part of Parliament's, no part of the English realm. Evil ministers artfully prejudiced the King against his devoted American subjects, despite the efforts of English whig reformers to whom Mason tendered his "most sincere and cordial thanks" for "their spirited and patriotic conduct in support of our constitutional rights and privileges." The ministry—the mass of the English people, too—were grievously misinformed on the historical justice of colonial claims. [53]

Mason persistently reminded Americans that shortly after the Glorious Revolution of 1688 Parliament had succeeded in subverting the constitutional balance of the British government. And through

52. George Mason, Extracts from the Virginia Charters, with some remarks on them made in the year 1773, ibid., 398–99 *n*.

53. George Mason, Fairfax County Resolutions, July 18, 1774, ibid., 418–27. See p. 155 for a discussion of Washington's identification with these Resolutions.

corruption, political bribery, and venality England had entered a moral decline, until "every town and village in the kingdom" was fouled. Standing armies—regiments had been in America since the Pontiac Rising of 1763—were a badge of this corruption. "Recollect the history of most nations of the world," urged Mason; "what havoc, desolation and destruction, have been perpetrated by standing armies!"[54] His antidote was the ancient Saxon militia, "the natural strength and only stable security of a free government," which would have the incidental virtue of relieving England of the need to tax Americans to support the standing army they did not want. If England refused to see the reasonableness of her colonists, then an American militia should be ready to fight for "the principles of the English Constitution." America had become "the only great nursery of freemen now left upon the face of the earth. Let us," concluded Mason, "cherish the sacred deposit."[55]

Mason's near neighbor, George Washington, gained fame for his defense of liberty by the sword rather than the pen. But although he did not play as prominent a role in formulating public opinion as Bland, Henry, Mason, Jefferson, or Richard Henry Lee, he was a well-read eighteenth-century gentleman-farmer with broad intellectual interests, and he eventually collected a library of some nine hundred volumes, a library replete with such authors as Vertot, Robertson, Burgh, Hume, and Mrs. Macaulay.[56] Robert Bell, the Philadelphia publisher, usually found Washington ready to support his subscription editions; and had Bell ever thought to reprint Joseph Addison's works, Washington would surely have been an eager customer. Wash-

54. Mason at the Virginia Convention, June 4, 1788, ibid., II, 398; June 19–23, 1788, ibid., II, 124–25; June 14, 1788, ibid., II, 409.

55. George Mason, Resolutions of the Fairfax County Committee, Jan. 17, 1775, ibid., I, 430, 432.

56. A. P. C. Griffin, ed., *A Catalogue of the Washington Collection in the Boston Athenaeum* (Boston, 1897).

ington particularly liked plays and history, and if the two were combined, so much the better. Addison's popular play *Cato* was one of
Washington's favorites. In a youthful letter to Sally Fairfax, he wished
he could play the part of Juba, the lover of Cato's daughter Marcia—
which role should naturally be the fair Sally's. And in the dark days of
Valley Forge, Washington scheduled a performance of the same *Cato*
to cheer his troops.[57] It is likely that Washington's taste in drama was
shared by Patrick Henry, whose famous request "Give me liberty or
give me death!" found a strikingly similar echo in Cato's remark

> It is not now a time to talk of aught
> But chains, or conquest; liberty or death.[58]

The historian whom Washington knew best was the widely read
Catherine Macaulay. He bought a set of her *History of England* for
Master Custis in 1769, and thanks to Richard Henry Lee, Washington later had the pleasure of meeting this representative of "the
foremost rank of writers."[59] At Lee's suggestion, Washington showed
Mrs. Macaulay the hospitality of Mount Vernon during her American visit in 1785. Washington was soon writing of a lady "whose
principles are so much and so justly admired by the friends of liberty
and of mankind," and there began a correspondence which was only
terminated by Mrs. Macaulay's death in the summer of 1791.[60]

Washington established no continental reputation as a writer or

57. See Samuel E. Morison, *The Young Man Washington* (Cambridge, Mass., 1932), 19–
21.

58. Joseph Addison, *Cato,* in Mrs. Elizabeth Inchbald, ed., *The British Theatre,* 25 vols.
(London, 1808), VIII, 31.

59. Richard Henry Lee to George Washington, May 3, 1785, James C. Ballagh, ed.,
The Letters of Richard Henry Lee, 2 vols. (N.Y., 1911–14), II, 352. For Lee's admiration of
Mrs. Macaulay, see Lee to Arthur Lee, Apr. 5, 1770, to Mrs. Macaulay, Nov. 29, 1771,
ibid., I, 44, 163; in the latter communication, Lee enclosed some colonial pamphlets and
invited Mrs. Macaulay to pass along to him "any other of her works that may be published."

60. Entries for June 4 and 8, 1785, John C. Fitzpatrick, ed., *Diaries of George Washington, 1748-1799,* 4 vols. (Boston, 1925), II, 381–82.

orator. Yet he was active in the political disputes long before the resort to arms. He opposed the Stamp Act strenuously, denouncing it as an "unconstitutional method of taxation."[61] When the courts in Virginia closed to avoid having to affix stamps to legal documents, Washington requested Mason, one of his constituents, to draft a scheme to expedite the processing of rent disputes without the use of stamped paper for the bond ordinarily required; but repeal of the Stamp Act made it unnecessary for Washington to introduce Mason's measure in the House of Burgesses.

In a letter which adumbrated the nonimportation agreement adopted by the Stamp Act Congress, Washington wrote in 1765 that "the eyes of our people, already beginning to open, will perceive that many luxuries which we lavish our substance to Great Britain for, can well be dispensed with whilst the necessaries of life are (mostly) to be had within ourselves. This consequently will introduce frugality, and be a necessary stimulation to industry. If Great Britain therefore loads her manufacturers with heavy taxes, will it not facilitate these measures? They will not compel us, I think, to give our money for their exports, whether we will or no; and certain I am none of their traders will part from them without a valuable consideration."[62]

Washington also collaborated with the more scholarly Mason in working out public policies in defense of colonial liberties. After the passage of the Townshend Acts, Washington, a member of the House of Burgesses, wrote Mason in 1769 for his opinion, and Mason recommended a nonimportation-nonexportation Association until the Acts were repealed. The Burgesses voted for nonimportation, and Washington entered into an association and directed his London merchant not to send him any taxed articles, "paper only excepted."[63]

61. George Washington to Francis Dandridge, Sept. 20, 1765, John C. Fitzpatrick, ed., *The Writings of George Washington . . . ,* 39 vols. (Washington, D.C., 1931–44), II, 425–26.

62. Ibid.

63. Washington to Robert Cary and Company, July 25, 1769, ibid., 512.

After the Boston Tea Party and Parliament's retaliatory Coercive Acts, Washington argued that "the Cause of Boston . . . now is and ever will be considered as the cause of America." He was convinced that the "Minds of People" in Virginia had never been more disturbed than by the "Invasion of our Rights and Privileges by the Mother Country." The ministry, he concluded, "are endeavouring by every piece of Art and despotism to fix the Shackles of Slavery upon us," but he warned that "the Ministry may rely on it that Americans will never be tax'd without their own consent."[64]

To oppose this "regular, systematic plan formed to fix the right and practice of taxation upon us," Washington and Mason collaborated on the formulation of the Fairfax Resolves, Mason spending the night at Mount Vernon on July 17, 1774, to work out the details in consultation with his neighbor. The Resolves, one of the most important pre-Revolutionary documents in Virginia, stated that "the most important and valuable part of the British Constitution, upon which its very existence depends, is, the fundamental principle of the people's being governed by no laws to which they have not given their consent by Representatives freely chosen by themselves, who are affected by the laws they enact equally with their constituents, to whom they are accountable, and whose burthens they share, in which consists the safety and happiness of the community."[65]

The Fairfax Resolves are usually ascribed to Mason, and the only manuscript copy is in his hand, but it is located in Washington's papers. Whatever his role in drafting the Resolves, Washington presided at the Alexandria meeting on July 18 when they were adopted; as the Fairfax delegate to the colonial convention in August he presented them in Williamsburg, where they were adopted; and as one

64. Washington to George William Fairfax, June 10, 1774, ibid., III, 224.

65. Rowland, *George Mason*, I, 426. For a discussion of Washington's connection with the Resolves, see Curtis P. Nettels, *George Washington and American Independence* (Boston, 1951), 89–92. There is no doubt that Washington contributed to their contents, that he was in full accord with their sentiments; in short, the Fairfax County Resolutions speak for Mason *and* Washington.

of the Virginia delegates to the First Continental Congress—along with Bland, Henry, Richard Henry Lee, Benjamin Harrison, Edmund Pendleton, and Peyton Randolph—he secured acceptance of the Fairfax plan, the basis for the Continental Association.[66]

Washington identified himself with the Fairfax Resolves because as he later wrote, "an innate spirit of freedom first told me, that the measures, which administration hath for some time been, and now are most violently pursuing, are repugnant to every principle of natural justice." But he added that "many abler heads than my own hath fully convinced me, that it is not only repugnant to natural right, but subversive of the laws and constitution of Great Britain itself." He was "satisfied then, that the acts of a British Parliament are no longer governed by the principles of justice, that it is trampling upon the valuable rights of Americans, confirmed to them by charter and the constitution they themselves boast of."[67]

For Washington there was never any doubt of the justice of the colonial cause. So long as Britain pursued her evident policy of premeditated, systematic tyranny, no man's life, liberty, or property would be secure.[68] The rights of Americans which he championed by force of arms were both "natural" and, above all, "constitutional." He was fully satisfied regarding the historical substance of American liberties. He knew that the colonists "as Englishmen" could not be justly deprived of their right to tax themselves. "The parliament of Great Britain," he reminded Bryan Fairfax in 1774, "hath no more right to put their hands into my pocket, without my consent, than I have to put my hands into yours for money." The right of taxation, he repeated, was the "essential" part of the English constitution.[69] No colonist should submit to its loss.[70] By 1775 he had decided that con-

66. Nettels, *Washington and American Independence*, 92–93.

67. Washington to Bryan Fairfax, Aug. 24, 1774, Fitzpatrick, ed., *Writings of Washington*, III, 240–41.

68. Washington to Captain Robert Mackenzie, Oct. 9, 1774, ibid., 245–46.

69. Washington to Bryan Fairfax, July 20, 1774, ibid., 231–33.

70. Washington to Mackenzie, Oct. 9, 1774, ibid., 246.

tinued petitions to Britain were futile, even demeaning: the colonies were contending not for a favor but a right. Grimly he concluded that "the once happy plains of America are either to be drenched with blood or inhabited by slaves."[71]

III

Southerners, like their associates in revolution to the North, were highly sensitive to their rights and liberties. Some—such as the Dulanys, Charles Carroll of Maryland, or William Henry Drayton of South Carolina—had received an important part of their political education in England. Others—such as Washington and his colleague Richard Henry Lee—enjoyed correspondence with contemporary English historians. They all read, they all became reasonably well "informed in the English, ancient and modern histories, the Law of Nations, and the rights" of their country.[72] They saw their constitutional inheritance, the ancient liberties of Englishmen, jeopardized by what Washington called "a systematic assertion of an arbitrary power." Their mother country, as Lee observed, was in the grip of a corruption "which has now [1776] swallowed up every thing but the forms of freedom in Great Britain" and threatened a similar fate for the colonies.[73] They sensed a mandate for action, a mandate from

71. Washington to George William Fairfax, May 31, 1775, ibid., 292. Washington conceded the melancholy nature of the alternatives, but asked rhetorically, "can a virtuous Man hesitate in his choice?"

72. John Drayton, *Memoirs of the American Revolution* . . . , 2 vols. (Charleston, 1821), I, xiii. William Henry Drayton remains a neglected figure, and the recent study by William M. Dabney and Marion Dargan, *William Henry Drayton and the American Revolution* (Albuquerque, 1962), does little to rescue the judge from undeserved obscurity, beyond reprinting Drayton's *Charge to the Grand Jury*, Apr. 23, 1776. Drayton's was a historical polemic, a comparison of the causes of the Glorious Revolution of 1688 and the new glorious revolution of 1776.

73. Washington to Mackenzie, Oct. 9, 1774, Fitzpatrick, ed., *Writings of Washington*, III, 245; Richard Henry Lee to [Edmund Pendleton?], May 12, 1776, Ballagh, ed., *Letters of Richard Henry Lee*, I, 191.

THE REVOLUTIONARY USE OF HISTORY

nature, from history—and for some a mandate from Heaven too.[74] Their emphases varied, but in the South as elsewhere history lent strength and persuasion to the Revolutionaries' argument. They determined, as Bland phrased it in 1766, to "enjoy the Freedom, and other Benefits of the *British* Constitution, to the latest Page in History!"[75]

74. William Henry Drayton, *Charge to the Grand Jury*, Apr. 23, 1776, Drayton, ed., *Memoirs*, II, 274: "The Almighty created America to be independent of Britain."
75. Bland, *Inquiry*, 29–30.

CHAPTER VIII

Thomas Jefferson and the Rights of Expatriated Men

"The earth Belongs always to the living generation," Jefferson reminded James Madison.[1] Thomas Jefferson is perhaps best known for his commitment to this belief. Dedicated to the proposition that man had a right to happiness and fulfillment in this world, Jefferson strove to emancipate the present from the tyranny of the past. The dead hand of custom and habit were not for Jefferson.

It was to the tyranny of the past that Jefferson was opposed, not to the past itself. He rejected oppressive custom, but not custom. Convinced of the intrinsic virtue of his fellow man, Jefferson searched for an explanation for the seeming corruption of that virtue. He saw history as an extension of political experience, as a guide to a perfectible future through a heightened awareness of the blemished past.

I

Jefferson probably read his first history book in the modest library of his father. In Peter Jefferson's collection young Thomas found Rapin's *History of England* in a two-volume folio edition, and he never ceased

---

1. Jefferson to James Madison, Sept. 6, 1789, Boyd et al., eds., *Jefferson Papers,* XV, 396.

singing its praises.[2] When he started buying books for himself, history soon emerged as his favorite category. The *Virginia Gazette* Day Books show Jefferson purchasing in March 1764 his first copy of David Hume's *History of England* (which he soon learned to detest), along with William Robertson's *History of Scotland*. Between 1762 and 1767 Jefferson studied law under the wise tutelage of George Wythe, gaining familiarity with works which combined historical and legal scholarship. When admitted to the bar he was well advanced in his studies of the *Reports* of Salkeld and Raymond and the *Institutes* of Coke.[3]

But his reading had indeed barely begun. By 1771, when he advised young Robert Skipwith on his book buying, Jefferson was able to include Sidney's *Discourses*, Bolingbroke's *Political Works*, Rollin's *Ancient History*, Stanyan's *Grecian History*, the Gordon translations of Tacitus and Sallust, as well as works by Clarendon, Hume, and Robertson. Into his Commonplace Book went passages from Dalrymple's *Essay on Feudal Property*, Spelman's *De Terminis Juridicis*, Kames's *Historical Law Tracts*, Sullivan's *Feudal Laws*, Blackstone's *Commentaries*, Molesworth's *Account of Denmark*, and the (to Jefferson) anonymously written *Historical Essay on the English Constitution*.[4] He had his own copies of William Petyt's *Ius Parliamentum*, Thorn-

2. Jefferson to George Washington Lewis, Oct. 25, 1825, Lipscomb and Bergh, eds., *Writings of Jefferson*, XVI, 125. The inventory of Peter Jefferson's property (including his library), filed after his death in Aug. 1757, is in the Albemarle County Will Book No. 2 which Marie Kimball cites in *Jefferson: The Road to Glory*, 13.

3. The *Virginia Gazette* Day Books disclose considerable book buying by Jefferson between 1764 and 1766; they are transcribed in William Peden's *Thomas Jefferson: Book Collector*. See also Peden's "Some Notes concerning Thomas Jefferson's Libraries," *William and Mary Quarterly*, 3d ser., I (1944): 265–74. Marie Kimball, by analysis of Jefferson's changing handwriting and identification of the "Pro Patria" paper used in his commonplacing, has deduced that the first 174 entries were made in 1766; see Kimball, *Jefferson: The Road to Glory*, 85–88.

4. Jefferson to Robert Skipwith, with a List of Books for a Private Library, Aug. 3, 1771, Boyd et al., eds., *Jefferson Papers*, I, 76–81. Jefferson's notes are in Chinard, ed., *Commonplace Book*, as follows: Dalrymple: 135–62; Spelman: 186–87, 189; Kames: 95–135; Sullivan: 233–34, 236–57; Blackstone: 193, 364–68; Molesworth: 213, 225–26; Hulme's *Historical Essay*: 296–98.

hagh Gurdon's *History of Parliament,* and Anthony Ellis's *Tracts on Liberty.*[5] Later he acquired copies of Henry Care's *English Liberties,* Rushworth's *Historical Collections,* Acherley's *Britannic Constitution,* Atkyn's *Power of Parliament,* Catherine Macaulay's popular *History of England,* Trenchard and Gordon's *Cato's Letters,* and—of course—Burgh's *Political Disquisitions.*[6] The list is not quite endless. But it is extraordinary for the representation Jefferson accorded the "True Whigs." These were books Jefferson bought not once but twice or three times, books he found essential to his political existence, books which served him beyond the realm of his practice of law. These books by introducing him to the mysteries of feudalism and constitutionalism led to a personal (but not unique) perspective on the rights of the American colonies and the Englishmen residing there.

In the 1760s and early 1770s the political content of his reading mounted sharply; indeed Jefferson's studies reflect his growing sensitivity to, and involvement in, his political environment. While studying law with Wythe in Williamsburg Jefferson breathed the air of the political controversy swirling about the bustling Virginia capital. He stood in the lobby of the Capitol building and heard Patrick Henry attack the Stamp Act in 1765. He knew, firsthand, the anger of the Burgesses at the Townshend Acts in 1767. When he secured election in 1769 as Burgess for Albemarle County, Jefferson brought experience as well as learning to his new responsibilities. He was ready to participate in Virginia's Nonimportation Resolutions in 1769 and was fully alert to the challenge presented by the Coercive Acts in 1774. When he learned of the oppressive measures directed at his Boston compatriots, Jefferson and Charles Lee "cooked up" (as Jefferson so nicely phrased it) some resolutions calling for a general day

5. These books were invoiced by Perkins, Buchanan, and Brown, Oct. 2, 1769, Boyd et al., eds., *Jefferson Papers,* I, 34.

6. Jefferson owned two copies of Care, and had *English Liberties* included in the University of Virginia library; Jefferson's initialed copy of Rushworth survives in the Library of Congress, as does Acherley, Atkyns, Macaulay, Trenchard and Gordon, and Burgh. See Sowerby, ed., *Catalogue of Jefferson's Library.* See also my "Thomas Jefferson's Use of the Past," *William and Mary Quarterly,* 3d ser., 15 (1958): 60–65.

of fasting and prayer on the day the Boston Port Act took effect. He hoped this would "give us one heart and one mind to oppose, by all just means, every injury to American Rights."[7] In the process of preparing his resolves Jefferson demonstrated his historical approach. He thought of the similarity of his own times to the days of the Puritan Revolution in seventeenth-century England and turned to John Rushworth's *Historical Collections* for help. In the pages of Rushworth Jefferson "rummaged over for the revolutionary precedents and forms of the Puritans of that day."[8] While Jefferson found Rushworth interesting, Governor Dunmore did not, and he dissolved the House of Burgesses. Before breaking up, the Burgesses held a lively meeting of their own at the Raleigh Tavern and issued a call for a Continental Congress to discuss the new British oppression.[9]

This move brought from Jefferson one of his most notable contributions to the literature of the American Revolution. He prepared a series of resolutions to present to a special Virginia convention meeting in August 1774; the resolutions would, if adopted, become instructions for the Virginia delegates to the forthcoming Congress in Philadelphia. Taken ill, Jefferson was unable to attend, but he sent two copies of his resolutions to Williamsburg. The convention took no official notice of his effort, but several members read the resolutions with enthusiasm. Without Jefferson's knowledge they had the manuscript published with the title *A Summary View of the Rights of British America.*[10] The *Summary View* laid the foundation of Jefferson's

---

7. Malone, *Jefferson the Virginian*, 92; Virginia Nonimportation Resolutions, 1769, Boyd et al., eds., *Jefferson Papers*, I, 27–31; John Pendleton Kennedy, ed., *Journals of the House of Burgesses of Virginia, 1773-1776* . . . (Richmond, 1905), 124.

8. Autobiography, Ford, ed., *Writings of Jefferson*, I, 10.

9. See Kimball, *Jefferson: The Road to Glory*, 234–37.

10. The best account of the political and biographical background to the *Summary View* is in Malone, *Jefferson the Virginian*, 180–81. For an interesting discussion of "Jefferson's *Summary View* as a Chart of Political Union" by Anthony M. Lewis, see the *William and Mary Quarterly*, 3d ser., 5 (1948): 34–51. [See also Peter Onuf, ed., *Jeffersonian Legacies* (1992); and Joseph J. Ellis, *American Sphinx: The Character of Thomas Jefferson* (1997). —T. C., 1997.]

Revolutionary reputation and was his most cogent and detailed examination of colonial rights before 1776.

In some ways, the *Summary View* is more representative of Jefferson's political thinking than the Declaration of Independence; it is a more personal expression of Jefferson's concept of Anglo-American relations. There has been criticism of the *Summary View* for the intemperance of its language and its lack of historical precision;[11] some scholars have commented on the lack of attention paid to the natural rights philosophy which Jefferson later expressed in the superbly simple opening paragraphs of the Declaration.[12] And yet the *Summary View* was an instant popular success with colonial patriots and sympathetic English whigs[13] because Jefferson was telling men what they wanted to believe and arguing the American cause in language immediately familiar. He assumed a working knowledge of history and did not seriously misjudge his unexpected audience; he took for granted the doctrine of natural rights, which was part and parcel of the eighteenth-century political atmosphere. He did not attempt to justify the colonial position with philosophy, but instead undertook a historical appraisal of the colonial case. In the process Jefferson, unlike a revolutionary, identified the good with the ancestral rather than with the purely rational.

In the *Summary View,* Jefferson supplied a most persuasive and felicitously phrased argument for resistance to British tyranny, and at the same time he provided a graphic illustration of the political uses of his careful reading of history. He established the tone of his essay at the outset. After a polite opening address to the King as "chief magistrate of the British Empire," the *Summary View* reminded George III of a history he seemed to have forgotten. Jefferson went back to his "Saxon ancestors" to point out how they "left their

---

11. Malone, *Jefferson the Virginian,* 182–84.

12. For example, see Carl L. Becker, *The Declaration of Independence; A Study in the History of Political Ideas* (N.Y., 1922), 278.

13. There is an excellent account of the reception given the *Summary View* in Boyd et al., eds., *Jefferson Papers,* I, 671–76.

native wilds and woods in the North of Europe, [and] had possessed themselves of the island of Britain." These ancient forefathers, he observed, had enjoyed the right of leaving their native land to establish new societies in the new world of England.[14] The transplanted Saxons had carried their free customs and political democracy with them, establishing in England "that system of laws which has so long been the glory and protection of that country." Jefferson noted that there was never any question of these Saxon settlers being subject to any form of allegiance or control by the mother country from which they had emigrated. These forefathers had "too firm a feeling of the rights derived to them from their ancestors to bow down the sovereignty of their state before such visionary pretensions." Jefferson declared pointedly that "no circumstance has occurred to distinguish materially the British from the Saxon emigration."

If the Saxon origins of English and American history held political lessons of merit, so too did the Saxon land system translated from ancient Germany to new settlements in England. Like the majority of the whig historians he consulted, Jefferson believed that in Saxon England "feudal holdings were certainly altogether unknown, and very few if any had been introduced at the time of the Norman conquest." His Saxon ancestors had held their lands and personal property "in absolute dominion, disencumbered with any superior, [and] answering nearly to the nature of those possessions which the Feudalist term Allodial." The responsibility for the obvious and tragic change in England Jefferson placed squarely upon "William the Norman"—just as did such favorite writers as Sir Henry Spelman and Sir John Dalrymple. Consequently Jefferson could and did insist that "feudal holdings were, therefore, but the exceptions out of the Saxon law of possession, under which all lands were held in absolute right." Feudalism for Jefferson was an alien thing, Norman in nature, established and maintained by force. A Norman conquest may have inflicted feudalism upon the bewildered and betrayed Saxons in En-

14. All references to the *Summary View* are to the text in ibid., 121–35.

gland, but Jefferson saw no reason why their modern descendants in America should suffer a similar fate. The ancient Saxons had made their settlements at their own expense, with no aid from the mother country, and thus were under no obligation. And so it was with the offspring of these same Saxons when they came to America: in both cases, argued Jefferson, "for themselves they fought, for themselves they conquered, and for themselves alone they have a right to hold."

An apparent weakness in Jefferson's appeal to whig history lay in the current, if temporary, fact of American submission to the British Crown, a weakness rather reminiscent of general whig embarrassment over the Norman conquest. The ancient Saxons had not indulged their Germanic forefathers so generously as to pretend to be politically dependent upon them; but, Jefferson explained, the early American colonists were "laborers, not lawyers,"[15] who had "thought proper to adopt that system of laws under which they had hitherto lived in the mother country." Therefore, the early Americans had graciously consented to continue a form of union with the mother country by submitting themselves to a common monarchy, which became the "central link connecting the several parts of the empire thus newly multiplied." Engrossed in winning existence from a strange and hostile land, the colonists had then been misled by crafty Crown lawyers into thinking that all American lands really did belong to the King. Accordingly, Americans had fallen into the grievous error of assuming they took their holdings from the British Crown, and as long as administration was mild, there was no occasion for the historic reality to be discovered. But recent efforts, begun in 1763, to restrict land grants and confine American settlements demonstrated that the time had come for fraud to be exposed, for a firm declaration that the King "has no right to grant lands of himself."

However, the issue of feudalism and land tenure was only one instance of the perils of historical ignorance, and Jefferson employed the *Summary View* as an instrument of whig enlightenment. He

15. Ibid., 133. Jefferson first wrote "farmers, not lawyers," see ibid., 137, note no. 35.

found the history of the British empire full of examples of similar invasions by both Crown and Parliament of the colonial rights so dearly acquired with the "lives, the labors and the fortunes of individual adventurers." And the list of British iniquities compiled by Jefferson was long indeed, demonstrating a continuous effort to reduce America to a modern version of feudal slavery. In each instance Jefferson reviewed the historical background and injustice involved, and with a fine impartiality indicted both British Crown and Parliament for an unrelieved record of arbitrary acts.

He blamed the Crown for continually authorizing the dissolution of colonial legislatures, a crime, Jefferson noted, for which the traitorous advisers of Richard II had suffered death. Jefferson recalled that since 1688, when the British constitution was supposedly restored "on it's free and antient principles," this power of dissolution had been rarely practiced in England. Since colonists were Englishmen equally entitled to ancient privileges, they were equally entitled to respect for their representative institutions.

Naturally the same argument applied to the suspension of the New York legislature over the recent Quartering Act controversy, although on this issue Jefferson chose to attack Parliament and denounced that body for an unwarranted assumption of authority. After all, as any well-read colonist knew, Parliament was now both corrupt and unrepresentative; if Americans submitted to the pretensions of the House of Commons, "we should suddenly be found the slaves, not of one, but of 160,000 tyrants," the limited electorate in Britain. Most of the recent acts of oppression Jefferson laid at Parliament's door and suggested that the King was influenced by "the partial representations of a few worthless ministerial dependents, whose constant office it has been to keep that government embroiled, and who by their treacheries hope to obtain the dignity of the British knighthood." The Administration of Justice Act, the Coercive Act which permitted trial of colonists in England, served to illustrate Jefferson's alarm at "parliamentary tyranny." Measures such as this were completely contrary to Magna Charta, since the accused

American would be "stripped of his privilege of trial by peers, of his vicinage."

What made Jefferson's indignation at the contemporary condition of English politics so impressive in the *Summary View* was his recollection of past difficulties. British interference with colonial trade and industry was not new; its history was painfully long and familiar, reaching back to the despotic Stuarts. Here was "a family of princes . . . whose treasonable crimes against their people brought on them afterwards the exertion of those sacred and sovereign rights of punishment, reserved in the hands of the people for cases of extreme necessity." But the execution of Charles I had not brought freedom for colonial trade; the Commonwealth Parliament proved equally capable of arbitrary acts, which were tragically maintained when Charles II was restored to the British throne. Once more American rights fell "a victim to arbitrary power."

For Jefferson, this record of Crown and Parliament presented an obvious message: "History has informed us that bodies of men as well as individuals are susceptible of the spirit of tyranny." And history also demonstrated to Jefferson that the British nation had so succumbed: "Single acts of tyranny may be ascribed to the accidental opinion of a day; but a series of oppressions, begun at a distinguished period, and pursued unalterably thro' every change of ministers, too plainly prove a deliberate, systematical plan of reducing us to slavery."

Jefferson even found danger in apparently harmless measures: setting up a colonial post office in Queen Anne's reign became just another device "for accommodating his majesty's ministers and favorites with the sale of a lucrative and easy office." This fitted perfectly with Jefferson's conclusions about England's political decline from the glory of Saxon times. The day had now arrived "when the representative body have lost the confidence of their constituents, when they have notoriously made sale of their most valuable rights, when they have assumed to themselves powers which the people never put into their hands."

If the British had forgotten that "the whole art of government consists in the art of being honest,"[16] Jefferson had not. The colonists were standing upon their historical rights as transplanted Englishmen; "expatriated men"[17] was Jefferson's later phrase claiming liberties sadly forgotten in the mother country. Clearly George III would not be permitted the role of another William the Norman and allowed to fasten a similar tyranny upon the Saxon emigrant in America. Jefferson concluded with an earnest plea to the King: "Let not the name of George III be a blot in the page of history."[18] In Jefferson's view, the King already had much for which to answer.

The warnings of Jefferson offered in his *Summary View* went unheeded. Indeed the King himself seemed bent upon destroying the empire, pursuing beliefs and policies that could only end in disaster. Jefferson was deeply disturbed by George III's address to Parliament in October 1775, a speech in which the King claimed for Britain complete credit for the establishment and survival of the American colonies.[19] Drawing upon Hakluyt and Raleigh for corroboration, Jefferson reviewed the colonization efforts of Gilbert and Raleigh. The historical record showed "no assistance from the crown," and any claim to the contrary was a "palpable untruth." Jefferson knew only contempt for "a king who can adopt falsehood." One might pity and even pardon error. But flagrant misstatements of historical fact Jefferson found intolerable. The King, his "weak ministers," and "wicked favorites" now joined Parliament as objects of Jefferson's scorn.[20] American separation from England had become a necessity.

For Jefferson drafting the Declaration of Independence did not demand any great originality of thought or scholarship. Its object was to rally its colonial readers, to set down for all to see the justifi-

16. Ibid., 134.

17. Jefferson to Judge Tyler, June 17, 1812, H. A. Washington, ed., *The Writings of Thomas Jefferson*, 9 vols. (N.Y., 1855), VI, 65.

18. *Summary View*, Boyd et al., eds., *Jefferson Papers*, I, 134.

19. Quoted in ibid., 284 *n*.

20. "Refutation of the Argument that the Colonies Were Established at the Expense of the British Nation" [after Jan. 19, 1776], ibid., 277–84. If Jefferson planned to publish this investigation, his intentions were not realized.

cation for the step the colonies were taking. As one recent writer has observed, Jefferson's famous and felicitous opening paragraphs were possibly "the least important part of the document."[21] The Declaration was to inform the world of the universality of the rights of Englishmen and to identify them with the rights of man. This it did, briefly, superbly. But much of the ensuing text discussed the specific violations of the English rights to which Jefferson was so committed. Indeed, the differences between the *Summary View* and the Declaration of Independence are mainly reflections of the pace of events during the intervening two years. The Declaration proclaimed what the *Summary View* had threatened: the independence of Englishmen in America, who like their Saxon ancestors had migrated, settled, and sought to live in freedom and in enjoyment of their inherited liberties. Where Jefferson had earlier attacked Parliament, he now focused upon the King as the major culprit. No longer would George III be excused as misled or misguided; he was now "a prince whose character is thus marked by every act which may define a tyrant . . . unfit to be the ruler of a people who mean to be free." And yet the British people—a term which would encompass Parliament—did not escape unnoticed. Theirs was the ultimate responsibility for legislative tyranny. "We have," Jefferson remarked, "reminded them of the circumstances of our emigration and settlement here." They had been warned of the usurpations practiced by their government at American expense. They had been told "that submission to their parliament was no part of our constitution, nor ever in idea, if history may be credited." And now came "the last stab to agonizing affection," the dispatch of "Scotch and foreign mercenaries to invade and deluge us in blood." Accordingly the link between Britain and her American colonies was ruptured: allegiance to the Crown, connection between "the people or parliament of Great Britain," both were repudiated and renounced.[22]

21. Elisha P. Douglass, *Rebels and Democrats* . . . (Chapel Hill, 1955), 314.

22. Jefferson's "original Rough draught" of the Declaration of Independence, Boyd et al., eds., *Jefferson Papers*, I, 423–27.

II

Independence did not signify any diminution in Jefferson's use of history. Having illustrated his belief in the rights of man with a historical substantiation of those rights in the face of British encroachment, Jefferson maintained his affection for both his Saxon ancestors and the wisdom his whig authors claimed for them. If tyranny came with the Norman conquest, and feudalism was its badge,[23] then every care was needed to rid Virginia of all vestiges of feudal practices. Even before the colonies formally announced their independence, Jefferson turned to the preparation of a suitable constitution for Virginia.

Jefferson hardly achieved the reputation for constitution writing later earned by his friend Madison, but he took his responsibility seriously, preparing three drafts of a frame of government intended to avoid the mistakes committed by Great Britain. In all versions Jefferson followed the recommendations of his whig historians, consciously seeking to "re-establish such antient principles as are friendly to the rights of the people."[24] The whig anxiety for annual parliaments[25] influenced Jefferson's decision for annual elections ("fresh without bribe") of both Senate and House of Representatives. To avoid potential dictators or hereditary monarchs, he planned an executive term of one year, the executive to be ineligible for re-election for five subsequent years. Even though he was given "the powers formerly held by the king," he was denied authority to veto legislation and deprived of the prerogatives resented in George III. Since feudal tenures had long ago crept into Virginia, Jefferson insisted that all such feudal appendages as quitrents, primogeniture, and entail should be swept aside: "Lands heretofore holden of the crown, and those hereafter to be appropriated shall be holden of none." And

23. Chinard, ed., *Commonplace Book,* 135–62, 186.
24. Virginia Constitution, 1776, Jefferson's First Draft [before June 13, 1776], Boyd et al., eds., *Jefferson Papers,* I, 339.
25. Hulme, *Historical Essay,* title page, *passim.*

standing armies in peacetime were forbidden; Jefferson preferred to encourage a revival of the Saxon system of a free militia by providing that "no freeman shall ever be debarred the use of arms." [26]

To Jefferson's distress, his Virginia colleagues were not ready to accept the lessons of whig history as completely as he, for the abolition of the feudal features he deplored did not take place immediately, though they came in time. [27] Edmund Pendleton, for example, argued that the quitrent system should merely be adapted so that the annual dues were paid to the state of Virginia. Pendleton thought Jefferson's proposal a radical "Innovation." [28] However, Jefferson believed that quitrents were dismal reminders of the misunderstanding that American lands were thought to be held of the Crown, and he wanted all land tenure on the same allodial basis enjoyed by the freedom-loving Saxons. This indeed was Jefferson's familiar yardstick, "the practice of our wise British ancestors." Quitrents were emblems of feudal tyranny, a means once of financing standing armies which his history showed to be a constant source of domestic insecurity. Appealing to his whig view of the past, Jefferson demanded of Pendleton: "Are we not the better for what we have hitherto abolished of the feudal system? Has not every restitution of the antient Saxon laws had happy effects? Is it not better now that we return at once into that happy system of our ancestors, the wisest and most perfect ever yet devised by the wit of man, as it stood before the 8th century?" Pendleton's response was illuminating: "I highly esteem the old Saxon laws in General," he conceded, "but cannot Suppose them wholly unalterable for the better after an experience of so many Centuries." After all, he added, these old Saxon laws were perhaps better

26. Virginia Constitution, 1776, Jefferson's First Draft [before June 13, 1776], Boyd et al., eds., *Jefferson Papers*, I, 340–41, 342–44.

27. Virginia ended entails in 1776, and primogeniture in 1785; there is now considerable doubt whether this brought the improvements hoped for by Jefferson.

28. Edmund Pendleton to Jefferson, Aug. 3, 1776, ibid., 484.

calculated "for a few, Hardy, virtuous men, than for a great Countrey made Opulent by commerce."[29]

Unwittingly, Pendleton touched one of the key concerns of whig historians generally and Jefferson particularly. Had Jefferson ever written further to his friend[30] he would have readily agreed that the Saxon system he wished to recreate was best suited to a simple agrarian state. Jefferson had no desire to see America become opulent from commerce or industry, for all his recent criticism of the British for interfering with both activities. In every historical instance, such opulence had led to luxury, corruption, and political and moral decadence, and whig writers like James Burgh had well advised him of the impact of luxury upon contemporary England. If the former mother country was a sample of a nation refined through commerce and made wealthy through trade, Jefferson knew enough history to want no part of such prosperity for America. Remaining convinced that the happy system of his Saxon ancestors was "the wisest and most perfect ever yet devised by the wit of man,"[31] he persistently labored for the revival of his historically tested utopia.

Perhaps typical of Jefferson's efforts was his sustained attack on the established church of Virginia, beginning in 1776. While in Jefferson's eyes the Anglican church's tax-supported and privileged ecclesiastical status was inherently wrong, there were also readily available historical reasons for disestablishment. Jefferson entered two such objections to the continued support of the Anglican church in Virginia, and both were derived from his study of the Saxon past. First, he knew from reading Sullivan's *Treatise on the Feudal Law* that "in the infancy of the Christian church . . . the clergy was supported by the voluntary contributions of the people," and that the state tax-

29. Jefferson to Edmund Pendleton, Aug. 13, 1776, and Edmund Pendleton to Jefferson, Aug. 26, 1776, ibid., 491–94, 507–8.

30. Jefferson and Pendleton agreed to continue their discussion when they met together in Williamsburg in Oct. 1776, but no further record of this debate is known to survive.

31. Jefferson to Edmund Pendleton, Aug. 13, 1776, ibid., 492.

supported system came later.[32] Since Jefferson thought Sullivan particularly partial to the clergy, he felt this information would carry great weight. Secondly, and of greater importance to Jefferson, there was the question of the historical foundation of the Anglican establishment.

When investigating his Saxon utopia, Jefferson became deeply concerned with the question of when Christian or ecclesiastical law became part of English common law. Reading widely and selectively into the subject, Jefferson took issue with such authorities as Sir Matthew Hale, Sir William Blackstone, William Lambarde, and Justice Fortescue Aland. He noted that Hale agreed that "christianity is parcel of the laws of England," but discounted this because Hale cited no authority, and in any case Hale was only "a sound lawyer when not biassed by his belief in Christianity or Witchcraft." Blackstone he rejected for quoting Hale, and both showed "the necessity of holding the judges and writers to a declaration of their authorities."[33]

Jefferson himself could find no evidence for the adoption of Christianity as part of common law during the period of its creative but unwritten development. Common law, commented Jefferson, "was introduced by the Saxons on their settlement in England, and altered from time to time by proper legislative authority from that to the date of the Magna Charta which terminates the period of the common law . . . and commences that of the Statute law." Since the Saxons had settled in England two hundred years before the introduction of Christianity, then some late grafting had taken place. For the record between the Saxon conversion to Christianity and Magna Charta, Jefferson found the compilations of Lambarde and Wilkins adequate, but he could not find when Christian law was taken into common law. Bracton was "valuable" since he wrote shortly after Magna Charta; yet although he was an ecclesiastic, and therefore suspect, significantly he did not mention the adoption of Chris-

32. Chinard, ed., *Commonplace Book*, 244–45.
33. Ibid., 352, 353.

tianity into common law. Fortescue Aland, "who possessed more Saxon learning than all the judges and writers before mentioned put together," came closer,[34] but it was a recent French writer who gave Jefferson his final answer.

David Houard's *Traités sur les coutumes Anglo-Normandes* contended that four chapters of Jewish law were appended to the body of King Alfred's codification of common law by "some pious copyist."[35] Thus the basic connection of ecclesiastical and common law derived from an "awkward Monkish fabrication," a fraud and forgery which to Jefferson was so obvious that English judges could only be accused of deliberately if piously avoiding the truth. Unfortunately, concluded Jefferson, the manner in which the clergy falsified the laws of Alfred was typical of "the alliance between Church and State in England," and judges have always been "accomplices in the frauds of the clergy."[36]

The thoroughness with which Jefferson undertook his research into the antiquity of ecclesiastical pretensions reflected his abiding devotion to what he believed to be the system of his abused Saxon ancestors. Indeed, it is likely that his original interest in Saxon history first stimulated the direction of this particular inquiry. For among the many whig works Jefferson consulted before writing his *Summary View* had been Hulme's *Historical Essay*. And Hulme had not only supplied Jefferson with quotable material on "our Saxon forefathers" and their "free constitution" but had also argued that the clergy "were foreign to the original institution, and only grafted themselves upon it."[37] In a very real sense Jefferson's campaign for the disestablishment of the Anglican church was part of his protracted endeavor to reestablish the true Saxon form of government. That Jefferson believed firmly the "Almighty God hath created the mind

34. Ibid., 354, 355.

35. David Houard, *Traités sur les coutumes Anglo-Normandes* . . . , 4 vols. (Paris, 1776), I, 87.

36. Chinard, ed., *Commonplace Book*, 362.

37. Ibid., 297–98; Hulme, *Historical Essay*, 38.

free"[38] is well known; that he found historical support for his belief is also true. In fact the same year that Jefferson first declared Virginians should "have full and free liberty of religious opinion: nor . . . be compelled to frequent or maintain any religious institution,"[39] he was also proposing a unique and symbolic seal for his new nation. The design suggested would feature representations of Hengist and Horsa, "the Saxon chiefs from whom we claim the honour of being descended, and whose political principles and form of government we have assumed."[40] Jefferson's affection for such a historical emblem was appreciated, but his plan was not accepted. Yet he was not discouraged and continued to work for a realization of his Saxon "heavenly city."

III

Jefferson's political career attained a pinnacle in 1776. He found the next decade less satisfying. He met with but limited success in his efforts to remodel his country in the image he desired, and his term as Governor of Virginia ended amid a flurry of criticism over his failure to prevent the British invasion. By September 1781 he was contemplating retirement from public life. To Edmund Randolph he confessed "I have . . . retired to my farm, my family and books from which I think nothing will ever more separate me."[41] In these circumstances he undertook his *Notes on Virginia,* an illuminating commentary on American life and history, and an enlightening review of the lessons he felt history continued to teach.[42]

38. Revisal of the Laws, 1776–1786: A Bill for Establishing Religious Freedom, Boyd et al., eds., *Jefferson Papers,* II, 545.

39. Virginia Constitution, 1776, Jefferson's Second Draft, ibid., I, 349.

40. John Adams to Abigail Adams, Aug. 14, 1776, Adams, ed., *Familiar Letters of John Adams,* 211.

41. Jefferson to Edmund Randolph, Sept. 16, 1781, Boyd et al., eds., *Jefferson Papers,* VI, 118.

42. Thomas Jefferson, *Notes on the State of Virginia,* ed. William Peden (Chapel Hill, 1955), xi.

Jefferson was anxious that the nation he helped to create prove successful in avoiding the economic, moral, and political pitfalls he saw afflicting Great Britain. His perspective on America was greatly affected by his perspective on his former mother country. In a Newtonian mood he observed that "human nature is the same on every side of the Atlantic, and will be alike influenced by the same causes." Recalling his Roman history, he noted that when "a heavy-handed unfeeling aristocracy" ruled a people made "desperate by poverty and wretchedness" the door was opened for a temporary tyrant who inevitably became perpetual. Potentially, this was the fate of divided Americans and decadent Englishmen, and a warning to both. The current trouble in Great Britain was simply explained, and in familiar whig terms: "The government of Great Britain has been corrupted, because but one man in ten has a right to vote for members of parliament. The sellers of the government therefore get nine-tenths of their price clear." Jefferson concluded that the main security against similar corruption in America must lie in numbers; the English example precluded a reliance upon government by the wealthy.[43]

Jefferson gave added point to his remarks in the *Notes* by referring to the present situation in Virginia. His suggestions for a state constitution had not, he felt, been adequately digested; the result was a legislature that looked dangerously uneven in representation. The homogeneous and somewhat unrepresentative Virginia Assembly with its 149 delegates and 24 senators now filled Jefferson with alarm. Relying upon the experience of history, he rendered his verdict that "173 despots would surely be as oppressive as one. . . . An elective despotism was not the government we fought for."[44]

Despotism was what the Revolution was about: there was no sense to substituting an American tyrant for an English one. Jefferson wished to avoid the demonstrable evils in the corrupted British constitution by dividing and balancing the branches and powers of

43. Peden, ed., *Notes on Virginia,* 121, 128, 149.
44. Ibid., 120.

government so that the known weaknesses of men might be circum-vented. With the example of British history ever before him, Jeffer-son urged that "the time to guard against corruption and tyranny, is before they shall have gotten hold of us." He frankly feared that the Virginia Assembly, like the Long Parliament in England, might "be deluded by the integrity of their own purposes. . . . They should look forward to a time, and that not a very distant one, when corruption in this, as in the country from which we derive our origin, will have seized the heads of government, and be spread by them through the body of the people." If corruption takes hold, if Virginians "will pur-chase the voices of the people," then they will pay the price as in Britain.[45]

Jefferson's fear of despotism was not wild or groundless. Under the stress and strain of war with Britain, some flirted with the idea of setting up a dictator in Virginia in June of 1781. Well-meaning men "had been seduced in their judgment by the example of an ancient Republic, whose constitution and circumstances were funda-mentally different." There were perils in learning Roman rather than British historical lessons. But in any case it was important to avoid the past and present troubles of others; Jefferson was sure that the logic of whig history dictated a dreadful collapse for the misguided and forgetful British. Well informed by writers like Thomas Gordon, Bolingbroke, and Burgh, Jefferson could see little help for his cor-rupted mother country: her stockjobbing, her enormous national debt, the erosion of the gains of 1688 — all combined with recent events to show that "the sun of her glory is fast descending to the horizon." England "seems passing to that awful dissolution, whose issue is not given human foresight to scan."[46] Nor was Jefferson's conclusion particularly extreme in its context: American newspapers were recently filled with reports of the terrible Gordon riots that broke out in London during June 1780. To a contemporary with a

45. Ibid., 121.
46. Ibid., 126–29, 65.

sound whig orientation, the news that London was temporarily in the hands of the city rabble seemed an omen of impending collapse.

Anxious to save America from such a fate, Jefferson did not limit himself to warnings and criticisms of constitutional failings: he was also aware of other aspects of England's recent history, such as the dependent character of her citizens huddled into industrial cities and deprived of the economic independence permitted a landowning nation. At least some of the corruption of English morals and politics came from manufacturing, in which large numbers depended for their substance on the "casualties and caprice of customers." American salvation could very well be found in her abundance of land "courting the industry of the husbandman." Jefferson urged that America rely upon the Old World for manufactures and avoid developing great industrial centers. Having just marked the menace of the London mob run wild at Lord George Gordon's foolish instigation, Jefferson was convinced that "the mobs of great cities add just so much to the support of pure government, as sores do to the strength of the human body." Cultivators of the soil, in contrast, were "the most virtuous and independent citizens."[47] As Jefferson later reminded John Adams, "the man of the old world was crowded within limits too small or overcharged, and steeped in the vices which that situation generates." American history should tell a different and potentially happier story, since "here men have choice of their labour, and so may safely and advantageously reserve to themselves a wholesome control over their public affairs, and a degree of freedom."[48]

Jefferson was not a particularly accurate prophet, but he was a patient observer. He was always ready to mark the progressive signs of a decline he knew must come; George III and his wicked ministers had spent "the fee simple of the kingdom, under pretence of governing it; their sinecures, pensions, priests, prelates, princes, and eternal wars, have mortgaged to its full value the last foot of their

47. Ibid., 164–65.
48. Jefferson to John Adams, Oct. 28, 1813, Cappon, ed., *Adams-Jefferson Letters*, II, 391.

soil."[49] He was convinced that a heavy national debt, such as endured by the collapsing British, was a national sin; "the modern theory of the perpetuation of debt," wrote a debt-ridden Jefferson in 1816, "has drenched the earth with blood."[50] He could allow that "the English have been a wise, a virtuous and truly estimable people"; the trouble was that "commerce and a corrupt government have rotted them to the core."[51] Reformation, possibly through "civil war, massacre," had to come, but the aftermath held distinctly good possibilities. "Their habits of law and order, their almost innate ideas of the vital elements of free government, of trial by jury, *habeas corpus,* freedom of the press, and representative government, make them capable of bearing a considerable portion of liberty," thought Jefferson generously.[52] But as he had remarked in his *Notes,* "the first settlers in this country [of Virginia] were emigrants from England," and the final outcome was a constitution that was "a composition of the freest principles of the English constitution."[53]

IV

Jefferson's enthusiasm for a nation of independent farmers and his awareness of the vast expanse of land available for this form of democratic preservation did not blind him to human realities. He knew that his new nation could survive only if its citizens were suitably informed of their precious heritage, their reason thus adequately armed. Helpful as economic self-sufficiency might be in fighting the evils of corruption, the foundation for a working democratic republic had to be an educated electorate. And by "educated" Jefferson

49. Jefferson to John Adams, Nov. 25, 1816, ibid., 496.
50. Jefferson to William H. Crawford, June 20, 1816, Ford, ed., *Writings of Jefferson,* X, 34.
51. Jefferson to James Ogilvie, Aug. 4, 1811, ibid., XIII, 69.
52. Jefferson to William Duane, Nov. 13, 1810, ibid., IX, 285.
53. Peden, ed., *Notes on Virginia,* 157, 84.

meant exposed to history, and the earlier the exposure, the safer the nation.

The extent of Jefferson's concern for properly educated youth was first indicated in 1778, when he submitted his famous "Bill for the More General Diffusion of Knowledge." The admitted reason was that "experience hath shewn, that even under the best forms, those entrusted with power have, in time . . . perverted it into tyranny." The purpose of the Bill was "to illuminate, as far as practicable, the minds of the people at large" and particularly to offer a reliable understanding of the past. Jefferson argued that with a "knowledge of those facts, which history exhibiteth," the people would thus enjoy the experience of other ages and countries and be better equipped "to know ambition under all its shapes, and prompt to exert their natural powers to defeat its purposes." From the first of the educational stages planned, Jefferson wanted an acquaintance "with Graecian, Roman, English, and American history,"[54] with students of promise given opportunity to continue their education on the college level.[55] And the first subject he suggested for advanced academic study was again history, "ancient and modern."[56]

Nothing was closer to Jefferson's heart in his last years than planning and working for a university, conveniently close to Monticello, where young Virginians would be suitably prepared for the outside political world. In a sense the University of Virginia was the climax to Jefferson's educational program, but it also served other important purposes. During his youth, Jefferson had disapproved a colonial tendency to go abroad for a college education. Going abroad for this

54. Revisal of the Laws, 1776–1786: A Bill for the More General Diffusion of Knowledge, Boyd et al., eds., *Jefferson Papers,* II, 526–27, 528.

55. Jefferson did not believe that all interested students should enter college; he wanted superior students to have superior training; his concept of equality was of opportunity, and he hoped the nation would develop its natural aristocracy of talent.

56. A Bill for the Establishment of District Colleges and University, sent to James Carrington Cabell, Oct. 24, 1817, cited in Saul K. Padover, ed., *The Complete Jefferson . . .* (N.Y., 1943), 1082.

purpose involved risks with which most whig writers were familiar. James Burgh had described the terrible temptations facing students at the English universities in the eighteenth century: Oxford and Cambridge were "little better than seminaries of vice."[57] Jefferson agreed. Education abroad exposed innocent American youths to "a fondness for European luxury and dissipation . . . a contempt for the simplicity of . . . [their] own country . . . a passion for whores, destructive of health." In England, the American "learns drinking, horse racing, and boxing. These are the pecularities of English education." Most menacing was the likelihood of contracting "a partiality for aristocracy or monarchy."[58] The foundation of the University of Virginia was Jefferson's antidote to such a disease. In Charlottesville, students were to have their minds safely enlightened and their morals cultivated along sound whig lines, developing "habits of reflection and correct action."[59]

This academic plan for moral cultivation was not just a polite form of historical indoctrination. Jefferson wanted a rounded education to be offered, including languages such as German, which had the distinct merit of being "of common descent with the language of our own country, a branch of the same original Gothic stock, and furnishes valuable illustrations for us." Even more important was Anglo-Saxon, "of peculiar value" because it helped us to better understand "our ancient common law, on which, as a stock, our whole system of law is engrafted." Further, Anglo-Saxon was "the first link in the chain of a historical review of our language," and was "already fraught with all the eminent science of our parent country."[60] And to be sure that proper principles of political philosophy developed with such tools, Jefferson wished students to master Locke's *Essay Concern-*

---

57. Burgh, *Political Disquisitions,* III, 154.
58. Jefferson to John Banister, Jr., Oct. 15, 1785, Boyd et al., eds., *Jefferson Papers,* VIII, 635–37.
59. Aims and Curriculum, Aug. 1–4, 1818, Padover, ed., *The Complete Jefferson,* 1098.
60. Ibid., 1102–3.

ing the True Original Extent, and End of Civil Government, and Algernon Sidney's *Discourses Concerning Government,* which he recommended for "the general principles of liberty and the rights of man."[61]

In a letter to George Washington Lewis, of the University of Virginia's faculty, Jefferson discussed details of the history curriculum.[62] He argued for the merits of ancient history, and the inclusion of Thucydides, Livy, Caesar, and Tacitus. But he devoted most attention to modern history, particularly that of England. Significantly, the one whig history included in Peter Jefferson's small library remained the first choice of his son Thomas Jefferson nearly seventy years later. "There is as yet no general history so faithful as Rapin's," Jefferson still insisted; only after Rapin should students read such unreliable historical heretics as David Hume.

Hume constantly drew Jefferson's irritated attacks as an apologist for the iniquities of the Stuarts: "he suppressed truths, advanced falsehoods, forged authorities, and falsified records." Hume disturbed Jefferson by the dangerous charm of his writing: "His pen revolutionized the public sentiment [in England] . . . more completely than the standing armies could ever have done." Along with "bewitching" style Hume offered a view of history totally opposed to Jefferson's, a view that argued "it was the people who encroached on the sovereign, not the sovereign who usurped on the rights of the people." When this dangerous Scotsman treated Saxon and Norman history, he twisted the facts, at least as Jefferson conceived them. The Saxon period, Jefferson carefully reminded his faculty members, exhibited "the genuine form and political principles of the people constituting the nation, and founded on the rights of man." The Norman regime,

61. The question of Jefferson's intention to indoctrinate rather than inform is discussed at length by Arthur Bestor in his excellent essay, "Thomas Jefferson and the Freedom of Books," in Robert B. Downs, ed., *Three Presidents and Their Books* (Urbana, Ill., 1955), and by Leonard Levy, *Jefferson and Civil Liberties: The Darker Side* (Cambridge, Mass., 1963), 142–57.

62. Jefferson to George Washington Lewis, Oct. 25, 1825, Lipscomb and Bergh, eds., *Writings of Jefferson,* XVI, 124–28.

on the other hand, was "built on conquest and physical force." The Conquest of 1066 settled nothing, because the English will "to recover the Saxon constitution continued unabated, and was at the bottom of all the unsuccessful insurrections which succeeded in subsequent times." This was the viewpoint of Jefferson's favorite whig historians, who had "always gone back to the Saxon period for the true principles of their constitution, while the Tories and Hume . . . date it from the Norman conquest." Students should not be allowed to read Hume without preparation in other works: "If first read, Hume makes an English Tory, from whence it is an easy step to American Toryism." Jefferson returned to the whig superiority of Rapin as supplying a needed basis of truth.

Fond of Rapin's *History* as he was, Jefferson conceded that it was a rather large dose for the average university student. But there were alternatives to tory historical seduction at the hands of Hume: another Scotsman, George Brodie, published in 1822 *A History of the British Empire from the Accession of Charles I. to the Restoration,* which included "a Particular Examination of Mr. Hume's Statements Relative to the Character of the English Government." Brodie offered a long and partisan review of Hume's tory failings, and like Jefferson, was convinced that "England at an early period, was distinguished for her freedom, and the comparative happiness of her people."[63] However, Brodie was a little too obvious, and much more attractive to Jefferson was John Baxter's older but rarer offering, *A New and Impartial History of England.* Jefferson bought his copy in 1805 and enjoyed recommending the book to his friends as "Hume's history republicanised."[64]

---

63. George Brodie, *A History of the British Empire* . . . , 4 vols. (Edinburgh, 1822), I, 11. For an evaluation of Brodie, see Thomas P. Peardon, *The Transition in English Historical Writing, 1760–1780* (N.Y., 1933), 202.

64. Jefferson to Bernard Moore, enclosed in Jefferson to John Minor, Aug. 30, 1814, Ford, ed., *Writings of Jefferson,* IX, 483 *n.* This list was first drafted about 1765, but the original version is lost; the copy sent to John Minor was revised in the light of recent publications, and so included the works of De Lolme, Burgh, and David Ramsay. Jefferson also included such authors as Ludlow, Macaulay, Locke, and Sidney.

He reported delightedly that when Baxter "comes to a fact falsified, he states it truly, and when to a suppression of truth he supplies it . . . [and] it is in fact an editio expurgata of Hume." For those who found Rapin difficult, Baxter was the best possible substitute.[65] This was not very surprising: Baxter's attitude toward history was also Jefferson's. "By a knowledge of the History of England," noted Baxter, "we are able to contrast the present with former times; to see where our liberties are invaded, or in danger; and learn, from example, how the evil is to be prevented."[66] Baxter had actually written an abridged version of Hume, changing words here, omitting some there, making over Hume's pages, as Jefferson said, into "sound history."[67]

If Baxter was to be of value in saving Americans from Hume's influence, his work had to be made available. Jefferson tried to secure an American edition, "and by reprinting it, place in the hands of our students an elementary history which may strengthen instead of weakening their affections to the republican principles of their own country and its constitution."[68] Failing in this, Jefferson tried to secure additional copies from England, if only to replace his copy which went to the Library of Congress on the sale of his second collection. Neither Mathew Carey, nor John Laval, nor even the American minister Richard Rush could oblige him with copies, in spite of his repeated requests, and Baxter remained a rarity in America.[69] It

65. Jefferson to Baron Alexander Von Humboldt, June 13, 1817. Lipscomb and Bergh, eds., *Writings of Jefferson*, XVI, 127–28.

66. John Baxter, *A New and Impartial History of England* . . . (London, ca. 1796), vi. No copy in the British museum; there is one in the New York Public Library and another in the Library of the University of Western Ontario; it is the latter copy which I have consulted.

67. Jefferson to William Duane, Aug. 12, 1810, Lipscomb and Bergh, eds., *Writings of Jefferson*, XII, 406. Jefferson said this several times: see his letters to John Norvell, June 14, 1807, Ford, ed., *Writings of Jefferson*, IX, 72, and to William Duane, Aug. 12, 1810, Lipscomb and Bergh, eds., *Writings of Jefferson*, XII, 406–7.

68. Jefferson to Mathew Carey, Nov. 22, 1818, cited in Sowerby, ed., *Catalogue of Jefferson's Library*, I, 176–77.

69. For a review of this correspondence, see ibid., I, 178–79.

was in vain that Jefferson urged a copy of Baxter for the University of Virginia library.[70] So impressed was Jefferson with Baxter's "method," that he suggested an extension of the practice as a guaranteed antidote to Hume's "poison." To the publisher Mathew Carey, Jefferson suggested reprinting Hume, and alongside in parallel columns placing the whig refutations, thus confronting Hume's "misrepresentations" with "authentic truths" from "honest writers" like Edmund Ludlow, Catherine Macaulay, and Rapin. After all, he wrote Carey, "the knowledge of our own history must be based on that of England";[71] in this manner a little historical learning need not be a dangerous thing.

No historian so exasperated Jefferson as did David Hume. Not only did Jefferson fret publicly over the menace Hume represented to innocent students at Charlottesville, but he continued to worry privately over Hume's pernicious influence. One occasion was an article that appeared in the *London Globe* in the spring of 1824 offering a quotation from Edmund Burke on David Hume: "I believe we shall all come to think at last with Mr. Hume," said Burke, "that an absolute monarchy is not so bad a thing as we supposed." This thought set Jefferson to reviewing Hume again, particularly his claim that the first two Stuart kings were not sinners, but sinned against by the people who willfully encroached upon the royal prerogative. Jefferson wrote in his Commonplace Book that Hume described Charles I as "a very virtuous prince and entirely worthy of the trust of his people," an opinion impossible for a good whig, and characteristic of Hume's Jacobite outlook. Hume's political philosophy offended Jefferson: his assertion that "it is seldom that the people gain anything by revolutions in government," his characterization of the theory of representative government as a noble dream "belied by all history

---

70. "President Jefferson's Catalogue of Books for the University of Virginia Library, 1825," in the Alderman Library, University of Virginia.

71. Jefferson to Mathew Carey, Nov. 22, 1818, Sowerby, ed., *Catalogue of Jefferson's Library*, I, 177.

and experience," his observation that "it is dangerous to weaken . . . the reverence which the multitude owe to authority" were all highly objectionable. Jefferson concluded that Hume's purpose was to instruct people in doctrines of obedience so they would mistakenly learn the impossibility of achieving freedom from the duty of their allegiance.[72] The very existence of the United States in 1824 seemed ample evidence of Hume's error. Beyond that, Jefferson was prepared to propagate the doctrine of disobedience and the right of revolution and to illustrate from history the justice revolutions had achieved.

V

Jefferson's last years were remarkable for the vigor with which he still conducted his extraordinary correspondence. In the summer of 1824 he received and replied to a letter from an unusual admirer, Major John Cartwright, the famed English radical.[73] The exchange of letters between these two octogenarians is a remarkable one on several counts: it illustrates the esteem in which Jefferson was held by surviving members of the English Real Whigs who had sympathized with the American Revolution; it confirms their agreement on the importance of history and its interpretation; and it reveals anew Jefferson's lasting commitment to the whig view of English history.

The excuse for Cartwright's communication was the publication of what was to be his final volume, *The English Constitution Produced and Illustrated.* Cartwright discussed at great length the "well-known existence of the Anglo-Saxon Elective Legislature, and the equally well understood Rights and Liberties out of which it naturally grew."

72. *London Globe,* Mar. 23, 1824; Jefferson's commentary is in Chinard, ed., *Commonplace Book,* 374–76.
73. Like James Otis, John Cartwright has long fascinated and frustrated scholars who felt the call to biography. In neither case is there sufficient material. A good short account of Cartwright is in C. B. Roylance Kent, *The English Radicals; an Historical Sketch* (London, 1899).

Repeatedly he stressed the pre-Norman origin of the English constitution he so ardently wished to restore in the early nineteenth century.[74] And Jefferson agreed completely with Cartwright's historical interpretation: "I think," Jefferson told Cartwright, "it has deduced the Constitution of the English nation from its rightful root. . . . Your derivation of it from the Anglo-Saxons seems to be made on legitimate principles."[75] Jefferson read Cartwright's work "with pleasure and much appreciation," and in acknowledging his enjoyment, he related his reasons.

The Saxons, Jefferson agreed, were the ancestors of present-day Englishmen. It is true that no written evidence of their constitution has been handed down, but "doubtless" they had one, and from their known history and laws "it may be inferred with considerable certainty." Jefferson conceded the Norman conquest, but insisted that "force cannot change right," that violence was part of recorded history but could not set aside historically established rights. Despite the Normans, "a perpetual claim was kept up by the nation, by their perpetual demand of a restoration of their Saxon laws." This was adequate evidence the Saxon system was "never relinquished by the will of the nation," and eventually, when the Stuarts were expelled, "the thread of pretended inheritance" was broken and the English regained their former rights. Admittedly not all such privileges were specified in the bills of rights, "yet the omission of the others was no renunciation of the right to assume their exercise also, whenever occasion should occur." After all, William and Mary "received no rights but those expressly granted."

Jefferson had no hesitation in avowing his historical allegiance: "It has ever appeared to me," he told Cartwright, "that the difference between the Whig and the Tory of England is, that the Whig deduces his rights from the Anglo-Saxon source, and the Tory from the Norman." The category for David Hume was inescapable: Hume re-

---

74. Cartwright, *The English Constitution*, 196.
75. Jefferson to Cartwright, June 5, 1824, Jefferson Papers, Library of Congress.

mained "the great apostle of Toryism," a "degenerate son of science," and a "traitor to his fellow men." And while Jefferson reminded Cartwright that the American Revolution was not confined by "the laws and institutions of a semi-barbarous ancestry," still he discussed the merits of a new division of local government that "would answer to the hundreds of your Saxon Alfred." Jefferson was as dedicated an admirer of his Saxon ancestors as he had ever been, still arguing that in the glorious days of Alfred there was no real alliance of church and state, that this was the work of judicial forgers: "What a conspiracy this, between Church and State!" exclaimed Jefferson, adding exuberantly, "Sing Tantara, rogues all, rogues all, Sing Tantarara, rogues all!" But Jefferson could look with genuine satisfaction at the elements of the Saxon system which he had helped restore in America. "The wit of man," he concluded, "cannot devise a more solid basis for a free, durable and well-administered republic."

Had Cartwright lived to reply, he would have enviously agreed with Jefferson. As he had remarked earlier, there were too many enemies to freedom in England, "hereditary Kings, privileged nobles, and time-serving priests," and yet England too might recover this same ancient glory if only, "by one comprehensive radical reform of her government," she would shake off "the *Norman Counterfeit*" and restore "her genuine Polity in all its purity." Cartwright did disclose to Jefferson his hope that with the ancient English constitution reestablished in America, the new nation might act like "a faithful mirror" upon the eyes and sympathy of his uninformed fellow countrymen.[76] And Jefferson, reading Cartwright's *English Constitution,* could find the same thought expressed more flatteringly: in the United States, "we have *Democracy* divested of its turbulence, its unsteadiness, its liability of being duped by Demagogues . . . while it yet retains its naturally genuine patriotism and disinterested devo-

76. Cartwright to Jefferson, Feb. 29, 1824, ibid.

tion to the public good. . . . Such *was* the government of a *Wittagen-mote,* executed by an *Alfred!* Such *is* the government of a Congress, executed by a Monroe!"[77]

VI

Jefferson himself provided a final footnote to his lifelong attachment to history. He was invited to participate in celebrations to be held in Washington on the fiftieth anniversary of the Declaration of Independence. Jefferson declined on account of failing health, but he offered some brief remarks on the meaning of independence. "All eyes are opened or opening to the rights of man," he wrote. "The general spread of the light of science has already laid open to every view the palpable truth that the mass of mankind has not been born with saddles on their backs, nor a favored few booted and spurred ready to ride them legitimately by the grace of God."[78]

This comprised Jefferson's last formal statement on democracy to his countrymen. But Jefferson's words were not his own. The phrases referring to mankind's freedom from saddles and spurs came directly from the dying speech of another revolutionary, Colonel Richard Rumbold, owner of the famous Rye House in which the deaths of Charles II and his Roman Catholic brother James were unsuccessfully plotted. Rumbold met his death on the scaffold, asserting that he was dying "in the Defence of the ancient Laws and Liberties." He was departing from "a deluded Generation, vail'd with Ignorance, that though Popery and Slavery be riding in upon them, do not perceive it."[79] He concluded with the observation employed by Jefferson: he

---

77. Cartwright, *The English Constitution,* 227.

78. Jefferson to Roger Weightman, June 24, 1826, Lipscomb and Bergh, eds., *Writings of Jefferson,* XVI, 182.

79. See Douglass Adair, "Rumbold's Dying Speech, 1685, and Jefferson's Last Words on Democracy, 1826," *William and Mary Quarterly,* 3d ser., 9 (1952): 526, 530.

223

did not believe, declared Rumbold, "that God made the greater part of Mankind with Saddles on their Backs, and Bridles in their Mouths, and some few booted and spurred to ride the rest."[80]

Just where Jefferson met with Rumbold's speech is uncertain. James Wilson had quoted it in his law lectures.[81] Bishop Burnet cited Rumbold in his *History of His Own Time*. Rapin drew from Burnet. So did James Burgh, who began his *Political Disquisitions* with Rumbold's "shrewd" saying.[82] Jefferson knew these authors intimately. English history was so much a part of Jefferson's intellectual existence that it seems singularly fitting that an English martyr's metaphor should also be the parting phrase of a successful American Revolutionary.

VII

The persistent and enduring affection for whig history that is so pronounced in Jefferson suggests a certain consistency in his historical thought and political action. It is abundantly clear that the whig historical approach had much that was attractive to Jefferson, although his receptivity probably varied with political necessity. Certainly it is more than pleasant to think of one's forefathers as exponents of democracy and liberty, and it was a comfort to subscribers to the Saxon myth to know that there had existed a political utopia in Saxon England. In fact the basis of whig history was largely this pre-Norman utopia, where there had been no menace from a standing army, no society organized for war on a feudal basis, and no land held other than allodially. This Saxon society, Jefferson learned, had been a society of law, unplagued by a shackling established church, a society governed originally by an elective monarchy and a popular assembly meeting in that original of parliaments, the annual Saxon witenagemot.

80. Rapin, *History of England,* II, 748.
81. Andrews, *Works of Wilson,* I, 66.
82. Burgh, *Political Disquisitions,* I, 3; Burnet's quotation is in *History of His Own Time,* 406.

This was the encouraging and sometimes inspiring view presented by the books Jefferson studied most carefully, books which contributed to his peculiar historical optimism, his belief in the "happy system" of his Saxon ancestors, his staunch faith that the past could be successfully adapted to the future in America. As he came increasingly to see the uniqueness of the United States by reason of its size and its unexploited land, history came to lack the immediate pertinence previously evident. He never needed history as desperately as when he sought guidance for the Revolution, but he was never dominated by it. History helped him understand his political and economic problems; it supplied a reassuringly empirical basis for argument.

It was Jefferson's ability to learn from and employ history for the present and future that contributed to his historical optimism. While he might repeat the historians he studied and admired, he did not see why history should repeat itself, and he did not subscribe to any cyclical theory which would deny man's perfectibility. The past for Thomas Jefferson was by no means the past portrayed by modern scholarship. What matters is that he was governed by what he believed happened in the days of his Saxon ancestors, and that he was optimistic enough to believe that this early version of democracy would be reestablished on an enduring basis in America.

CHAPTER IX

The Whig Historical Tradition and the Origins of the American Revolution

In seventeenth-century England men found history peculiarly instructive and useful. By the eighteenth century, history had become the practical study for gentlemen on both sides of the Atlantic. Americans praised history as "the least fallible guide," and their "oracle of truth."[1] The British colonies may have been predominantly agricultural but they produced a society with remarkably bookish (if not literary) tastes. Shelf after shelf of historical studies in college libraries, booksellers' shops, library societies, lawyers' offices, and personal libraries attest to the measure of the colonists' historical interest and opportunity. Their study of history was a vital part of their intellectual environment. With history the Revolutionary generation of Americans sought to extend its political experience; with assistance from the past, Americans determined their future.

I

The colonial focus was on the history of the mother country. "The history of Great Britain," remarked John Jay in *The Federalist,* "is the

---

1. Such comments abound in *The Federalist;* see Jacob E. Cooke's annotated edition (Middletown, Conn., 1961), *Federalist* No. 6 (Hamilton), 32, and *Federalist* No. 20 (Madison), 128.

one with which we are in general the best acquainted."[2] To know English history was to know America's origins. And to know English history in the mid-eighteenth century was to know history as it was written and sometimes made by Englishmen of the "True *Whig*" persuasion, so designated by Robert Molesworth. These were the writers, so aptly called "Commonwealthmen" by Caroline Robbins, who justified political action against the Stuarts in the seventeenth century by appeals to the antiquity of the privileges sought. These were the writers who offered a historical justification of the Glorious Revolution, reveled briefly in its accomplishment, and then found to their horror that after 1688 neither England's government nor its society remained true to its professed purposes. They became fearful for the future of their country as they saw the love of luxury increase and attachment to virtue diminish. The power and ambition of the Crown was not yet curbed; Parliament threatened a new despotism as dire as that of the Stuarts—indeed, threatened a despotism made worse by an alliance with the Crown at the expense of the people.

What these radical whig historians and critics said about their government and society made sense to many Americans. Well read on the golden age of their Saxon ancestors, colonial patriots thoughtfully noted the contrast presented in the whig portrayal of modern England. There seemed to be a conspiracy to defraud Englishmen of their constitutional rights overseas as well as at home. John Adams was quite specific: "the conspiracy . . . against the Public Liberty," he declared in 1774, "was first regularly formed, and begun to be executed, in 1763 or 4."[3] The American interpretation of English history colored colonial explanations of events and furnished Americans with an arsenal of arguments that eventually transformed a rebellion into a revolution.

Independence—which required revolution—was not initially intended by the colonial leaders. As Clinton Rossiter observed when studying their political theory, "however radical the principles of the

2. *Federalist* No. 5 (Jay), 24.
3. John Adams, Diary, Mar. 6, 1774, Butterfield, ed., *Adams Papers,* II, 90.

Revolution may have seemed to the rest of the world, in the minds of the colonists they were thoroughly preservative and respectful of the past."[4] Their respect for the past brought them to their rebellious and finally revolutionary posture. The last stage of their journey was the most difficult and also the most carefully related to history: on the eve of independence colonists were consulting such whig oracles as Hulme's *Historical Essay on the English Constitution* (it was "invaluable"), noting anew how the Saxons secured "the free election of their magistrates and governors; without which our ancestors thought all our liberties were but a *species* of bondage." Comparisons were irresistible: "How different from, and how much superior to, our present form of government, was the Saxon, or old constitution of England!"[5] The language of history was commonplace: "Provoke us not too far!!" warned a Rhode Islander; "*Runymede* is still to be found, as we may there assert our rights."[6] Mounting doubt about England's interest in this common legacy of liberty played its part in the colonial decision. "Cassandra," writing in March 1776, cited Hulme and Burgh as he contended that "the British constitution is so effectually undermined by the influence of the crown, that the people of Britain have no security for the enjoyment of their *own liberties*." He concluded that "Americans can never be safe in being dependent on such a state [as Britain]." Englishmen in the mother country had "lost the distinguishing character between freemen and slaves."[7] A New Englander employed more colorful phrasing: England was no longer "in a Condition at present to Suckle us, being pregnant with Vermin that corrupt her Milk, and convert her Blood and Juices into Poison."[8]

4. Rossiter, *Seedtime of the Republic*, 448.

5. *Maryland Gazette* (Annapolis), May 2, 1776.

6. *Newport Mercury*, Sept. 7, 1772.

7. *Maryland Gazette* (Annapolis), May 2, 1776. "Cassandra" was James Cannon, mathematics tutor at the College of Philadelphia; his essays first appeared in the *Pennsylvania Evening Post* (Philadelphia). His chief critic was the Reverend William Smith, Provost of the College, who wrote as "Cato" in the *Pennsylvania Ledger* (Philadelphia). For a review of this exchange, see Schlesinger, *Prelude to Independence*, 262–63.

8. *Connecticut Courant* (Hartford), June 5, 1774 (reprinted from the *Pennsylvania Packet* [Philadelphia]).

Revolution became both a preventative and a preservative course of action. Americans wanted to prevent the spread of "the poison of corruption" to their own shores.[9] ("May placemen and pensioners never find seats in American senates" was one toast drunk in June 1776.[10]) Americans wanted to preserve their inherited rights and liberties. And above all they wanted to maintain their *virtue*. For whig historians and colonial readers Clio was a highly moral muse. Virtue was considered as important to the body politic as virginity to a young maiden. Americans were repeatedly told that they represented a last outpost of English freedom, that they were the last sentinels of English virtue. They labored thus under "a double obligation"— to preserve their own virtue and in so doing "rouse the dormant spirit of liberty in England, give a check to luxury and a spring to virtue."[11] Joseph Warren in his 1775 "Massacre" oration expressed a widespread hope "that *Britain's* liberty, as well as *ours*, will eventually be preserved by the virtue of America."[12]

Sincerely imbued as they were with a sense of imperial public service as well as historical obligation, many Americans were much encouraged by the historical commentaries crossing the Atlantic: John Dickinson's exchange with Edward Dilly, Richard Henry Lee's correspondence with Catherine Macaulay, the Boston Sons of Liberty letters to John Wilkes—all brought comfort, information, and an enhanced awareness of common history and common purpose.[13] "Thank God," ran a letter of Wilkes carried by the *Maryland Gazette,* "our Ancestors were Heroes and Patriots, not *prudent* Men. Russell and Sydney were considered by the Townshends of their Age

---

9. *Newport Mercury,* July 1, 1776.

10. Ibid.

11. *Connecticut Courant* (Hartford), Feb. 15, 1774.

12. Oration of Dr. Joseph Warren, Mar. 6, 1775, Hezekiah Niles, ed., *Principles and Acts of the Revolution . . .* (Baltimore, 1822), 21.

13. For evidence of the admiration Wilkes excited in New Englanders, see The Committee of the Sons of Liberty [Benjamin Kent, Thomas Young, Benjamin Church, Jr., John Adams, Joseph Warren] to John Wilkes, June 6, 1768, in Massachusetts Historical Society, *Proceedings* 47 (1914): 191–92.

as *imprudent* Men. They risked all for liberty."[14] When Wilkes campaigned in 1774, Americans read of his ambition for electoral reform, the "restoration" of Saxon annual parliaments, and a reversal of the ministerial policies toward the colonies.[15] (He likened critics of the American cause to Charles I's infamous attack on Parliament in 1628.[16]) Several years before the Declaration of Independence Wilkes was reported asking publicly whether "in a few years the independent Americans may not celebrate the glorious era of the revolution of 1775, as we do that of 1688?"[17]

And yet the final decision was distinctively American. Real Whigs in England might sympathize with the colonists, but there were few who looked for American independence. The whig purpose was limited to offering colonial virtue as a mirror for the mother country. The repetitive historical reviews of corruption, the unrepresentative character of the House of Commons, and the unholy conspiracy of Crown and Parliament against the ancient English constitution were intended to educate and enlighten, to create the climate for redress and reform at home. Neither a Hulme nor a Blackstone countenanced colonial claims to self-government under the cloak of English constitutional rights; they might deplore some consequences of the Glorious Revolution, but as Charles H. McIlwain has observed, for them prerogative was such of the ancient discretionary rights of the Crown as Parliament chose to leave untouched.[18] Whigs questioned the wisdom but rarely doubted the authority of Parliament. They might offer a justification for certain colonial claims to redress

14. *Maryland Gazette* (Annapolis), Apr. 26, 1770.

15. Ibid., Jan. 23, 1772.

16. Ibid., Jan. 18, 1776.

17. *New-York Gazette; and Weekly Mercury,* June 10, 1773.

18. McIlwain, *The American Revolution: A Constitutional Interpretation,* 2. The value of McIlwain's study remains uncontested, even though his approach awaits scholarly exploitation; however, the constitutional correctness of the colonial case matters less than their belief in that correctness.

of grievances but they preferred not to counsel revolution at home or in America.

The colonists were selective in their use of whig history. They seized and made their own, specific concepts and ideas only. They took seventeenth-century historical arguments against the Stuarts and directed these arguments against the eighteenth-century Parliament. They wrenched whig history from its monarchical framework and gave emphasis to the revolutionary acts of the Puritan Revolution of the 1640s—something English historians rarely cared to do. The American achievement was one of adaptation and translation. They used whig history, they used whig arguments, but their borrowing fed ideas and led to decisions appropriate only to the colonial circumstances. Had the Founding Fathers remained totally true to the English whig historical tradition they would never have produced a revolution—and their counterparts in England did not.

In the process of seeking to educate Grenville, Townshend, and North, Americans educated themselves. Persuaded of the historical reality of their constitutional claims, convinced that political depravity had indeed "swallowed up all the virtue of the island of Great-Britain,"[19] Americans moved beyond protest, beyond mere resistance, to revolution. And yet the Declaration of Independence pretended to nothing new. It offered only "the common sense of the subject," its authority resting "on the harmonizing sentiments of the day, whether expressed in conversation, in letters, printed essays, or the elementary books of public right." It presented the record of "absolute tyranny" as a brief for the contention that British governmental *purpose* was intrinsically at fault, precluding any likelihood of reform.[20] The constitution so admired and respected by Americans no longer existed in Britain; the natural rights of mankind, once

19. *Connecticut Courant* (Hartford), June 5, 1774.
20. See Becker, *The Declaration of Independence*, 25–26, 14–15.

secure under British law, now lacked protection.[21] In these circumstances the purpose of government itself demanded restatement.

It was this identification of English rights with natural rights that made relatively easy the transition from history to political theory. Hitherto colonists had hesitated to trust themselves to philosophical abstractions, notwithstanding their acceptance of Locke's libertarian principles. Many had felt, as James Duane expressed it in 1774, that "the Law of Nature . . . will be a feeble support." He felt more secure grounding his rights on the laws and constitution of the mother country, "without recurring to the Law of Nature."[22] But by the summer of 1776 there seemed no choice but to appeal to the natural rights which the British constitution had once embodied but no longer supported. Americans knew that historically sovereignty lay with the people rather than with any law-making power; the time had come for the people to exercise that sovereignty; the time had come to address the future rather than the past.

The Revolution came with Americans abandoning the conservative, evolutionary progress normally advocated by their whig friends. But the whig interpretation of history had served significantly. It had shown, as one Pennsylvanian noted, that "whether you be *English, Irish, Germans,* or *Swedes,* whether you be churchmen presbyterians, quakers, or of any other denomination of religion, whatsoever, you are by your residence, and the laws of your country, freemen and not slaves." It had shown Americans that they were "entitled to all the liberties of *Englishmen* and the freedom of this constitu-

---

21. "The glory of the British Government," announced the *Connecticut Gazette* (New Haven) as early as Apr. 10, 1756, is that the "natural Rights of Mankind, are secured by the Laws of the Land." See Rossiter, *Seedtime of the Republic,* 143. When John Adams reminded readers of the *Boston-Gazette,* Jan. 27, 1776, that "all men are born equal," he also told them that "the drift of British constitution is to preserve as much of this equality as is compatible with the people's security." The rights of men were God-given, but supported by the British constitution.

22. John Adams, "Notes of Debates in the Continental Congress," Sept. 8, 1774, in Butterfield, ed., *Adams Papers,* II, 129.

tion."[23] It allowed Americans to approach the issue of independence gradually, almost obliquely. In insisting upon rights which their history showed were deeply embedded in antiquity, American Revolutionaries argued that their stand was essentially conservative; it was the corrupted mother country which was pursuing a radical course of action, pressing innovations and encroachments upon her long-suffering colonies. Independence was in large measure the product of the historical concepts of the men who made it, men who furnished intellectual as well as political leadership to a new nation.

II

The first publication of the Declaration of Independence in book form took place early in July 1776. It was an integral part of a little volume prepared by one "Demophilus" entitled *The Genuine Principles of the Ancient Saxon, or English Constitution.*[24] It was, claimed the author, "carefully collected from the best AUTHORITIES; with some OBSERVATIONS, on their peculiar fitness, for the UNITED COLONIES in general, and PENNSYLVANIA in particular." The title page also carried two quotations. The first was from Sidney: "All human Constitutions are subject to Corruption, and must perish, unless they are 'timely renewed' by reducing them to their first Principles."[25] The second, even more familiar, came from Hulme's *Historical Essay:* "Where ANNUAL ELECTION ends, TYRANNY begins."[26] Almost three-quarters of the book comprised excerpts

23. *Pennsylvania Journal* (Philadelphia), Sept. 28, 1758, quoted by Rossiter, *Seedtime of the Republic,* 143.

24. "Demophilus," *The Genuine Principles of the Ancient Saxon, or English Constitution* (Philadelphia, 1776), published between July 8–15, 1776, by Robert Bell. "Demophilus" has not been identified positively, but he may well have been George Bryan; see also the *Pennsylvania Gazette,* March 19, 1777, for a further contribution from this Saxon-oriented constitutionalist.

25. The quotation from Sidney is taken from his *Discourses,* I, 206.

26. See title page, Hulme, *Historical Essay;* as noted in chap. 5, John Adams was fond of this maxim.

from Hulme. Americans were reminded how their Saxon ancestors "founded their government on the common rights of mankind. They made the elective power of the people the first principle of the constitution."[27] The point could hardly be missed: "the old Saxon form of government, will be the best model, that human wisdom, improved by experience, has left . . . to copy."[28]

Whig history survived. But with a few notable exceptions, it failed to excite American interest and allegiance. Once independence was declared and institutionalized, the whig view of English history became less prominent in the American mind. When the colonists' quarrel with England began, they already had much of what English whig writers had long sought for themselves. A major objective of the American Revolution was the maintenance of liberties already enjoyed.

After independence new tasks created new needs, new interests. When Americans contemplated a new federal union in 1787 they found other aspects of their historical education of value. They gave renewed attention to their classical literature. Polybius now came into his own as an authority on the Greek city-states, and American constitution-makers pored over his pages, studying again the causes of the dissolution of ancient republics.[29] They reviewed European history, mainly for examples of modern confederations, such as the Dutch. Sir William Temple's *Observations upon the United Provinces of the Netherlands* enjoyed a new vogue (none of the delegates in Phila-

27. Hulme, *Historical Essay*, 6–7, cited by "Demophilus," *Genuine Principles*, 5.

28. "Demophilus," *Genuine Principles*, 17.

29. For a recent study of the impact of the Greek and Roman ideas on the Founding Fathers, see Richard M. Gummere, *The American Colonial Mind and the Classical Tradition; Essays in Comparative Culture* (Cambridge, Mass., 1963); for his discussion of Polybius and the Constitution, see 177–78. Probably the most incisive study of intellectual origins of the 1787 Constitution is Douglass Adair, "The Intellectual Origins of Jeffersonian Democracy: Republicanism, the Class Struggle, and the Virtuous Farmer" (Ph.D. diss., Yale University, 1943). But no one has done for the Founding Fathers what Harold T. Parker did for the French Revolutionaries of the 1780s and 1790s—see his *The Cult of Antiquity and the French Revolutionaries* (Chicago, 1937).

delphia read Dutch), and Franklin, Wilson, Madison, and Benjamin Rush were among those looking to the Dutch experience for constitutional wisdom, arguing that the Dutch confederacy, like the American government under the Articles of Confederation, was both ineffective and unjust.[30] Yet English history was hardly neglected—the English constitution still excited admiration—and there persisted the confident feeling that Americans could profit from the English experience "without paying the price which it cost them."[31] "Happy that country which can avail itself of the misfortunes of others," commented John Marshall.[32] In a distinctive way the new federal union was as much a product of history as the Revolution itself;[33] but the Constitution of 1787 reflected different needs and problems and was accordingly the subject of a broader historical canvas.

III

History is made in the minds of men, and in the eighteenth century there were men whose minds were filled with history. The history made by the American Revolutionaries was in part the product of the history they read, in part the product of their translation

30. See William H. Riker, "Dutch and American Federalism," *Journal of the History of Ideas* 18 (1957): 499–508.

31. John Jay, *Federalist* No. 5, ed. Cooke, 24.

32. John Marshall, June 19, 1788, Jonathan Elliot, ed., *Debates in the Several State Conventions on the Adoption of the Federal Constitution . . .* (Philadelphia, 1881), III, 225.

33. Naroll, in his *Clio and the Constitution*, offers an arithmetical approach to the use of history in Philadelphia in 1787. He notes nearly 400 references to historical events, of which about 100 were to British history, mostly post-1688, about 70 to European history, about 70 to ancient history, and the balance to post-1763 American history. He finds Anglo-Saxon political experience furnishing material for 55 per cent of all historical references. Obviously such statistics are of little help without further investigation into the actual use and meaning of the history employed. But there seems no reason to dispute Naroll's contention that the delegates did not trifle with history: "they seldom used a historical reference as an ornament, a rhetorical flourish or a display of knowledge." Ibid., 71. Edward McNall Burns in "The Philosophy of the Founding Fathers," *The Historian* 16 (1954): 142, argues for a profound influence of "the lessons of antiquity."

of a whiggish Clio into "an expression of the American mind"[34] of universal significance. The historical principles of whiggery relating to the right of resistance, royal prerogative, and civil liberty were basic ingredients in the colonial constitutional theory of the pre-Revolutionary period. Americans read history in a highly selective manner, shrewdly sorting out and altering to American requirements whiggish views in support of their doctrines on their rights as Englishmen. They were, as Franklin put it, "Whigs in a Reign when Whiggism is out of Fashion."[35]

34. Jefferson to Richard Henry Lee, May 8, 1825, Washington, ed., *Writings of Jefferson,* VII, 407.

35. Franklin to the Printer of the *Publick Ledger* (London), n.d., Franklin Papers, L, Pt. 1, fol. 8, American Philosophical Society. It might be observed that Benjamin Rush, a personal acquaintance of Mrs. Macaulay and James Burgh, accepted the view in *Cato's Letters* that "in England the whigs in power are always tories, and the tories out of power are always whigs." See Rush to William Gordon, Dec. 10, 1778, Lyman H. Butterfield, ed., *Letters of Benjamin Rush,* 2 vols. (Princeton, 1951), I, 221-22. Reflecting on his experiences in London in 1768 and 1769, Rush decided "the ministry read history not to avoid blunders, but to adopt and imitate them." See "Letters, Facts and Observations upon a variety of subjects," Rush Manuscripts, Library Company of Philadelphia.

The Saxon Myth Dies Hard

F or all its inaccuracies, the interpretation of English history presented by the Real Whigs proved remarkably durable. In the
mid-nineteenth century Americans were praising Algernon Sidney
as "one of the noblest martyrs of that liberty which the progress of
civilization and the developments of time seem to point out as the
heritage of the Anglo-Saxon race."[1] And another scholar carefully
identified the Goths as "the noblest branch of the Caucasian race."
"We are," he added, "their children."[2]

The crux of the whig view was the concept of Germanic superiority and the peculiarly felicitous capacity of the Anglo-Saxon
for democratic ways; these ideas remained popular throughout the
nineteenth century. At the Johns Hopkins University, America's first
great center of graduate study, Herbert Baxter Adams put forward
his germ theory of American history. Keenly alive to "the possibility
of tracing the great stream of American democracy to its earlier English source," Professor Adams asserted that it was from the primitive
Teutonic constitution that American democracy derived.[3] Woodrow

---

1. George Van Santvoord, *Life of Algernon Sidney* (N.Y., 1854), 333.

2. George Perkins Marsh, *The Goths in New-England . . .* (Middlebury, Vt., 1843), 13–
14.

3. W. Stull Holt, ed., *Historical Scholarship in the United States, 1876–1901 As Revealed in
the Correspondence of Herbert B. Adams* (Baltimore, 1938), 113–14.

Wilson, one of Adams's many notable students, commented that the only examples he knew of successful democracy were in governments "begotten of English race," and where "the old Teutonic habit has had the same persistency as in England."[4]

In Berlin, American historian John Burgess, who received his training under the great Rudolf Gneist, learned of "the great struggle for liberty conducted by the English subsequent to the Norman Conquest." Burgess in turn preached Saxon democracy and its moral for Americans.[5] John Fiske's social Darwinism was in the same vein as the Teutonism of Burgess,[6] and evolutionary thought led to a racist adaptation of the whig concept of the noble Saxon. Imperialists reached back into their past, Josiah Strong proclaiming that "the Anglo-Saxon holds in his hands the destinies of mankind." Strong believed Anglo-Saxons "a race of unequaled energy," and representative of "the largest liberty, the purest Christianity, the highest civilizations." In the Darwinian struggle for existence, Strong found the fitter Saxons had survived owing to "their traditions of civil liberty."[7]

In England, the radical Charles Dilke surveyed his world and forecast that the Anglo-Saxon race was the only one which could maintain its freedom.[8] Well-intentioned politicians like Dilke's friend Joseph Chamberlain spoke proudly of "the greatness and importance of the destiny which is reserved for the Anglo-Saxons";[9] he sought to cultivate a union of the Saxon Powers—America, Britain, and Germany. America's Mr. Dooley was sceptical: "You an' me, Hinnisey, has got to bring on this here Anglo-Saxon 'lieance." To Mr. Hennessy's enquiry, Mr. Dooley explained that "an Anglo-Saxon

4. Woodrow Wilson, "Democracy," in *Harper's Encyclopedia of United States History*, 10 vols. (N.Y., 1902).

5. Rudolf Gneist, *The English Parliament* . . . , trans. Jenery Shee (London, 1886), 86.

6. See Julius W. Pratt, *The Expansionists of 1898* . . . (Baltimore, 1936), chap. 1, for a discussion of the views of Fiske, Burgess, and Strong. See also Edward N. Saveth, *American Historians and European Immigrants, 1875-1925* (N.Y., 1948).

7. Josiah Strong, *Our Country* . . . (N.Y., 1885), 179, 174.

8. Sir Charles W. Dilke, *Greater Britain* . . . (London, 1869), v–vi.

9. Joseph Chamberlain, *Foreign and Colonial Speeches* (London, 1897), 6.

is a German that's forgot who was his parents."[10] But in Europe, von Treitschke was both certain and proud of his ancestry and wrote at length of the glories he and his nation derived therefrom. Houston Stewart Chamberlain was sufficiently carried away to propose that Jesus Christ must have been of the Germanic race.[11]

No one factor can explain completely these racial perversions, but apart from the powerful influence of Darwinian thought, some responsibility rests with those major nineteenth-century historians who lent their names to enough of the Saxon myth to dignify its degeneration into racial and nationalistic causes. "The strong man and the strong nation," explained William Stubbs, "feel the pulsation of the past in the life of the present."

According to Bishop Stubbs, "it is to Ancient Germany that we must look for the earliest traces of our forefathers, for the best part of almost all of us originally were German."[12] Stubbs subscribed to the Tacitus interpretation of a noble and democratic Germanic race who transferred their liberal customs to England. Professor Petit-Dutaillis has explained Stubbs's attitude in terms that make the Bishop seem very nationalistic indeed: "He belonged to the liberal generation which had seen and assisted in the attainment of electoral reforms in England. . . . He had formed himself in his youth under the discipline of the patriotic German scholars who saw in the primitive German institutions the source of all human independence. He thought he saw in the development of the English Constitution the magnificent and unique expansion of those germs of self-government, and England was for him the messenger of liberty to the world."[13]

Historians like Edward Freeman, John Green, John Kemble, and

---

10. Finley Peter Dunne, *Mr. Dooley in Peace and War* (Boston, 1909), 54.

11. Houston Stewart Chamberlain, *The Foundations of the Nineteenth Century* (London, 1911); see Arnold J. Toynbee, *A Study of History,* 12 vols. (London, 1948–61), I, 207–71, for a study and discussion of racial and environmental factors in civilizations.

12. William Stubbs, *Lectures on Early English History,* ed. Arthur Hassall (London, 1906), 2–12.

13. Charles Petit-Dutaillis, *Studies and Notes Supplementary to Stubbs' Constitutional History* (Manchester, 1908), xii–xiii.

even Henry Adams joined Bishop Stubbs in his conviction that the Anglo-Saxons had enjoyed a democratic society. Henry Adams was deeply interested in "the primitive popular assembly, parliament, law-court and army in one; which embraced every free man, rich or poor." He noted how "among all German races, none have clung with sturdier independence or more tenacious conservatism to their ancient customs and liberties, than the great Saxon confederation."[14] Tacitus remained a largely unquestioned source. A nonfeudal land tenure and the elective German kingship were carried from the Saxon woods to England to bless that island until the arrival of the Normans. Late-nineteenth-century scholars had relatively few doubts on this subject.

Carl Stephenson has commented that to accept the nineteenth-century interpretation of Anglo-Saxon society, a historian had "first to read into comparatively late sources a meaning which they never had and then apply that misinterpretation to an imaginary society of a thousand years earlier."[15] Tacitus has received a closer examination today. Scholars now agree that the *Germania* depicted a warrior peasant far different from that claimed by the whig historians. Tacitus described the German people as dominated by a class of warriors who saw agriculture as degrading for them personally and lived off the produce of the lower peasants. Tacitus may have found the Germans a happy contrast to contemporary Rome, but Saxon society was certainly not the democratic one envisaged by Jefferson and the whigs. As a society, in fact, the Saxon was less agrarian than military, and the personal tie which bound peasant to lord involved the performance of a customary service nearly as rigid as that brought in by the Normans. On the credit side for the whigs, it must be emphasized that there was no professional class of knights sustained by military benefices in pre-Conquest England.

The true meaning of the term *witan* eluded the early historians:

14. Henry Adams, *Essays in Anglo-Saxon Law* (Boston, 1876), 1, 6.
15. Carl Stephenson, "The Problem of the Common Man in Early Medieval Europe," *American Historical Review* 51 (1946): 419.

Sir Frank Stenton claims the Saxon councils were composed, not of all classes, but of the upper ranks of the aristocracy, along with ecclesiastics when the church became established. The best that Stenton has found is "the character of a constitutional monarchy," which was "extremely narrow in form."[16]

Other features of the whig interpretation have also been subjected to reexamination. The idea of the breach in English historical development occasioned by the Norman Conquest was less popular in the nineteenth than in the eighteenth century. Stubbs began the emancipation from this broken-continuity concept of the whigs, and his influence is evident in Stenton, although such notable scholars as J. H. Round and G. B. Adams continued to argue that the Conquest did interrupt English historical development.

In G. B. Adams's view the English constitution rested wholly upon the feudal foundations laid by the Normans. The Saxons had been approaching a feudalistic state before the Conquest, but "beneath the superficial similarity, there was a great difference." According to Adams, the Normans possessed a more centralized absolutism and imposed this upon the Saxons; he explained the similar legislative machinery that ensued as due to the Saxon Chronicles' habit of persistently calling the Norman *curia regis* by the old name of witenagemot. The real institutional difference, Adams insisted, was very wide, despite this feudalistic similarity. But there was no real compromise with the whig interpretation: "The origin of the English limited monarchy is to be sought not in the primitive German state, nor in the idea of an elective monarchy or a coronation oath, nor in the survival of institutions of local freedom to exert increasing influence on the central government."[17]

16. Frank M. Stenton, *Anglo-Saxon England* (Oxford, Eng., 1947), 546. At the beginning of the twentieth century, H. Munro Chadwick conducted a scholarly analysis the findings of which were in direct contrast to those of Stubbs, Freeman, et al. See his *Studies on Anglo-Saxon Institutions* and *The Origin of the English Nation* (Cambridge, Eng., 1905, 1907).

17. George Burton Adams, *The Origin of the English Constitution* (New Haven, 1912), 3 n, 79, 185.

Today the prevailing tendency is to view the post-1066 Anglo-Norman state as unique, the result of many antecedents, Saxon, Flemish, Danish, and Breton.[18] Most of the later features of whig history have been explored and revealed as false oversimplifications which endured because people wanted to believe. The myth of Magna Charta has been attacked by scholars distressed over extravagant claims made on its behalf. The feudal character of the document is now widely recognized. Its limitations may be disputed, but no longer in the political language of the 1680s.[19] Most scholars see the Charter as a grant of privileges on the part of King John to the freemen of England and agree that it could not apply to the mass of a people still thoroughly servile.[20] As Faith Thompson has commented, the famous Charter which was so important to seventeenth- and eighteenth-century lawyers and historians "meant many things to many groups, varying greatly from age to age in actual content [meaning] and realistic value."[21]

Certainly few whig writers underestimated the Charter's significance as a support for their claims. But, according to Professor Herbert Butterfield, such "wrong history" may well have been of great political advantage to England, if not to her historical erudition. Whig writers, by providing liberty with the steadying alliance of history and tradition, performed a service that the French (for example) sadly lacked. Revolts in England have been relatively quiet and sober affairs. At least a partial explanation is the manner in which the whig historians brought history, with its substantiation of man's

18. See, for example, H. R. Loyn, *Anglo-Saxon England and the Norman Conquest* (London, 1962), chap. 1.

19. See William Sharp McKechnie, *Magna Carta, A Commentary on the Great Charter of King John . . .* , 2d ed. (Glasgow, 1914); Max Radin, "The Myth of Magna Carta," *Harvard Law Review* 60 (1947): 1060–91; S. B. Chrimes, *English Constitutional Ideas in the Fifteenth Century* (Cambridge, Eng., 1936), xvii.

20. Carl Stephenson, *Medieval History . . .* (N.Y., 1955), 556.

21. Faith Thompson, *Magna Carta,* 375.

rights, to the aid of political radicalism. Thus neither Englishmen at home or in America underwent the rigors known to France between 1789–93.[22] Viewed in this light, it is possibly the world's misfortune that myths are becoming intellectual curiosities.

22. Butterfield, *Englishman and His History*, 7.

History in the Colonial Library

The listings which follow can assist in charting the historio-graphical environment of the American colonists and the character of their historical resources. Although these lists are samples only, even this partial survey should supply the flavor of the colonists' interest in history and the nature of their reading. The frequency with which a given title recurs does not prove much in isolation; a book which crops up rarely may yet be of startling significance to a Thomas Jefferson or a Richard Bland. Nevertheless, the lists serve as a rough indication of the colonists' common exposure when seeking historical knowledge.

In some instances, however, the lists make a point of their own. David Hall's orders to William Strahan reflect how the market for history books was enlarging. The catalogues of the Library Company of Philadelphia show the persisting interests of the stockholders in history. And Jefferson's book lists, with their repetition of titles, show his enduring attachment to particular history books.

The lists include some works which might not be catalogued as history today, but which nevertheless had a historical significance for eighteenth-century colonists. There may be special meaning in the frequent priority accorded Sidney's *Discourses* over Locke's *Treatises on Civil Government*. While these lists accurately reflect the colonial absorption in English history, they also confirm the availability of diversified histories dealing with revolutions and, as Edwin Wolf has put it, "the mutability of kings and states." The popularity of Abbé Vertot is particularly eloquent testimony to this interest. A comparable reading of the English governing classes at this same period might throw additional light on Anglo-American misunderstandings.

The form of the listings below follows substantially the form employed in the original, and where the identity of a book remains obvious, the original misspellings and minor title variations are retained. For purposes of typographical clarity, there is an effort at consistent italicizing of titles, which was not the case in the originals. Entries marked with an asterisk have not been identified.

The entries are grouped under geographical categories: New England; New York, New Jersey, and Pennsylvania; and the Southern Colonies.

I. COLLEGE CATALOGUES
A. Harvard College

I. LIBRARY CATALOGUE OF 1723

Clarendon's *History of the Rebellion*
Coke's *Institutes*
Cambden's *Britannia*
Harrington's *Oceana*
Rushworth's *Historical Collections*
John Speed's *History of Great Britain*
Potter's *Greek Antiquities*

2. ADDED BETWEEN 1725 AND 1735

Burnet: *History of Own Time*
Selden's *Works*
Tyrril's *History of England*
Rapin's *History of England*

3. ADDED BY 1773

James Burgh: *Dignity of Human Nature*
Cato's Letters
Echard's *Ecclesiastical History*
Gordon's *Tacitus*
    "   *Sallust,* with Cicero's Orations against Cataline.
Hampden's Tryal
David Hume's *History of England* 6 v.
[White] Kennett's *Complete History of England* 3 v. fol.
Basil Kennett: *Roman Antiquities*
John Locke: All his works. 3 v. fol.
Ludlow's *Memoirs*
Catherine Macaulay's *History of England* 5 v.
Milton: All his works
Molesworth: *Account of Denmark and Sweden*
William Molyneux: *Case of Ireland, being bound by the Parliament of England*
Edw[ard] W. Montagu: *Rise and Fall of Republicks*
Montesquieu, *Oeuvres*
Henry Neville *on Government*
John Oldmixon, *History of England*
Puffendorf: *History of Sweden*
    "   *Law of Nature and Nations*
    "   *Intro. to the History of Europe*
William Robertson: *History of Scotland*
    "   "   *History of the Emperor Charles V.*
Rollin's *Roman History*
Rycaut's *Ottoman Empire*
Temple Stanyan's *Greek History*
Sydney *on Government*
Sir William Temple's *Works*
James Tyrrel *on the Ancient Constitution of the English Government.* fol.

4. ADDED BETWEEN 1773 AND 1790

William Guthrie's *General History of England* 3 v.
Hottoman's (Fr.) *Franco Gallia* two editions: 1573 and 1586

A second set of Hume's *History of England* 1786

Three editions of Catherine Macaulay's *History of England:* 2 v. 1763, 5 v.
1776, 4 v. 1769

[Second copy of] Molesworth's *Account of Denmark* (both 1738 editions)

[Second set of] Rapin's *History of England* (first, 1726, second, 1732)

Roger Acherley: *Brittanic Constitution* 1741

      "   "   *Free Parliaments* 1731

Nathaniel Bacon: *Historical & political discourse on the laws.* . . . 1760 edn.

      "   "   *Discourse of the uniformity of the govt. of England* 1647
edn.

Rob. Brady: *A ful & clear answ. to a book written by W. Petit esq.* 1681

James Burgh: *Political Disquisitions* London 1774 2 sets.

Dalrymple: *Essay towards a general hist. of feudal property in Eng.* 1759

Ellys: *Tracts on Liberty* 1765

[Henry] Care *British Liberties, with an essay on political Liberty and view of
the constitution of Great-Britain* London 1766

J. Locke: *Two Treatises on govt.* London 1698 & 6th ed. 1764 2 sets.

M. Nedham: *Excellencie of a Free State* London 1767 2 copies

H[enry] Nevil: *Plato Redivivus* London, 1681, 1698, 1763. 3 copies.

Wm Petit: *Ancient Right of the commons of Eng. asserted* 1680

Granville Sharp *Declaration of the People's Right* 1775

Algernon Sidney: *Discourses concerning govt.* London 1751, 1763. 2 copies.

Samuel Squire: *Enquiry into the foundation of the english constitution.*

G[ilbert] Stuart: *Dissertation concerning antiquity of the English constitution*
London, 1753

      "   "   *Historical Essay on the english constitution* Lond. 1771 [1]

Frank Sullivan: *Lectures on the feudal law* London, 1772.

J. Tyrrell: *Bibliotheca politica* London, 1727

Walter Moyle: *Works,* 2 v. London, 1726; 3 v. London, 1726, 1727. 2 sets.

Wm. Temple: *Observations on the United Netherlands* London, 1690.

      "   "   *Works* London, 1720; London, 1740. 2 sets.

John Wilkes *North Briton,* 2 v. London, 1763

---

1. This item was not Stuart's but the anonymously published essay now ascribed to
Obadiah Hulme. It was a similar error — in favor of Allan Ramsay — which attracted sufficient notice at Columbia, later, to be copied generally.

B. Yale College

1. LIBRARY CATALOGUE OF 1743

Puffendorf's *History of Europe*
Cambden's *Brittania* 2 v. fol.
Rushworth's *Historical Collections*
Clarendon's *History of the Rebellion*
Sir Thomas Smith's *de Republica Anglorum*
Buchanani Rerum Scotarum fol.
Echard's *Roman History* 5 v.
Taciti Opera 2 v.
Potter's *Greek Antiquities*

2. ADDED BY 1755

Raleigh's *History of the World*
*The History of King Henry VII**
   "   "   "   " *Charles I**
   "   "   "   " *Charles II**
   "   "   " *Oliver Cromwell**
   "   "   " *King William III**
   "   "   " *Queen Anne**
Ricaut's *Turkish History*
Sir William Temple's *Works* 2 v. fol.
The Antient and Modern Whigg

3. ADDED BY 1791

Macaulay's *History of England* 5 v.

C. The College of New Jersey

LIBRARY CATALOGUE OF JANUARY 29, 1760

Burnet's *History of his own Times*
   "   *History of the Reformation*
Clarendon's *History of the Rebellion* 6 v.
Cato's Letters
Eachard's *Eccleciastical History* 2 v.
   "   *Roman History* 5 v.

*History of the House of the Stewarts**
Puffendorf's *Introduction to the History of Europe*
Potter's *Antiquities of Greece* 2 v.
Rapin's *History of England*, with Tindal's *Continuation*. 5 v. 3 sets in all.
Sidney *on Government*
Tacitus, Englished by several Hands, 3 v.
Sir William Temple, *Letters & Observations on the United Provinces* 3 v.

D. Rhode Island College

LIBRARY CATALOGUE OF 1782

Oldmixon's *History of England*
Clarendon's *History of the Rebellion*
Burnet's *History of his own Times*
Universal History 8 v.
Robertson's *History of Scotland* 2 v.
Mrs. Macaulay's *History of England* 3 v.
Puffendorf's *History*

II. SOCIAL OR PUBLIC LIBRARIES

A. New England

1. SAYBROOK, LYME AND GUILFORD, CONNECTICUT

Library Catalogue, 1737

Burnet's *History of his own Time*
Camden's *Britannia*
Locke *on Education*
Rollin's *Ancient History*
Rapin's *History of England*

2. REDWOOD-LIBRARY, NEWPORT, RHODE ISLAND

Library Catalogue, 1750

Acherley's *Britannic Constitution*
Burnet's *History of the Reformation* 3 v.
    " *History of His own Times* 2 v.

Camden's *Britannia* 2 v.
Hale's *Pleas of the Crown*
Hawkin's *Pleas of the Crown*
Kennet's *History of England* 3 v.
Locke's *Works* 3 v.
Rawleigh's *History of the World*
Rapin's *History of England* 2 v. fol.
Tindal's *Continuation of Rapin* 3 v.
Selden's *Works* 6 v. (in Latin)
Spelman's *Works* (in English)
Temple's *Works* 2 v.
Buchanan's *History of Scotland* 3 v.
Puffendorf's *History of Sweden*
Voltaire's *History of Charles XII*
Molesworth's *Account of Denmark and Sweden*
Echard's *Ecclesiastical History* 2 v.
Potter's *Antiquities of Greece*

3. PROVIDENCE LIBRARY, PROVIDENCE, RHODE ISLAND

Library Catalogue, 1768

Bolingbroke's *Letters on History*
     "   *Letters on Patriotism*
Buchanan's *History of Scotland*
Burnet's *History of the Reformation*
  "   *History of His Own Times*
Clarendon's *History of the Rebellion*
Echard's *Roman History*
Gordon's *Tacitus* 5 v.
    "   *Sallust*
Hume's *History of the Stuarts*
Life of Alfred
Locke's *Works* 3 v.
Ludlow's *Memoirs*
Machiavel's *Works*
Modern Universal History

Molesworth's *History of Denmark*
Montague *on Ancient Republics*
Plutarch's *Lives*
Puffendorf's *History of Sweden*
     "   *Intro. to History of Europe*
Raleigh's *History* abridged
Rapin's *History of England* 21 vol.
Ricaut's *History of the Turks*
Rise and Fall of the Romans, by Montesquieu
Rollin's *Ancient History*
Montesquieu *Spirit of Laws*
Temple's *Works* 2 v.

B. New York, New Jersey, and Pennsylvania

I. NEW YORK SOCIETY LIBRARY

Library Catalogue, 1754

Buchanan's *History of Scotland*
Guthrie's *History of England*
Harrington's *Oceana*
Locke's *Works* 3 v.
Ludlow's *Memoirs*
Rapin's *History of England*
Rushworth's *Historical Collections*
Sidney *on Government*
Tyrrel's *History of England* 5 v.
Temple's *Works* 2 v.
Vertot's *Revolutions of Sweden*
     "   "   " *Spain*
     "   "   " *Rome*
     "   "   " *Portugal*
Smollett's *History of England* 3 v.
Bolingbroke *on Patriotism*
     "   *Works* 5 v.
Gordon's *Tacitus* 4 v.
Rollin's *Roman History* 2 sets

Burnet's *History of his own Times*
Cato's *Letters* 4 v.
Independent Whig 4 v.

2. BURLINGTON, NEW JERSEY, LIBRARY COMPANY

Library Catalogue, 1758

Sidney, *Discourses on Government* fol.
Rapin's *History of England* 2 v. fol. 1743
Independent Whig 4 copies
Cato's *Letters* 4 v. 1737
Henry Care's *English Liberties* 5th ed. 2 copies
Burgh's *Britain's Remembrancer* 7th ed., 1748
Burnet's *History of His Own Time* 4 v. London, 1753
Edmund Ludlow, *Memoirs* 3rd ed., 3 v. Edinburgh, 1751

3. LIBRARY COMPANY OF PHILADELPHIA

a. *Library Catalogue, 1733*[2]

The Annals and History of Tacitus, translated by Mr. Gordon. 2 v. 1728
Wood's *Institutes of the Laws of England* 1728
Sidney's *Discourses on Government* 1704
Puffendorf's *Law of Nature and Nations,* translated by Basil Kennett, 1729
      "   *Introduction to the History of the principal Kingdoms and States of Europe* 1728
De Rapin Thoyras, *The History of England* 15 v. 1731
Vertot, *The History of the Revolutions that happened in the Government of the Roman Republick* 2 v. 1732
    "   *The History of the Revolution in Sweden* 1729
    "   *The History of the Revolutions in Spain* 5 v. 1724
    "   *The Revolutions of Portugal* 1724
    "   *A Critical History of the Establishment of the Bretons among the Gauls* 2 v. 1722

---

2. This initial catalogue no longer exists, and the following historical selection is drawn from the compilation by Edwin Wolf 2nd. Catalogues were published in 1735, 1741, 1746, 1757, 1764, 1770, and 1775.

Plutarch's *Lives* 8 v. 1727

Chevalier Ramsay, *The Travels of Cyrus* 2 v. 1728

De Voltaire, *The History of Charles XII King of Sweden* 1732

Joseph Addison, *Miscellaneous Works* 3 v. 1726

b. *Added by 1764*

Camden's *Britannia* 2 v.

Harrington's *Oceana* 1737

Temple's *Works* 2 v. 1738

Locke's *Works* 3 v. 1740

Rushworth's *Collections* 1721

Acherley's *Britannic Constitution* 1727

Raleigh's *History of the World* 2 v. 1733

Rycaut's *Ottoman Empire*

Burnet's *History of his Own Time* 2 v. 1734

William Robertson's *History of Scotland* 2 v. 1759

David Hume, *History of England . . . to 1688* 6 v. 1762

Molesworth, *Account of Denmark* 1738 Second copy, 1694

Hotman, *Franco-Gallia,* translated by Molesworth 1721

Potter, *Antiquities of Greece*

Rollin, *Roman History* 10 v. 1744

Clarendon, *History of the Rebellion* 2 v. 1720 2 sets

Buchanan's *History of Scotland* 2 v. 1733

Temple Stanyan, *Grecian History* 2 v. 1739

Walter Moyle, *Works* 2 v. 1726

Bolingbroke, *Dissertation on Parties* 1743

Thornhagh Gurdon, *History of the High Court of Parliament* 2 v. 1731

Care's *English Liberties* 1719

Locke's *Treatises on Government* 1698

John Chamberlayne, *The Present State of Great Britain* 1729

Verstegan, *Restitution of Decayed Antiquities* Antwerp, 1605

Bolingbroke, *Letters on the Study and Use of History* 2 v. 1752

Tacitus, *Works,* translated by Thomas Gordon. 2nd ed., 4 v. 1737

Samuel Puffendorf, *Compleat History of Sweden* London, 1702

E. W. Montagu, *Reflections on the Rise and Fall of the antient Republics* 1759

John Dalrymple, *History of Feudal Property* 3d. ed., 1758

Independent Whig 3 v. 1735

Cato's Letters 4 v.

c. Added by 1770

N[athaniel] Bacon's *Discourses of the Laws and Government of England* 5th ed. 1760

Care's *British [sic] Liberties* 1767

Burgh's *Dignity of Human Nature*

Wharton *True Briton* 2 v. 1723

Milton, *History of England* 1677

Echard, *History of England*

Mascou, *History of the ancient Germans* 2 v. 1738

Sidney, *Discourses on Government* 2 v. 1750

Ellis: *Liberty of Subjects in England* 1765 *Tracts on Liberty*

Ludlow: *Memoirs* 3 v. 1698

Macaulay: *History of England* 4 v. 1767

Robertson's *History of Scotland* 4th ed. 1761

Temple's *Works* 4 v. 1757

Warner's *History of Civil War in Ireland* 2d ed. vol. 1 only 1768

Rapin's *History of England* 1st ed., 30 v. 1728; 4th ed., 21 v. 1757

d. Added by 1775

Robertson's *History of Charles V.* 3 v. Robert Bell's Philadelphia edition

Allan Ramsay *An Essay on the Constitution of England* 1766

[Obadiah Hulme] *An Historical Essay on the English Constitution* London, 1771. "Where Annual Election Ends, There Slavery Begins."

Molyneux, *The Case of Ireland being bound by Acts of Parliament, Stated* London, 1770

Francis Sullivan, *History of Feudal Law* London, 1772

4. UNION LIBRARY COMPANY OF PHILADELPHIA

a. Library Catalogue, 1754

Raleigh's *History of the World*
Puffendorf's *Introduction to the History of Europe*
Tacitus, *Annals* 3 v. London, 1698. "Made *English* by several Hands."
Temple's *Introduction to the History of England* 2 v. London, 1699
Vertot: *History of the Revolution in Sweden*
　　　　 "　　　 "　 "　 "　　　 "　　 "　*Roman Republic*
　　　　 "　　　 "　 "　 "　　　 "　　 "　*Portugal*
Locke's *Human Understanding* London, 1748
　　　 "　 *Thoughts concerning Education* London, 1696
Rapin: *History of England* 28 v. London, 1728
Buchanan's *History of Scotland* 2 v. 1738
Henry Care: *English Liberties* 4th ed. London, 1719
Independent Whig 7th ed., 3 v. London, 1743. 2 sets.
Molesworth, *Account of Denmark,* 5th ed., London, 1745
Cato's Letters, 4 v. London, 1724

b. Added by 1765

Kennet: *Antiquities of Rome* 3 sets.
Burnet's *Abridgement of his own times:* also unabridged in 4 v.
Rushworth's *Collections* 1659 2 sets.
Smollett's *History of England*
Sidney's *Discourses*
Temple's *Observations on the United Provinces*

5. ASSOCIATION LIBRARY COMPANY OF PHILADELPHIA

Library Catalogue, 1765

Cato's Letters
Guthrie's *History of England*
Gordon's *Annals of Tacitus*
Clarendon's *History of the Rebellion*
Vertot: *Revolutions of Sweden*
　　　 "　　　 "　　 "　*Portugal*
Buchanan's *History of Scotland*

Independent Whig
Locke's *Works*
Smollet, *History of England*
Warner's *History of Ireland*

6. JULIANA LIBRARY-COMPANY, LANCASTER, PENNSYLVANIA

Library Catalogue, 1766

Rapin's *History of England & Continuation* 1743, 1758
Cambden's *Britannia*
Sidney's *Discourses on Government* 1751
Locke's *Essay concerning Human Understanding* 2 v. 1753
Kennet's *Antiquities of Rome* 1717
Molesworth's *Account of Denmark* 1694
Bolingbroke: *Letters on Patriotism & Parties* 1749
Temple's *Observations on the United Provinces* 1705
Locke, *On Education* 1752
   "   *Two Treatises on Government* 1713 (Given by Mr. Christopher Marshall)
Rollin's *Roman History* 16 v. Dublin, 1740

C. The Southern Colonies

1. CHARLESTOWN LIBRARY SOCIETY

a. *Library Catalogue, 1750*

Acherley's *Britannic Constitution*
Nathaniel Bacon's *Discourse on the Laws and Government of England*
Burnet's *Hist. of His Own Times*
Harrington, *Oceana*
Rapin's *History of England,* and Tindal's *Continuation*
Milton's *Works*
Clarendon's *History of the Civil Wars*
Hakwell's *Modus Tenendi Parliamentum*
Independent Whig 4 v.
[Montagu?] *Reflections on the Grandeur and Decension of the Romans*
Clarke's *Essay upon Study*
Rollin's *Antient History*

257

Cato's Letters 4 v.

Gordon's *Sallust*

Rollin's *Roman History*

Gordon's *Tacitus*

Kennett's *Antiquities of Rome*

Vertot, *Revolutions in Rome*

    "   *Revolutions in Sweden*

Hale's *Original Institution of Parliaments*

Bolingbroke's *Dissertation on Parties*

Locke's *Works* 3 v.

Raleigh's *History of the World* 2 v. 2 sets

Potter's *Antiquities of Greece*

Montesquieu's *Spirit of Laws* 2 v.

Fortescue, *The Difference between an absolute and limited Monarchy*

Atkyan's *Parliamentary Tracts*

Petyt's *Ancient Right of the Commons*

b. *Catalogue, 1770 (As above, but added:)*

Rushworth's *Historical Collections*

Temple's *Works*

Bolingbroke's *Works* 1754 5 v.

Blackstone's *Commentaries* 4 v. Oxford, 1768

Hume's *History of England* 6 v. 1762

Robertson's *History of Scotland* 1759

    "   *Reign of Charles V* 3 v. 1769

Smollett's *History of England* 4 v. 1757

Warner's *History of rebellion and civil wars in Ireland* 1767

Bolingbroke's *Letters on Study and Use of History* 2 v. 1752

Fletcher (of Salton) *Political Works* 1732

Goldsmith's *Roman History* 1769

Hotoman's *Franco-Gallia* 1721

Horn's *Mirror of Justices* 1768

Hakewell's *Modus Tenendi* 1671

Montague *on ancient republicks* 1760

Molesworth's *Account of Denmark*

Petyt's *Ancient Right of the Commons* 1680

Samuel Squire's *Enquiry into the Foundation of the English Constitution* 1745

Sidney's *Discourses on Government* 2 v. Edinburgh, 1750

Dalrymple *Feudal Property* 1759

Macaulay's *History of England* 1769

Stanyan's *Grecian History* 1751

III. PRIVATE LIBRARIES

A. New England

1. SAMUEL LEE, BOSTON

Library Catalogue, 1693 (MS in Massachusetts Historical Society)

Raleigh's *History of the World*

Langhorn's *Introduction to the History of England*

Petit's *Ancient Right of the Commons of England*

Tacitus

2. GEORGE CURWIN, "LATE OF SALEM"

Auction List, 1718 (Photostat in Historical Society of Pennsylvania)

Care's *English Liberties*

Sir William Temple's *History of the Netherlands*

Potter's *Antiquities of Greece*

3. JOHN ADAMS, BOSTON

a. Library Catalogue, 1790 (MS in Massachusetts Historical Society)

Acherley, *Brittannic Constitution*

Blackstone's *Commentaries*

      "   *Law Tracts*

Coke's *Institutes*

    "   *Reports*

Hale's *History of the Pleas of the Crown* 2 copies

Hawkins' *Pleas of the Crown*

Montesquieu, *Spirit of Laws*

Puffendorf, *Law of Nature and Nations* 1729
Rushworth's *Historical Collections* 2 sets
Seldeni, *Opera*
Sharpe's *Declaration of the People's Rights*
Wood's *Institutes*
Burnet's *History of his own time* 2 sets
Buchanan's *historia Scot*
Caesar's *Commentaries*
Clarendon's *History of the Rebellion*
Davila's *Civil wars of france*
Echard's *Roman History*
Guiccardini's *History of Italy*
Gordon's *Tacitus* 2 sets
    "   *Sallust*
Hume's *History of England* 8 v.
Rollin's *Histoire Romaine* 16 v.
Littleton's *History of Henry II* 6 v.
Ludlow's *Memoirs* 3 v. only
[Blackburne, ed.,] *Memoirs of Thomas Hollis*
Macaulay's *History of England* 5 v.
Machiavel's *Works* 4 v.
Molesworth's *Account of Denmark*
Plutarch, *Lives* 5 v.
    "   *Oeuvres*
    "   *Opera*
Potter's *Antiquities of Greece* 2 sets
Puffendorf, *History of Sweden* 1702
Robertson's *History of Scotland* 2 sets
Sheridan's *History of Revolution in Sweden*
Smollett's *History of England* 16 v.
Temple's *Observations on the United Provinces*
Tacitus *on Germany.* Aikin.
Tyrrell's *History of England.* 1st and 5th vols. only
Temple's *Works* 1st vol.
Harrington's *Works* 2 sets

Bolingbroke, *Letters on Patriotism*

Locke *on Government* 1694

Milton's *historical political & miscellaneous Works* 3 v. fol.

Montagu *on Republics*

Burgh *Political disquisitions.* 2 v. 3rd vol. missing. [Presentation copies from the author.]

Sidney *on Government* 2 v.

Addison's *Works* 4 v.

Locke's *Works* 3 v. fol.

Bolinbroke's *Works* 11 v.

b. *Added between 1790 and 1826* [3]

John Cartwright, *The English Constitution* 1823 2 copies, sent by the author

Cato's Letters

Edward Spelman, *Roman Antiquities* 1768

Sir John Fortescue, *De Laudibus legum Angliae*

John Gillies, *History of Ancient Greece* 1786 2 v.

Thomas Gordon, *A Cordial for Low Spirits* 3 v. 1743

Gordon and Trenchard, *Independent Whig* 2 v. 1782

Kames's *Historical Law Tracts* 1761

     "   *British Antiquities* 1763

John Jebb, *Works* ed. John Disney 1787 3 v.

Marchamont Nedham, *Excellencie of a free state* 1747 Gift from Brand Hollis

Henry Neville, *Plato Redivivus* 1681. Gift from Brand Hollis

John Oldmixon, *History of England* 1730

Rapin's *History of England* 1732–33 2 v. fol.

---

3. The Adams books are mainly distributed among three repositories: the Stone Library back of the Adams mansion at Quincy; the Boston Athenaeum; most are at the Boston Public Library. The BPL issued a catalogue of its holdings of Adams books in 1917; in 1938 Henry Adams and Worthington C. Ford issued *A Catalogue of the Books of John Quincy Adams Deposited in the Boston Athenaeum,* which identified the books of John Adams and indicates when they have his marginal comments. It would seem that several of the following works were in Adams's hands in the 1770s and 1780s, and he failed to list them in his 1790 catalogue.

Robertson, *History of the reign of Charles V* 1777
Rollin, *Ancient History*
John Somers's *The Judgement of whole kingdoms* 12th ed. Boston, 1774

B. New York and Pennsylvania

I. JOHN MONTGOMERY, NEW YORK

Sale List of Library, 1732 (MS in New York Public Library)

Clarendon's *History*
Rushworth's *Collections*
[Sir William Temple?] *History of Holland*
Vertot, *Revolutions of Rome*
    "   *History of Malta*
    "   *History of Spain*
    "   *Revolutions of Sweden*
    "   *Revolutions of Portugal*
    "   *Revolutions d'Angleterre*
History of Greece
Caesar's Commentaries
Tacitus
Sallust
Harrington's *Works*
Tyrrell's *General History of England*
Raleigh's *History of the World*
Sir William Temple's *Works*
Milton's *Works*
Sidney *On Government*
Ludlow's *Memoirs*
True Brittain Philip, Duke of Wharton
Locke's *Works*
Cato's Letters
Ricaut's *Ottoman Empire*
Rapin's *History of England*
Baker's *Chronicle*
Moyle's *Works*
History of Charles V William Robertson

2. JAMES LOGAN, PHILADELPHIA

Library Catalogue, 1760 (MS in the Library Company of Philadelphia)

Burnet's *History of the Reformation*
Brady, *Introduction to old English History* 1684
   "   *Complete History of England* 2 v. 1685
Buchanan, *Opera* Edinburgh, 1715
Camden: *Britannia*
Herbert: *Henry VII* 1672
Harrington: *Oceana* 1656
Rapin: *History of England* 2 v. 1732
Paul Rycaut: *Present State of the Ottoman Empire* 1670
John Speed: *History of Great-Britain*
Tacitus: *Opera* Antwerp, 1607
James Tyrell: *General History of England* 1700
Bullstrode Whitlocke: *History of England* 1713
   "   "   *Memorials* 1682
Davila: *Historia delle Guerre civili di Francia* in lione, 1641
Guiccardini: *Historia d'Italia* Venice, 1589 2 v.
Vertot: *Histoire des Revolutions de la Republique Romaine* Lay Haye, 1724
Buchanan: *De jure regni apud Scotos* 1594
Clarendon: *History of the Rebellion* 1705 6 v.
Molesworth: *Account of Denmark* 1694
Echard: *Roman History* 1695 2 v.
Hotoman: *Franco-Gallia* 1665
Ludlow: *Memoirs*
Potter's *Antiquities of Greece* 1722 2 v.
Puffendorf: *Introduction to the History of Europe* 1728
   "   *Present State of Germany* 1696
Raleigh: *History of the World,* abridged 1698
Sir William Temple: *Observations upon the Provinces of the Netherlands*
   1673
Vertot: *History of Revolutions in Sweden* 1721
   "   *History of Revolutions in Portugal*
Spelman's *Posthumous Works* Oxford, 1698
Selden's *Opera* 3 v. 1726

3. BENJAMIN RUSH, PHILADELPHIA

Library Catalogue, 1790 (MS in the Library Company of Philadelphia)

Rollin's *Roman History*
Goldsmith's *Roman History*
Rappin *History of England*
Universal History
Macaulay's *History of England*
Robertson's *History of Charles the Vth*
Goldsmith's *History of England*
De Lolme's *English Constitution*
Political Disquisitions James Burgh
Harrington, *Oceana*
Vertot, *Revolutions of Portugal*
Sharp's *Declaration of the People's Rights*
Bolingbroke's *Letters on Patriotism*
Kennett's *Antiquities*
Tacitus, *Opera*

C. The Southern Colonies

1. ROBERT "KING" CARTER, COROTOMAN,
LANCASTER COUNTY, VIRGINIA

Library Catalogue, 1732 (Louis B. Wright, "The Gentleman's Library in Early Virginia," Huntington Library Quarterly, 1 [1937], 3-61)

Coke *on Littleton* 1628
Coke's *Institutes*
Nathaniel Bacon, *An Historical & Political Discourse* 1689
Sidney's *Discourses* 1698
Baker's *Chronicles* 1643
Burnet's *History of his Own Time* 1724–34
Camden's *Britannia* 1586
Clarendon's *History of the Rebellion* 1702–4
Echard's *Roman History* 1698–99
Sir William Temple, *Introduction to the History of England* 1695
Ludlow's *Memoirs* 1698–99

Puffendorf's *Introduction to the history of Europe* 1699
Rushworth's *Historical Collections* 1680–1701
Rapin's *History of England* 15 v. 1725–31
Tacitus, *Works,* translated by Thomas Gordon 1728–31

2. WILLIAM DUNLOP, PRINCE WILLIAM COUNTY, VIRGINIA

"William Dunlop's Library" May 25, 1740 (William and Mary College
Quarterly, *1st Ser., 15 [1907], 275–79)*

Rapin *History of England*
Burnet's *History of his Own Time*
Temple's *Works*
    " 　*Memoirs*
Rollin's *Historie Ancienne*

3. WILLIAM BYRD II, WESTOVER, CHARLES CITY COUNTY, VIRGINIA

(Byrd died in 1744, and the catalogue of his library was compiled subsequently;
MS in the Library Company of Philadelphia)

Brady's *History of England*
Baker's *Chronicle*
Cambden's *Britannia*
Harrington's *Oceana*
Clarendon's *History of the Rebellion*
Ludlow's *Memoirs*
Molesworth's *Account of Denmark*
Temple's *Memoirs*
Milton's *History of England*
Echard's *History of the Revolution*
Potter's *Antiquities of Greece*
Vertot's *Revolutions of Sweden*
Rushworth's *Historical Collections* 7 vol.
Kames's *Antiquities of England British Antiquities*
Coke's *Institutes*
Bracton, *de Legibus*
Seldeni, *Fleta*
Fortescue's *Laws of England*

Mirror of Justice [Andrew Horn?]

Hale's *Common Law*

Henry Care's *English Liberty* 2 copies

Bolingbroke *Dissertation upon Parties*

James Burgh *Britain's Remembrancer*

Locke *on Government*

Tacitus *Opera* 4 vol.

4. "COUNCILLOR" ROBERT CARTER, NOMINI HALL,
WESTMORELAND COUNTY, VIRGINIA

Library Catalogue, 1772 (William and Mary College Quarterly, *1st Ser., 10 [1902], 232–41; 11 [1903], 21–28; grandson of "King" Carter, "Councillor" Carter died in 1804; he had over 1500 volumes in his library by 1774.)*

Postlethwayt's *Dictionary of Trade and Commerce*

Locke's *Works* 3 v.

Temple's *Works* 2 v.

Ackerley's *Britannick Constitution*

Spelman's *Works*

Bacon's *Government Historical Discourse*

Raleigh's *History of the World*

Cooke *on Littleton*

Sidney *on Government*

Blackstone's *Commentaries*

Universal History 21 v. & supplement

Bolingbroke *Dissertation upon Parties*

Buchanan's *History of Scotland*

Echard's *Roman History*

Hale's *History of the Common Law*

Kaims's *Law Tracts*

Montesquieu's *Spirit of Laws* 2 v.

Kennet's *Roman Antiquities* 2 sets

Salmon's *History of England*

Molesworth's *Account of Denmark*

Smollet's *History of England* 10 v.

Littleton's *History of Henry VII* 3 v.

Locke *on human understanding*

Oldcastle's *Remarks on the History of England.* Reprinted from
   The Craftsman, written by Bolingbroke

Potter's *Greek Antiquities*

Robertson's *History of Scotland* 2 v.

Thoyras [Rapin], *History of England*

Gordon's *Tacitus* 4 v.

Voltaire *History of Charles XII of Sweden* 3 v.

Sarpi *History of the Council of Trent*

Hume's *History of England* 8 v.

Vertot's *Revolutions of Sweden*

Littleton's *Life of Henry II* 2 v.

Burnet's *History of his own Time of England* 6 v.

Plutarch's *Lives* 7 v.

Addison's *Works* 3 v.

Trenchard's *Tracts* 2 v.

5. THOMAS JEFFERSON, MONTICELLO, ALBEMARLE COUNTY, VIRGINIA

   *a. The First Library (burned at Shadwell, 1770; this list compiled from books
   inherited from Peter Jefferson, 1757, from the* Virginia Gazette Day Books
   *for the 1760s, and the invoice from Messrs Perkins, Buchanan and Brown,
   October, 1769. See Boyd et al., eds.,* Jefferson Papers, *I, 34.)*

   David Hume's *History of England*

   William Robertson's *History of Scotland*

   Coke's *Institutes*

   Kames's *Historical Law Tracts*

   Dalrymple's *Essay on Feudal Property*

   Matthew Hale's *History of the Common Law*

   William Petyt, *Jus Parliamentum*

   Thornhagh Gurdon's *History of Parliaments*

   Locke, *On Government*

   Ellis, *Tracts on Liberty*

   Warner's *History of Ireland*

        "   *History of the Civil Wars in Ireland*

   Montesquieu, *Oeuvres*

b. The Second (Main) Library 1770–1815

    (1) Jefferson's list for Robert Skipwith, August 3, 1771 (Boyd et al., eds., *Jefferson Papers*, I, 79–80) indicates his familiarity with the following items *not* noted in the first library.

Sidney *on Government*

Ld. Bolingbroke's *political works* 5 v.

Blackstone's *Commentaries* 4 v.

Rollin's *Antient history. Eng.* 13 v.

Stanyan's *Graecian history* 2 v.

Livy. (the late translation)

Sallust by Gordon

Tacitus by Gordon

Vertot's *Revolutions of Rome* Eng.

Plutarch's *Lives* by Langhorns 6 v.

Robertson's *History of Charles the Vth* 3 v.

Clarendon's *history of the rebellion* 6 v.

Locke *on Education*

    (2) Added by 1783 (All the above items were included in the 1783 manuscript catalogue Jefferson prepared prior to his expected voyage to France. Original in the Massachusetts Historical Society. In addition the following historical works were listed.) [4]

Goldsmith's *Roman History*

Kennet's *Antiquities of Rome*

Universal History

Raleigh's *History of the World*

Pelloutier's *Histoire des Celtes*

Ld Molesworth's edition of *Franco-Gallia* [TJ wanted but did not yet own a copy]

    "   "   *account of Denmark*

Cambden's *Britannia*

Verstegan's *Antiquities*

---

4. The entire collection that made up Jefferson's enormous second library is expertly catalogued in E. Millicent Sowerby, ed., *The Catalogue of the Library of Thomas Jefferson*, 5 vols.

Temple's *Introduction to the history of England*
Brady's *History of England*
Tyrrel's *History of England*
Speed's *History of England*
Baker's *Chronicle*
Rapin's *Histoire d'Angleterre*
Temple's *Works*
Kennet's compilation of a *History of England, 1060–1702*
Guthrie's *History of England, 54 A.C.–1702*
Bish. Burnet's *History of his own times*
Blackburne, ed., *Memoirs of Thomas Hollis*
Mrs. Macaulay's *History of England, 1603–1742*
Chamberlayne's *Present State of Great Britain* (1759)
Care's *English Liberties* 2 copies
Fortescue *on Monarchy*
Acherley's *Britannic Constitution*
Sommers' *rights of king & people*
Nathaniel Bacon *on government of England* 2 copies
De Lolme *sur la constitution d'Angleterre*
[Hulme] *An Historical Essay on the English Constitution*
Stuart's *historical dissertation on the antiquity of the British constitution*
Burgh's *Political Disquisitions*
Rushworth's *Historical Collections*
Spelman's *Works*
Gordon and Trenchard, *Cato's Letters*
     "   "   "   *Independent Whig*
Wharton *True Briton*
St. Amand's *historical essay on parliament*
Petyt's *Antient Rights of the Commons of England*
Selden *on the judicature of parliaments*
Parliamentary and Political Tracts by Atkyns and others
Wilkes' *Speeches*

c. *The Third Library, 1815–26*
   (From Nathaniel Poor's auction list, *President Jefferson's Library*
   [Washington, D.C., 1829])

Gillies, *History of Greece* 4 v.

Potter's *Antiquities of Greece* 2 v.

Rollin's *Ancient History* 9th volume

Vertot's *Roman History*

Tacitus Cronovii et Gordon, Lat. Eng. 8 v. [this was TJ's third
   collated version]

Echard's *Roman History* 5th vol.

The Universal History, Ancient 20 v.

Guicciardini, *Istoria d'Italia* 2 v.

Davila, *Guerre civile de Francia* 6 v.

Milot's *History of France* 3d vol.

Voltaire, *Histoire de Charles XII*

Puffendorf's *Introduction to History*

Cambden's *Britannia*

Verstegan's *Original of Nations*

Baker's *Chronicle*

Rapin's *History of England* 15 v.

Rushworth's *Historical Collections* 2d vol. fol.

Fox's *History of James II*

Burnet's *History of his own Times* 6 v.

Blackstone's *Commentaries* 4 v.

Spelmani Glossarium fol.

d. The *"Fourth" Library, 1824*
   (Jefferson's catalogue for the University of Virginia, completed
   September 1824, formed the base for the *1828 Catalogue of the Library
   of the University of Virginia,* ed. William H. Peden [Charlottesville, Va.,
   1945])

   Stanyan's *Grecian History*

   Potter's *Antiquities of Greece*

   Vertot's *Revolutions de Rome*

   Gordon's *Tacitus*

   Basil Kennet's *Roman Antiquities*

   The Universal History

   Vertot's *Revolutions de Portugal*

Pelloutier, *Histoire des Celtes*
Ld Molesworth's *Account of Denmark*
Camden's *Britannia* by Gibson
Milton's *History of England*
Brady's *History of England*
Tyrrel's *History of England*
Speed's *History of England*
Clarendon's *History of the Rebellion*
Temple's *Works*
Rapin's *History of England*
John Baxter's *New and Impartial History of England*
Guthrie's *History of England* and continuation
Burnet's *History of own times*
Macaulay's *History of England*
Buchanan's *History of Scotland*
Robertson's *History of Scotland*
Warner's *History of Ireland*
Dalrymple's *Essay on Feudal Property*
Sullivan's *Lectures on Feudal Law*
Kaims's *Historical Law Tracts*
    "   *British Antiquities*
Spelman's *English Works*
Filmer *on Government*
Sidney *on Government*
Nedham's *Excellencie of a free state*
Nathaniel Bacon *On the government of England*
Acherley's *Britiannic Constitution*
Tyrrell's *Bibliotheca Politica*
Sir Thomas Smith, *De republica Anglorum*
Coke, *Third Part of the Institutes of the Laws of England*
    "   *Fourth Part of the Institutes of the Laws of England*
Kames, *Historical Law Tracts*
Sir John Dalrymple: *Essay towards a general history of Feudal Property*
Hale's *History of the Common Law*
Warner's *History of Ireland*

Pelloutier, *Histoire des Celtes*
   "   *Histoire des Galates*
Stanyan, *Grecian History*
Raleigh, *History of the World*
Malachy Postlethwayt, *The Universal Dictionary of Trade and Commerce*
   1751
Spelman, *De Terminis Juridicis*
   "   *Glossarium Archailogicum*
William Somner, *A Treatise of Gavelkind*
Blackstone, *Commentaries*
Abraham Stanyan, *An account of Switzerland* 1714
William Camden, *Britannia*
William Temple, *Observations upon the United Provinces*
Paul Henry Mallet, *Introduction a l'histoire de Danemark*
William Guthrie, *History of England*
Robert Molesworth, *An account of Denmark*
Vertot, *Histoire des Revolutions de Suède*
Voltaire, *Charles XII*
Thomas Salmon, *Modern History*
[Obadiah Hulme] *Historical Essay on the English Constitution, from the
   Saxon establishment* 1771
Squire's *Enquiry into the Constitution of the Anglo-Saxon Government*
   1753
Sharpe, *Declaration of the right of the people in legislation* 1774
Care's *British Liberties* 1767
Care's *English Liberties* by Nelson 1719
Ellys *on the Spiritual and Temperal Liberties of England* 1763
Gilbert Stuart: *Dissertation on the Antiquity of the English Constitution*
   1790
Burgh's *Political Disquisitions* 1774
De Lolme's *Constitution of England*
Fortescue *on Monarchy*
Sommers' *Judgement on the rights of Kings and People* 1771
Rushworth's *Historical Collections* 1659
Bolingbroke's *Political Writings*

Gordon & Trenchard's *Cato's Letters* 1724
Gurdon's *History of Parliament* 1731
Petyt's *Ancient Rights of the Commons* 1680
    " *Jus Parliamentum* 1739

e. *Historical Works on which Jefferson made notes*
(From *The Commonplace Book of Thomas Jefferson,* ed. Gilbert Chinard; Chinard observed "it is remarkable that . . . political philosophers occupy so little space.")

William Robertson, *History of the Reign of the Emperor Charles V*
Francis Stoughton Sullivan, *An Historical Treatise on the Feudal Laws*
Montesquieu, *Esprit des Lois* (TJ: "has done mischief everywhere.")
[Hulme,] *An historical Essay on the English Constitution*
Fortescue, *De Laudibus Legum Angliae*
David Hume, *History of England*

6. JOHN MACKENZIE, CHARLESTON, SOUTH CAROLINA

(*A Catalogue of Books Given and Devised by John Mackenzie Esquire to the Charleston Library Society . . . . [Charleston, 1772]*)

Burnet's *History of own Times* 2 v. 1724
Camden's *Britannia* 2 v. 1753
Clarendon's *History of the Rebellion* 1759 Oxford, 1721 2 sets
Harrington, *Oceana* 1747
Locke's *Works* 3 v. 1759
Raleigh's *History of the World* 2 v. 1736
Rapin's *History of England* 2 v. fol. 1743
Sidney's *Discourse* 1751
Bacon Nathaniel, *on the Laws & Government of England* 1760
Blackstone, *Commentaries* 1770 Oxford
Bracton, *De Legibus* 1640
Hume's *History of England* 6 v. 1762
Lyttleton's *Henry II* 2 v. 1760
Tacitus 2 v. 1721
Warner's *History of Ireland* 1763
    " *History of Rebellion and Civil Wars in Ireland* 1767

Bolingbroke's *Dissertation on Parties* 1743
Buchanan's *History of Scotland* 1722 2 v.
Chamberlain's *Present State of Britain* 1755
Coke's *Reports* 7 v. 1738
Dalrymple *on Feudal Property* 1758
Kames's *Historical Law Tracts* 1761 Edinburgh
Macaulay, *History of England* 4 v. 1769
Molesworth, *Account of Denmark* 1738
Montagu, *Rise and Fall of ancient Republicks* 1759
Plutarch's *Lives* 6 v. 1758
Potter's *Antiquities of Greece*
Smollett's *History of England* 7 v. 1758
Stanyan's *Grecian History* 2 v. 1751
Temple's *Works* 1757
Cato's Letters 4 v. 1755
Fletcher of Salton's *Political works* Glasgow 1749
Gordon's *Tacitus* 5 v. 1753
Rollin's *ancient history* 12 v. 1749

IV. THE BOOK TRADE

A. New England

I. JOHN MEIN, BOSTON PUBLISHER AND BOOKSELLER

1765 Catalogue (Original in Massachusetts Historical Society)

Rollin's *Ancient History*
Hume's *History of England* to 1688 8 v.
Robertson's *History of Scotland*
Potter's *Antiquities of Greece*
Kennett's *Antiquities of Rome*
Burnet's *History of his own Time*
Ludlow's *Memoirs*
Vertot's *Revolutions of Portugal*
Buchanan's *History of Scotland* 2 v.
Sidney *on Government*

Locke *on Human Understanding*
Temple's *Works*
Kaims's *Law Tracts*

2. HENRY KNOX, BOSTON BOOKSELLER

*1773 Catalogue (*A Catalogue of Books Imported and to be Sold *[Boston, 1773])*

Addison's *Cato, a Tragedy*
Blackstone's *Commentaries*
      "   *Tracts chiefly relating to the Antiquities and Laws of England*
Burgh's *Dignity of Human Nature* 2 v.
Cato's Letters 4 v.
Hume's *History of England* 8 v.
Hawkins *Pleas of the Crown*
Hutchinson's *Hist. of Mass.* 2 v.
History of Magna Charta
Independent Whig 4 v.
Kennet's *Roman Antiquities*
Locke *on Govt.*
   "   *on Education*
   "   *on Human Understanding*
Macaulay's (Mrs.) *History of England* 4 v.
Rappin's *Summary of the History of Eng.* 3 v.
Rollin's *Ancient History* 7 v.
   "   *Roman History*
Trenchard and Gordon's *Tracts* 2 v.

3. JOHN FOSTER CONDY, BOOKSELLER, UNION STREET, BOSTON

*1774 Booklist (*Advertised "To be sold," Boston-Gazette, *Jan. 3 and 10, 1774)*

Blackstone's *Commentaries,* 5 vol.
Robertson's *History of Charles the 5th* 3 vols.
Hutchinson's *History of Mass. Bay* 3 vols.
Lord Sommers *On Nations and King's* [sic]

4. JOHN LANGDON, BOOKSELLER IN CORNHILL, BOSTON

*1774 Advertisement (*Boston-Gazette, *Feb. 7, 1774) Advertises "the 12th edition of Lord Somers* Judgment of whole Kingdoms and Nations," *with remark that ten editions have been issued in London in less than twelve months. The 11th edition was published in Philadelphia in 1773, followed closely by this 12th edition from Newport, R.I., in 1774.*

5. SMITH AND COIT, HARTFORD BOOKSELLERS, 1772

a. *1772 Advertisement* (Connecticut Courant, *July 28, 1772; see also issues of Aug. 3, Aug. 11, 1772)*

Kimber's *History of England*
Rapin's *History of England* Abridg'd
Robinson's [*sic*] *History of Scotland*
Rollin's *Ancient History*
Cato's Letters
Independent Whig
Locke *on Government*
   "   *on Education*

b. *1773 Advertisement* (Connecticut Courant, *July 5 and 13, 1773)*

As above, but adding
Goldsmith's *History of England*

c. *1776 Advertisement* (Connecticut Courant, *Feb. 12, 1776)*

As above, but adding
Blackstone's *Commentaries*
Mrs. Macaulay's *History of England*

6. HEZEKIAH MERRILL, HARTFORD BOOKSELLER, AND APOTHECARY

1773 Advertisement ("Just imported from London," Connecticut Courant, *May 11, 1773; see also issue of Dec. 21, 1773)*

Kimber's *History of England*
Robinson's [*sic*] *History of Scotland*
   "   *History of Charles V*
Rollin's *Antient History*

B. New York and Pennsylvania

I. GARRAT NOEL AND EBENEZER HAZARD, BOOKSELLERS, NEW YORK

1771 Catalogue (Catalogue of Books *[N.Y. 1771]*)

1st category: "History, Voyages, and Travels &c."
Buchanan's *History of Scotland* 2 vols.
Caesar's *Commentaries,* tr. Prof, Duncan 2 v.
Goldsmith's *Roman History* 2 v.
Hutchinson's *History of Mass. Bay* 3 v.
Hume's *History of England* 8 v.
Kennet's *Antiquities of Rome*
Littleton's *History of King Henry II* 4 v.
Livy's *Roman History* tr. with Notes 8 v.
Mrs. Macaulay's *History of England* 4 v.
Robertson's *Hist. of Scotland* 2 v.
    "   *Hist. of Charles V*
Rollin's *Roman History* 10 v.
    "   *Antient History* 12 v.
Vertot's *Revolutions of Sweden and Portugal*
"Law" category
Henry Care's *British Liberties, or the Freeborn Subject's Inheritance*
Dalrymple *on Feudal Property*
Kaims's *Historical Law Tracts*
"Misc." category
Burgh's *Dignity of Human Nature* 2 v.
Bolingbroke's *Collection of Political Tracts*
Home's Lord Kames *Essays concerning British Antiquities*
Locke *on Government*
    "   *on Education*
"Pamphlets" category
North Briton Extraordinary

2. NOEL AND HAZARD, NEW YORK BOOKSELLERS

1773 Advertisement ("Imported in the last vessels, and to be sold by Noel and Hazard," *Rivington's* New-York Gazetteer, *July 1, 1773)*

Goldsmith's *Roman History*
    "   *History of England*

3. JOHN DONALDSON, NEW YORK BOOKSELLER

1773 Advertisement (Rivington's New-York Gazetteer, *Sept. 9, 1773)*

Lord Bolingbroke's *Miscellaneous Works* 4 vols.
Rollin's *Ancient History*
Vertot's *Revolutions of Rome*

4. SAMUEL LONDON, SHIP-CHANDLER AND BOOKSELLER, NEW YORK

1773 Advertisement (Rivington's New-York Gazetteer, *July 8, 1773)*

Hume's, M'Caulay's, &c. *Histories of England*
Robertson's *Hist. of Scotland*
Others "too numerous to insert particulars here."

5. WILLIAM GREEN, NEW YORK BOOKSELLER

a. 1775 Advertisement (Rivington's New-York Gazetteer, *May 11, 1775)*

*The Chronicles of the King's of England . . . down to His present Majesty,
George III* "This excellent History contains a true Description of royal
Life and Manners."

b. 1775 Advertisement (Rivington's New-York Gazetteer, *June 22, 1775)*

"*Political Disquisitions* by J. Burgh, Gentleman. 2 v. price 20/- Pa.
peculiarly necessary at this time for all friends of Constitutional Liberty, whether Britons or Americans." [Long quotation from Burgh's
Preface follows.]

6. JAMES RIVINGTON, BOOKSELLER AND PUBLISHER

1775 Advertisement (Rivington's New-York Gazetteer, *Nov. 23, 1775)*

Advertisement for the complete *Political Disquisitions* by James Burgh
(Robert Bell's Philadelphia edition), which shows "how, and by what
means, the royal, ministerial, and Parliamentary managers cajole, tempt,
and bribe the people to commit suicide on their own liberties. . . .
The perusal of the work at this important period, will be attended
with the most salutary and certain advantages, if the inhabitants of

America will be so rational, as to act wisely, in taking warning from the folly of others. . . ."

7. ANDREW BRADFORD, BOOKSELLER, SECOND STREET, PHILADELPHIA

1731 Advertisement (American Weekly Mercury, *Dec. 28, 1731)*

Burnet's *History of His Own Time*
Temple's *Observations on the United Provinces*

8. DAVID HALL, PHILADELPHIA BOOKSELLER

a. *Book orders to William Strahan, 1751–1765 (From David Hall Letterbooks, American Philosophical Society)*

(1) Order of Mar. 28, 1751 (Letterbook #1)
Locke *on Understanding*
Addison's *Works*
Raleigh's *History of the World* (abridged)

(2) Order of Jan. 3, 1754 (Letterbook #1)
Gordon's *Tacitus*
Locke *on Education*

(3) Order of Aug. 7, 1754 (Letterbook #1)
3 Copies Kennet's *Roman Antiquities*
3 Copies Locke *on Government*
3 Copies *Cato's Letters*

(4) Order of Jan. 3, 1755 (Letterbook #1)
2 Copies Gordon's *Tacitus*

(5) Order of Apr. 4, 1757 (Letterbook #1)
Sidney *on Government*
Gordon's *Tacitus*
Cato's Letters
Locke *on Education*

(6) Order of Dec. 22, 1760 (Letterbook #2)
Sidney *on Government*
Montague's *Rise and Fall of Republicks*
3 Copies Rollin's *Ancient History*
3 Copies   "   *Roman History*

6 Copies *Cato's Letters*
6 Copies *Independent Whig*

(7) Order of May 10, 1762 (Letterbook #2)
Burgh *Britain's Remembrancer* 6 copies
Locke *on Government* 6 copies
Cato's Letters 3 copies

(8) Order of Mar. 3, 1763 (Letterbook #2)
Cato's Letters 3 copies

(9) Order of Dec. 17, 1764 (Letterbook #2)
3 copies of Sidney *on Government*

b. *Book Order for the Library Company of Philadelphia (In May 1763 David Hall reported to Strahan that he was now buying for the Library Company of Philadelphia and requested only "the latest and best Editions.")*

(1) Order of May 14, 1763 (Letterbook #2)
N[athaniel] Bacon *on the Government of England*
Postlethwaite's *Dictionary of Trade and Commerce*
Ralph's *History of England*
Tindal's *Continuation* of Rapin's *from George II*
Hume's *History of England*
Blackstone's *Law Tracts*
Also "For Mr. Thomas Mifflin" Rapin's *History of England* & Tindal's
    contin.

(2) Order of May 3, 1764 (Letterbook #3)
Coke *upon Littleton* "for a customer"
Hume's *History of England*
Gordon's *Tacitus*

(3) Order of Dec. 20, 1764 (Letterbook #3)
"Orders for the Amicable Library Co."
2 Copies of Henry Care's *English Liberties*

(4) Order of Dec. 16, 1765 (Letterbook #3)
3 copies Sidney *on Government*
1 copy Macaulay's *History of England*

c. *Sale List, 1765 (Broadside, on deposit in the Library Company of Philadelphia)*

Kennet's *Roman Antiquities*
Locke, *On Government*
Puffendorf's *Introduction to the History of Europe*
Vertot's *Revolutions of Rome*
Sidney *on government*
Gordon's *Tacitus*
Bolingbroke's *Letters on Patriotism*
Fletcher's *Works*
Cato's Letters

d. *Sale List, 1768 (Broadside, on deposit in the Library Company of Philadelphia)*

Vertot *Revolutions of Sweden* [listed twice]
Robertson's & Buchanan's *History of Scotland*
Sidney *on Government* [listed twice]
Hume's *History of England*
Vertot's *revolutions of Rome*
Kames's *British Antiquities*
Gordon's *Tacitus*
Cato's Letters
Tacitus *Opera*

e. *Sale List, 1769 (Broadside, on deposit in the Library Company of Philadelphia)*

Coke *on Littleton*
   " 2nd, 3d, 4th *Institutes*
Rapin's *History of England*
Sydney *on Government*
Blackstone's *Great Charter*
    " 1st, 3rd, 4th vols. of *Commentaries*
Vertot *Revolutions of Sweden*
Lyttleton's *History of Henry II*
Hume's *Letters on History of England*

Buchanan's *History of Scotland*
Cato's Letters
Independent Whig
Fletcher's *Political Works*

9. RIVINGTON AND BROWN, BOOKSELLERS, NEW YORK
AND PHILADELPHIA

   a. 1762 Catalogue (A Catalogue of Books, *1762, original in the Historical Society of Pennsylvania)*

Locke's *Works*
Bolingbroke's *Works*
Stanyan's *Grecian History*
Temple's *Works*
Montagu's *Rise and Fall of antient Republicks*
Rapin and Tindal, *History of England* ("with Cuts")
Echard's *Roman History*
"*The Annal of Tacitus,* an Author of singular Wisdom and Energy, elegantly Translated, by Mr. Gordon, the author of *Cato's* Letters, and the Independent Whig."
Harrington's *Oceana* (Toland)
Hume's *History of Britain* "a Work of first Class"
Kames's *Historical Law Tracts*

   b. 1762 "A Library of a Gentleman of genteel Taste" (Rivington and Brown's Catalogue, *1762, beginning page 83)*

Rapin's *History of England* 2 v. fol.
Cambden's *Britannia* 2 v.
Temple's *Works* 2 v.
Burnet's *History of Own Times* 2 v.
Gordon's *Tacitus*
Kennett's *Antiquities*
Echard's *Roman History*
Independent Whig

10. WILLIAM BRADFORD, BOOKSELLER, PHILADELPHIA

a. *1760 Catalogue* (Catalogue of Books "Just Imported from London. To be sold at the London Coffee House, Philadelphia," *1760, original in the Historical Society of Pennsylvania*)

Rapin's *History of England*
Burnet's *History of Own Times*
Smollett's *History of England*
Independent Whig 4 v.
Cato's Letters 4 v.
Echard's *Roman History*
Temple's *Works*
Rollin's *Antient History*
   "   *Roman History*
Gordon's *Tacitus*
Buchanan's *History of Scotland*

b. *Auction Sale List, 1769 (Broadside, on deposit in the Historical Society of Pennsylvania)*

Burnet, *History of his Own Times*
Rapin's *History of England*
Clarendon's *History of the Rebellion*
Sidney *on Government*
Bolingbroke, *Works*
Vertot's *Revolutions of Spain*
Harrington's *Works*
Temple's *Works*
Locke's *Works*
Bolingbroke's *Dissertation on Parties*
Robertson's *History of Charles V*
Hume's *History of England*
Bolingbroke *on Study, on Patriotism*
Molesworth's *Account of Denmark*
Rollin's *Ancient History*
Cato's Letters

11. ROBERT MCGILL, MARKET STREET BOOKSELLER, PHILADELPHIA

1773 and 1775 Advertisement (Pennsylvania Gazette, Sept. 22, 1773, Nov. 3, 1775)

Rollin's *Ancient History*
Robertson's *History of Charles V*
"   *History of Scotland*
Moyle's *Tracts*
Kennet's *Antiquities of Rome*

12. ROBERT BELL, BOOKSELLER AND PUBLISHER, PHILADELPHIA

1771 Auction Advertisement (Pennsylvania Packet, Dec. 2, 1771)

"Amongst which are . . . Mrs. Macaulay's history of England."

C. The Southern Colonies

1. DIXON AND HUNTER, WILLIAMSBURG, VIRGINIA

1775 Catalogue ("A Catalogue of Books for Sale," Virginia Gazette, Nov. 25, 1775: Dixon and Hunter published the Gazette; their advertisement covered the entire front page and much of the second.)

Blackstone's *Commentaries*
Buchanan's *History of Scotland* 2 v.
Care's *British Liberties, or the Free Born Subject's Inheritance*
Kennett's *Antiquities of Rome*
Locke's *Essay on the Human Understanding*
Robertson's *History of Scotland*
Rapin's *History of England* 21 v.
Wharton *True Briton* 2 v.
Temple's *Works* 4 v.
Bolingbroke's *Miscellaneous Works* 4 v.
Rollin's *Ancient History*

2. WILLIAM AIKMAN, BOOKSELLER, ANNAPOLIS, MARYLAND

1774 and 1775 Advertisement (Maryland Gazette, June 23, 1774; see also issues of Nov. 17, 1774, Feb. 16, 1775, and July 20, 1775)

Hume's *History of England*
Macaulay's *History of England*

Goldsmith's *History of England*
Littleton's *Henry II*
Blackstone's *Commentaries*
Bolingbroke's *Works* (London, 1754)

3. GEORGE WOOD, "STATIONER AND BOOKBINDER IN
ELLIOTT-STREET, CHARLESTON"

1768 Advertisement (South-Carolina Gazette, May 18, 1768) "He likewise
has a collection of curious books, consisting of histories, voyages,
travels, lives, memoirs, novels, plays, etc., which are lent out to
read. . . ."

A catalogue (not located) was available at Wood's shop.

4. NICHOLAS LANGFORD, BOOKSELLER IN BROAD STREET, CHARLESTON

a. 1768 Advertisement (South-Carolina Gazette, Aug. 22, 1768)

"Lately imported from London. . . . A neat and choice Collection
of Books."

b. 1769 Advertisement ("His second collection of choice and useful
BOOKS," *South-Carolina Gazette, Nov. 23, 1769)*

Robertson's *Life of Emperor Charles V*
Dodsley's *Annual Register*
Hume's Robertson's and Macauley's *Histories*

5. FRANCIS NICHOLSON, BOOKSELLER IN KING STREET, CHARLESTON

1768 Advertisement (South-Carolina Gazette, Oct. 3, 1768)

"Just Imported in the *Friendship.* . . . A Neat Collection of New Books;
Consisting of Law, Physick, History and Divinity." Catalogue at the
shop.

6. ROBERT WELLS, BOOKSELLER, CHARLESTON

1771 Advertisement (South-Carolina Gazette, May 23, 1771)

Advertises a "grand Feast of HISTORICAL ENTERTAINMENT,"
namely the third volume of William Robertson's "celebrated" *History of
Charles V.* Boasts also of constantly maintaining "the LARGEST and
most COMPLETE STOCK of BOOKS to be met with in America."

7. SAMUEL GIFFORD, BOOKSELLER, CHARLESTON

1772 Advertisement (South-Carolina Gazette, *Nov. 26, 1772)*

"Lately arrived from London . . . has taken a Store in Broad-Street Charleston . . . which he has opened as a Circulating Library." The fee is £1 per year, or 12/-per six months, and 3d for a catalogue. New books can be kept four days, others up to one month.

Index

Acherley, Roger, 42, 45, 248; and John Adams, 103, 127, 259; in private libraries, 195, 259, 266, 269, 271; in social libraries, 250, 254, 257

Act of Settlement, 1701, 183

Act of Union, 1707, 114

Adams, Charles Francis, 106

Adams, G. B., 241

Adams, Henry, 240

Adams, Herbert Baxter, 237

Adams, John: on American Revolution, xxi, 3, 120; on value of history, 6, 103–6, 120–21; on reading, 11; library of, 13–14, 102–4, 259–62; and Thomas Jefferson, 14, 100–101, 104, 106, 126–28, 212–13; as book collector, 14–16; and James Burgh, 23, 104, 112, 117, 118, 120, 121, 261; on common law, 30; and Thomas Gordon, 31, 103, 260, 261; and Tacitus, 31–32, 260; and Rapin, 32–33; and De Lolme, 40; and New England clergy, 71–72; on Jonathan Mayhew, 72–73, 75; on James Otis, 84; and Sam Adams, 89; and Boston Massacre trial, 94, 111; historical education of, 100–105; and Bolingbroke, 101, 103, 105, 108, 127, 261; and Sir William Blackstone, 102, 103, 111, 259; and Montesquieu, 101, 259; and John Milton, 102, 104, 109, 261; and Algernon Sidney, 102, 103, 109, 111, 127, 261; and Lord Kames, 103, 107, 261; and Sir Edward Coke, 103, 111, 114–15, 127, 259; and John Trenchard, 103, 261; and Matthew Hale, 103 n. 8, 259; and Lord Clarendon, 103, 127, 260; and John Locke, 103, 109, 261; and Catherine Macaulay, 104, 112, 121, 260; and Rapin, 103, 112, 127, 261; and James Harrington, 103, 109, 111 n. 29, 116, 118, 127, 260; and Gilbert Burnet, 103, 111 n. 29, 127, 260; and David Hume, 103, 125, 127, 260; and Nathaniel Bacon, 103, 127; and Marchamont Nedham, 104, 261; reaction to Stamp Act crisis, 105–10; and William Robertson, 106, 260, 262; exchange with William Brattle, 112; and dispute between governor and General Court, 113–14; *Novanglus,* papers of, 114–18, 145; and William Hawkins, 115, 259; position of, 1776–79, 118–21; and William Temple, 121, 260; *Defence of the Constitutions,* 122–26; and John Cartwright, 125, 127, 261; and Julius Caesar, 125, 260; position of, in later life, 126–28; continuity of position of, 127–28; on John Dickinson, 143–44; and Benjamin Franklin, 155; and Richard Bland, 174; sees English conspiracy against liberty, 227; sees natural rights in English constitution, 232 n. 21

Adams, John Quincy, 120–21

Thomas Jefferson, 194, 268, 271; in social libraries, 251, 254, 256, 258; in private libraries, 260, 263, 265, 266, 268, 271, 272; his books advertised for sale, 274, 283
Molyneux, William, 12, 66, 247, 255
Monmouth, Duke of. *See* Scott, James, Duke of Monmouth
Monroe, James, 223
Montagu, Edward, 27, 95, 247, 261; in social libraries, 17, 252, 255, 257, 258; his books advertised for sale, 274, 279, 282
Montesquieu, Charles Louis Secondat de, 101, 247, 254, 258; in private libraries, 259, 266, 267, 273
Montgomery, John, 262
Monticello, 214
Mount Vernon, 189
Moyle, Walter, 10, 27, 248, 262, 284; in social libraries, 17, 254
Murray, John, Earl of Dunmore, 196

Naroll, Raoul, 122 n. 57, 235 n. 33
Natural laws, 93, 232–33
Natural rights, 93, 116–17, 146, 190–91, 231–33
Navigation Acts, Prussian, 157
Nedham, Marchamont, 72, 104, 248, 261, 220
Neville, Henry, 247, 248, 261
New Hampshire, 163
New Jersey, 142
New Jersey, College of, 12–13, 249–50
Newport, R.I., 18
Newton, Isaac, 5
New-York Gazetteer, 21, 277–78
New York Society Library, 18, 252–53
Nicholson, Francis, 285
Niles, Hezekiah, 3

Noel, Garrat, 21, 277–78
Non-importation agreements, 188, 195
Norman Conquest. *See* England, Norman Conquest
Norris, Isaac, Jr., 15
North, Frederick, Lord North, 98, 141, 231
North Carolina, 16, 120

Oldcastle, Humphry, 267
Oldmixon, John, 247, 250, 261
Olive Branch Petition, 141
Otis, James, 71, 82–88, 138
Oxford University, 215

Paine, Thomas, 151
Parliament, 8, 51, 57–59, 62–63, 67, 154; and general warrants, 83–84, 84–85; and James Otis, 86–88; and Sam Adams, 92–93; and John Adams, 112, 113–14, 115–16, 117; and John Dickinson, 134–36, 140, 142; and James Wilson, 145–50; and Benjamin Franklin, 160–61; and Charles Carroll, 167–68, 170–72; and Daniel Dulany, Jr., 173; and Richard Bland, 176, 179; and Patrick Henry, 182–83; and George Mason, 185–86; and George Washington, 190–91; and Thomas Jefferson, 200–201; and Declaration of Independence, 202–3; and "*True Whigs,*" 227; and Real Whigs, 230. *See also* Elections, annual; House of Commons; House of Lords; Long Parliament
Parson's Cause, 181, 182
Patten, William, 79
Pelloutier, Simon, 268, 271, 272
Peloponnesian War, 184
Pendleton, Edmund, 190, 205

The typeface used for this book is Bembo, produced by Monotype in 1929. It is based on a roman cut at Venice by Francesco Griffo in 1495. The companion italic is based on a font designed in Venice in the 1520s by Giovanni Tagliente. Bembo is a graceful and versatile face of genuine Renaissance structure.

This book is printed on paper that is acid-free and meets the requirements of the American National Standard for Permanence of Paper for Printed Library Materials, z39.48-1992. ♾

Book design by Louise OFarrell, Gainesville, Florida

Typography by Tseng Information Systems, Inc., Durham, North Carolina

Printed and bound by Worzalla Publishing Co., Stevens Point, Wisconsin